Goo...

Tha...

If you're looking for a professional, technical or managerial position, you'll get hundreds of leads from **How To Find A Good Job In Seattle.** No other career guide tells you about

- 1,150 employers in business, government, education and nonprofits in Seattle, Tacoma, Bellevue, Everett, Bremerton and Olympia;

- 230 joblines accessible from anywhere;

- Nearly 250 professional associations that offer job banks and networking;

- Local publications that can help you further research the Northwest job market; and

- Free and inexpensive career-search and placement services.

How To Find A Good Job In Seattle also tells you about

- Internships and part-time, seasonal and free-lance work;

- Resumes and cover letters that'll make you stand out in the crowd; and

- The noncash benefits (and the hidden costs!) of jobs.

Plus: no-nonsense advice from headhunters and personnel managers.

How To Find A Good Job In Seattle is an invaluable part of your job search whether you're looking for a first job or a senior executive's position. It's better than any other directory because it's written by a native—someone with 20 years of experience in the Puget Sound job market.

How To
Find
A Good Job
In Seattle

Second Edition

Linda Carlson

Barrett Street Productions
P.O. Box 99642
Seattle WA 98199
(206) 284-8202

Copyright © 1993 by Linda Carlson
All rights reserved
Printed in the United States of America

Library of Congress Catalog Card Number: 92-73581

ISBN 0-9627122-1-3

Cover design by Virginia Hand Graphic Design

Introduction

Welcome to the Puget Sound job market! Finding a job in the Seattle area can be a challenge. That's where this book can help.

If you're looking for a professional, managerial or technical position, you'll find hundreds of ideas in **How To Find A Good Job In Seattle.**

Rather than simply list the largest employers in the Northwest, this book suggests a wide variety of employers likely to have white-collar and skilled positions. You'll also find information on job search classes and support groups, helpful publications and local professional associations.

Unlike many other career guides, **How To Find A Good Job In Seattle** is not a compilation of other directories. All of the information in this book is based on telephone interviews conducted in mid-1992. Every telephone number has actually been called by the author. (Information is always subject to change, unfortunately; prior to submitting resumes, you should call employers to verify the accuracy of names and addresses.)

We look forward to your comments about **How To Find A Good Job In Seattle**. Please use the form on page 375 to tell us what you found most valuable.

Contents

1. Counseling and Job-Search Help: Free and Inexpensive Programs

At its most basic, job-hunting means reading the ads, writing a good resume and filling out applications. But there's much more you can and should do. If you've been out of the 8-to-5 world for long or if it's been years since you looked for a job, a job-search workshop or career counseling may be helpful.

In this chapter, you'll find examples of free or inexpensive workshops and career counseling. Some programs have age, income or residence requirements; others are open to everyone.

Washington State Employment Security Department
The state operates 28 Job Service Centers across Washington; besides processing claims for unemployment benefits, these centers offer job-placement help. Assistance is not based on income; everyone is eligible. Services vary by centers; however, all offer a computerized job matching service; job listings; workshops; and referrals to other resources (for example, to training or to veterans' programs). Each center also offers a disability, older worker and veterans placement specialist. The state also operates Job Service Center branches that focus on placement and counseling; these branches do not handle unemployment claims. Employment Security offers other programs for the unemployed, including unemployed middle managers. Programs available at press time are described later in this chapter; for information on new programs, call your job service center.

Community Colleges
Most of the state's community colleges have offices to help adults reentering the workplace or returning to college. Although these are often called "women's centers," they usually serve both men and women. Some schools have "displaced homemakers" programs that

focus on those returning to the job market because of separation, death or divorce. Most community colleges also have counseling or career placement offices. Course offerings vary every quarter.

Bellevue Community College Women's Center: 641-2279

Through its Women's Center, BCC offers a free 50-hour course for displaced homemakers. These "job readiness" classes are offered twice each quarter and include testing, confidence-building, career discovery, resume writing and interviewing techniques. Other free services of the Women's Resource Center include a job board, where openings are posted, and a job book, where openings are compiled. "Peer counselors" are also available to provide the initial counseling for those considering a career change, a return to school or reentry to the work force. If you'd like help with your resume, you can attend one of BCC's occasional resume workshops (about $15 each) or be referred to a private resume specialist ($35-$85 for each one-hour session).

Edmonds Community College

Women's Center: 672-6309
Career Center: 771-1624
Student Employment Office: 771-7445
Continuing Education: 771-1517

The Women's Center offers counseling, a career discovery and research class, referrals to other community job-search resources, a job board and support groups ($10 for an eight-week session) on personal and career issues. There's also a displaced homemaker program run in conjunction with Pathways for Women. The Career Center provides a variety of job-search resources and the Student Employment Office can help you with your resume, even if you're not a student. Continuing Education also offers an occasional career-oriented class.

Everett Community College: 259-7151

You'll find three resources here: a "job club," where job-seekers (men and women) can consult a career specialist during free monthly meetings; a career center, with the SIGI program and other career-search materials; and a counseling center, which offers life planning and career search classes. To learn about the job club, ask the operator for the Women's Center; for classes, ask for the counseling center.

Green River Community College

833-9111
Toll-free from Seattle: 464-6133

Re-entering the job market or going back to school? Visit GRCC's

Women's Center (Ext. 402), which offers a job board, referrals to community resources and occasional classes. The Educational Planning Center (Ext. 274) can provide information on career exploration, assertiveness training and self-esteem courses; administer interest inventories; and offer free individual counseling. The Student Employment Office (Ext. 306) is open to the public. Its staff can help you prepare a resume and refer you to the computer lab, where you can word process your resume. On a quarterly basis it also offers a four-session "Job Hunters' Workshop."

Highline Community College Women's Programs:
878-3710, Ext. 340
Here you'll find personal and academic counseling as well as a job search specialist. If you're returning to school while on public assistance, you can attend "Making It Work," a self-help group. A displaced homemakers' program is offered in cooperation with Lake Washington Technical College. There's also an annual career fair with speakers and employers' booths.

North Seattle Community College
Career and Employment Center: 527-3685
Women's Center: 527-3696
Continuing Education: 527-3705
Whether or not you're a student, you're welcome to check the listings at the placement center. The Women's Center offers a variety of programs, including support groups. You'll also find career development and planning programs and a job search workshop (including one by the author of this book) taught through Continuing Education.

Olympic College
Career and Job Information Center: 478-4702
Continuing Education: 478-4839
Counseling and Testing: 478-4561
You need not be an Olympic student to enroll in the free resume-writing, interview skills and career development workshops offered by the Career and Job Information Center, which also provides a resource library and the job announcements from the Bremerton Job Service Center. Occasional classes on career search topics are also offered through Continuing Education. And if you're considering a return to school, testing and advice is available through Counseling and Testing.

Pierce College
Career Center: 964-6590
Continuing Education: 964-6600
Whether or not you're enrolled at Pierce, you're welcome to use the materials in the Career Center and check the job board. Pierce also offers testing, workshops and a popular credit course, "Human Relations and Career Planning." A special needs counselor is available for those who have learning or physical disabilities.

Seattle Central Community College Women's Programs: 587-3854
Workshops include one using "SIGI-Plus," an interactive program that suggests career options based on your interests, skills and education. There is a special class for welfare recipients interested in attending college. Other services include a weekly lecture series that meets at noon in room BE 1110. Topics include work-related concerns, personal growth and social issues. There's a resource center, with career information, a job book and information on scholarships. Counseling and referrals to other community job-search resources are also available.

Shoreline Community College
Women's Programs: 546-4606
Employment and Placement: 546-4610
Lectures, workshops and support groups are among the programs offered by the women's center. Topics include "Life Planning and Re-Entry for Women," "Finding Money for College," and "Writing A Resume That Works." There's also a new program to help single mothers aged 18-30 get into and complete educational programs; it's called, "On The Way To Self-Sufficiency." Another new service: a grant-funded "special populations coordinator" who advises vocational students, especially those who are "dislocated workers" (in other words, those unemployed due to significant changes in their industries), gender minorities and ethnic and racial minorities. The Student Employment and Placement Center helps community members as well as SCC students and alumni.

South Seattle Community College
Career Development: 764-5304
Continuing Education: 764-5339
Senior Adult Education: 764-5395
Career Information and Employment Services: 764-5805
Career Development offers resume, career change and re-entry workshops and support groups. The Senior Adult Education program, in cooperation with the Mayor's office, offers job search classes for

those 50 and older. For help with career planning, SSCC offers a credit psychology course that includes testing and assessment. Tuition waivers are available for low-income applicants.

Tacoma Community College
Career Services Center: 566-5027
Counseling Center: 566-5122
The career center has a job board, a library and the WOIS system. Individual counseling is also available. Through the Counseling Center, you can enroll in career development courses.

Senior Centers
If you're 50 or older and would like to change jobs or return to work, either full-time or part-time, you'll find help at several community senior centers. Services vary by center, but most include "Positions Available," usually for part-time handyman or home care jobs. For more information, call: Northshore (Seattle), 486-4564; Greenwood (Seattle), 461-7841; Edmonds (south Snohomish and north King counties), 778-3838 or 774-2921; Des Moines, 878-1642; Pike Market Senior Employment Program, 728-4262; and Maple Valley Community Center Senior Outreach Program, 432-1272.

ANEW (Apprenticeship and Nontraditional Employment for Women): 235-2212
This five-month skills training course prepares women for entry-level employment in such trades as carpentry, plumbing, roofing, and electrical maintenance. The program includes classes and hands-on experience in trade and industrial skills at Renton Technical College. Weight training, strength building, career counseling and employment referral are also provided. Eligibility requirements include age (22 or older) and residency in Seattle or King County. For more information about income qualifications and program content, call about the weekly orientation sessions.

The Center for Career Alternatives: 723-2286
A private nonprofit serving King County residents, the center offers two-week workshops for low-income job-seekers 16 and older. Topics include how to complete job applications and write resumes, interviewing techniques, and career planning. Call for information on qualifications, the intake process and an orientation session.

Center for Human Services: 546-2411
This nonprofit offers free job-search training for youth 14-19 in schools and community centers. For more information about arranging such a program in your community, call the program coordinator.

Clover Park Technical College Continuing Education: 589-5671
This vo-tech school offers a free 11-week course, "Getting Ready for the Job Market." It's intended for career changers, re-entering homemakers and others—men and women.

Community Information Line
461-3200
Toll-free within Washington: (800) 621-INFO
This Crisis Clinic service provides information on hundreds of nonprofit and government training and employment programs, including those for youth, senior citizens, displaced homemakers, the disadvantaged and ethnic groups. No referrals to for-profit programs or job openings. The line is staffed weekdays between 9 and 5.

Everett Public Library Career Center: 259-8012
Computerized assessment programs, job resource information and material on training and education are available from career adviser Anita Johansen. Job search skills classes are also offered regularly.

Experience-Plus
If you are 55 or older and are underemployed or have been unemployed for at least two months, you may qualify for the Employment Security Department's Experience-Plus program. Intended to help people who do not have four-year college degrees, the program offers as much as six months of training at a community or technical college; job search assistance; and referrals to other agencies. The focus is on enhancing existing skills; retraining is limited to people who require career changes for health reasons or because their previous occupations no longer exist. There are income and residency criteria. For more information, contact the Experience-Plus program manager at one of the locations noted. (Some Experience-Plus programs are offered outside Job Service Centers under different names.) For Seattle and King County residents, call the Rainier Job Service Center, 721-4488; Tacoma and Pierce County, Older Workers' Program, 591-5450; Bremerton and Kitsap County, the Kitsap Job Training Center, 478-4620; Olympia and Thurston County, Thurston County Employment and Training Division, 786-5586; and Everett and Snohomish County, 55+, OI Job Connections, 258-2766.

Focus: 329-7918
This Seattle group provides inexpensive resume review and interviewing skills workshops each month. For details, see *"Professional Associations: How to Network Even If You Know No One."*

Forty Plus of Puget Sound: 450-0040
A membership organization oriented to those who are 40 or older and

have earned at least $35,000 in a professional, managerial, executive or administrative position, Forty Plus is more completely described in "*Professional Associations: How to Network Even If You Know No One.*" There is an initiation fee (at press time, $300 for the unemployed and $400 for the employed), $50 monthly dues and, for the unemployed, a 16-hour-per-week volunteer work commitment. Services include an intensive class for new members, using the national Forty Plus curriculum on marketing yourself. Members can also use offices equipped with personal computers, telephones, fax and copy machines, and an answering service. Contact Forty Plus regarding its free orientation sessions.

Green Thumb Employment and Training: 776-4684
A federally-funded program for low-income older workers, Green Thumb serves nine counties from its western Washington office; in this area, there are Green Thumb participants in Snohomish, King and Thurston counties. Similar to the Senior Community Service Employment Programs, Green Thumb provides on-job site training, usually in government agencies.

Jewish Family Services: 461-3240
Through its Vocational Guidance Program, which has offices both in Seattle and Bellevue, JFS offers individual career planning and job counseling, testing, coordination of information interviews, support groups, workshops and referrals to other JFS and community services. The programs are open to all adults. Fees are on a sliding scale, ranging from $15 to $65 per hour; some financial assistance is available.

Job Search Skills Training
Designed for people who have suffered job-related injuries and made claims through the Department of Labor and Industries, this program is available in all Job Service Centers.

King County Human Services, Community Services Division
Employment Training Program: 296-5220
Veterans' Programs: 296-7656
Women's Programs: 296-5240
King County's job-training and job-search programs, some limited to those who live within King County but outside Seattle, include Employment Training, the umbrella for the Veterans' Program and the Work Training Program. The Veterans' Programs office, which is staffed by veterans who served in Vietnam or Korea, offers informal counseling, help with resumes, skills assessment and job placement. You'll need a copy of your DD214. The Women's Programs office

maintains files of job announcements and information on other job-search resources and works with the other programs listed below. The Work Training Program provides help for adults, youth and teen parents. Eligibility requirements vary, but in general, you must live in King County outside Seattle and be either low-income or disabled. Services include:

For adults:
Helping qualified participants find and obtain jobs; on-the-job skills training for adults entering new occupations; job counseling, both individual and group; educational help, including high school completion, GED and short-term vocational programs; and help with child care, transportation and work clothing.

For youth:
Individual job counseling, help with your job search skills, educational and skills assessment, tutoring and referral to GED and high school completion programs. To participate in year around programs, you must be between 16 and 21 years of age; during the summer, 14 and 15-year-olds may also participate. If you're applying only for a summer job, call 296-5220 between mid-March and June 1.

For teen parents:
Help completing your education, job counseling, help finding part-time or full-time work, pre- and postnatal medical services, parenting education, counseling and peer support groups and child care as needed. You're eligible if you're a teenager and pregnant or a parent, if you live in Renton, Auburn, Enumclaw, Shoreline, Highline or Bellevue and meet income or disability requirements.

King County Library System Community Relations: 684-6606
All branches of this library system have some career-search materials; the six larger facilities (Burien, Fairwood, Federal Way Regional, Bellevue, Kent Regional and Shoreline) also have microfiche files on major employers. Ask librarians to direct you to these and other resources. Free job-search workshops are offered occasionally.

Kirkland Job Center: 827-8696, 455-7210
Located in the Lake Washington Technical College placement center, this is a branch of the Employment Security Department. Free placement counseling is available and the administrator will help set up interviews for job-seekers. No unemployment claims. Call for hours.

Lake Washington Technical College
Women's Center: 828-5647
Library: 828-5645
The women's center at this Kirkland school offers a free displaced homemakers program. It also runs programs to help women complete training in nontraditional industries (for example, diesel mechanics). At press time, the women's center had a state grant to assist single parents and displaced homemakers with child care and transportation costs and tuition waivers while in school. Men and women at any career level can also receive referrals to community job-search resources. The LWTC library offers handouts, videos and workshops on resume writing and interview skills. For information, contact Jeffrey Keuss.

Maple Valley Community Center: 432-1272
Youth aged 12 to 20 can participate in an employment search workshop coordinated by Pete Ryan; it provides training in completing applications, interview skills and work skills. Ryan also maintains a job-seeker registry and a jobs listing.

Mercer Island Jobline: 236-3530
The City of Mercer Island and King County fund this program, which matches jobs and job-seekers, primarily youth and senior citizens. Priority goes to Mercer Island residents.

Metrocenter YMCA: 382-5011
GED preparation and job training are two of the Y's programs. GED classes are open to everyone, regardless of age. The job training programs, which often include both coursework and work experience, are designed for young people 16-21. The Y also offers an employment specialist who can help you one-on-one. Call for information on eligibility and the intake process.

National Pacific Asian Resource Center on Aging: 624-1221
A nonprofit federally-funded agency, this center offers two programs for those 55 and older. The first, the Senior Community Service Employment Program, is similar to that offered by the AARP; on-job training is provided for low-income residents of King County. The Resource Center's program differs only in that it targets (but does not restrict its help to) Pacific Asians. The second offering, the Senior Environmental Program, has no income or residency requirements. It places skilled and professional workers (ranging from secretaries to chemical engineers) in positions in the Environmental Protection Agency. Each job placement is for a minimum of one year.

Operation Improvement
From Everett: 258-2766
From Seattle: 745-2636
Operation Improvement provides free and low-cost employment services to Snohomish County residents 18 and older. If you're 55 or older, you can receive special help through the "55+" program. Services include job search workshops and seminars, support services (such as financial help with day care and transportation), vocational training through community colleges and technical colleges, GED-exam preparation and assistance with basic math and reading skills. Programs vary in length from two weeks to two years.

Pathways for Women: 774-9843
This group runs three different programs: Saturday workshops on such topics as self-esteem, decision-making and assertiveness; displaced homemakers programs; and job clubs, open to everyone in the job market. Fees for the workshops vary; the displaced homemakers program and job club are free.

Pierce County Library: 536-6500
You'll find information on Tacoma-area employers as well as resume-writing and job-search guides in the reference sections of several branches. The two largest reference sections are in the Lakewood and South Hill facilities. For information about programs, call the Public Services or Public Information departments.

Redmond Project Employment: 827-8696
Funded by the City of Redmond, this program helps un- and under-employed Redmond residents. Services include a job-finding workshop and placement help.

City of Seattle
Mayor's Office for Senior Citizens: 684-0500
Seattle Veterans Action Center: 684-4708
Through the Mayor's Office for Senior Citizens, those older than 55 can use "The Age 55+ Employment Resource Center," which offers a job bank, job referral service, jobs hotline (684-0477), individual counseling, two-day job search workshops and prescreening of candidates for employers. There are only two eligibility requirements: age and residency in King County. The Veterans Action Center maintains a job bank.

Seattle Pacific University
Continuing Education: 281-2121
Career Development Center: 281-2018

Occasional classes in job search skills are offered by the Continuing Education office. Although most Career Development Center programs are for SPU students and alumni, the public can visit the library, located on the second floor of the student union at Third and Bertona. SPU also publishes a job bulletin. See *"Job Bulletins and Valuable Publications."*

Seattle Public Library Education Department: 386-4620
The "Career Information and Job Search Center" section of the Education Department (second floor) maintains job-search materials and State of Washington job announcements. The Business and Science Department (also on the second floor) has annual reports, files of clippings from newspapers and many directories, including *Contacts Influential.* The main library and most branches also have WOIS, the Washington Occupation Information System. Many branches also have copies of directories like *Contacts Influential* and *Advanced Technology in Washington State*; these are often kept in the librarian's desk or behind the counter.

Seattle University
Career Development Center: 296-6080
Evening Programs and Continuing Education: 296-5920
If you attended SU or one of several other Jesuit institutions, you can use the career center. It's also open to SU staff and faculty. Through Evening Programs and Continuing Education, SU offers "Leadership Synthesis," which sponsors occasional speakers of interest to job-seekers.

Senior Community Service Employment Program
Seattle: 624-6698
Kent: 859-1818
Funded by the American Association of Retired Persons (AARP), this program for low-income people 55 and older provides on-job training in nonprofits, advice on such job search concerns as resumes and referrals to community resources. The agency also employs job developers, who contact employers for information on positions available.

Senior Services of Seattle/King County: 448-3110
For senior citizens and their families, this office provides referrals to appropriate agencies, arranges home visits if necessary and follows up to make sure you receive the help you need. If you're a senior seeking work, the office staff can refer you to job banks and training programs for which you qualify.

Tacoma Public Library
Quick Info: 591-5666
Community Relations: 591-5688
Want to know the largest companies, public and private, in Tacoma, Seattle and Everett? You'll find detailed descriptions when you use "Infotrac," a CD-based general business file at the main branch's reference desk on the first floor. The main branch also receives some 800 magazines and trade journals and 150 newspapers to help you in researching prospective employers and job locations. There's a career information file, with resume-writing and other job-search materials. A more limited selection of publications and newspapers is available at the Moore and McCormick branches.

Thurston County Job Search Network: 786-5416
A list of local joblines, a typewriter and individual resume counseling are some of the services offered by this Thurston County-funded office. County residents have priority. If you're interested in working for the state, attend one of the workshops explaining the state hiring process. At press time, a job bank for older workers was being established. All services are free.

University of Washington
Women's Information Center: 685-1090
Placement Center: 543-9104
Extension: 543-3900
At the Women's Information Center there are job boards and a library with articles and books that can help you write a resume. You can also obtain information on the agencies and programs that provide aptitude and vocational testing. And you can visit the center to refer to its directory of women's organizations and professional associations. There's also a file on women-owned businesses. All of these programs are open to the public—men and women. If you're planning to return to school, you can receive help from the staff of re-entry counselors. The placement center is open only to degree-pursuing UW students, but it publishes job bulletins available to anyone by subscription. See *"Job Bulletins and Valuable Publications."* UW Extension offers career counseling and a variety of courses and tests. For a fee ($35 per month), you can also use the Resource Center, which offers SIGI-Plus and resume-writing computer programs; a videotape library, with materials on local companies and job-search techniques; and reference materials, including *Contacts Influential* and the WOIS books.

Youth Employment Project: 547-2220

Individual job coaching and referrals to jobs are provided to University District youth 14-22 by this program, funded by the Northwest Children's Fund and the City of Seattle and operated by the Center for Human Services.

University YWCA : 632-4747

Besides workshops on the job search process, the Y offers a job resource room, individual counseling and job search support groups. Presentations by community members cover different industries and job functions. Fees are based on income. The support groups are for women only; all other programs are open to the public.

YWCA of Seattle-King County

Downtown Seattle: 461-4862
Eastside: 644-7361
North Seattle: 364-6810
East Cherry: 461-8480

Each Y office offers employment help, including assessments by a career specialist, one-to-one counseling, help with resume writing, interviewing techniques and job search skills, job listings from area employers and a typewriter to use for preparing your own resume or job applications. Low-income job-seekers are eligible for free individual counseling. At the downtown Seattle office, you'll find brown-bag lunch talks on career-change and job-search topics. If you live in Bothell or the Shoreline area, you can see the career specialist when she visits your area. Call the North Seattle office for a schedule. If you are a low-income single head of household, you may qualify for the Y's "Project Self-Sufficiency." Call the East Cherry office for information on this program, which provides help with training, housing and placement for as long as two years. The Y also offers vocational testing, which is helpful if you're considering a career change. Fees are based on income. For details, call the downtown Seattle office.

YWCA of Tacoma-Pierce County: 272-4181

This Y also offers a career resource center open to the public. Here you'll find many job postings and classes in job-search techniques.

YWCA of Thurston County: 352-0593

A displaced homemakers program, job assistance help and an interview clothes bank are among the offerings of this Y.

Washington Human Development: 762-5192

Migrant farm workers and minority and low-income job-seekers can receive clerical and word processing training and job-search skills through this program funded by the Seattle-King County Private Industry Council. The six-month training program is open-ended; you can start it at any time. Participants receive several weeks of assistance upon completing the program. Call for eligibility requirements.

Washington Women's Employment and Education
Kent: 859-3718
Tacoma: 627-0527

WWEE provides help for low-income women and men who face barriers (often resulting from personal crises) to completing their education and obtaining work. This nonprofit provides referrals (for example, to counseling or drug abuse programs) as part of the initial screening. Eligible applicants are enrolled in an intensive three-week program which includes at least a year of followup as participants pursue training or job placement. WWEE can help participants obtain child care, housing, clothing, transportation, and scholarship and loan applications. For eligibility information, call for a telephone interview.

WOIS, Washington Occupation Information System: 754-8222

More than 1,300 careers that exist in Washington state and the training required for these positions are described in the computer program and books produced by a nonprofit. Updated annually, WOIS also provides information on all accredited post-secondary schools, including colleges, universities, vo-tech schools and private vocational courses. The computer program includes a self-assessment component that allows you to match your interests and skills with those required by specific jobs. WOIS is available in most community colleges, usually through the career placement or counseling office. Some schools charge a $5 or $10 fee to use the program. WOIS is also available free in most branches of the Seattle and King County libraries and in many Job Service Centers and Employment Security offices.

Workforce: 684-7390

For Seattle-area residents, the Employment Security Department and the Private Industry Council cosponsor a program to help displaced workers. There are no income or education criteria for Workforce; many participants are former middle managers unemployed due to industry changes or company closures. You may be eligible for help through this program if you have been laid off due to technological change; through a mass plant closure; or due to foreign competition. You may also be eligible if you have been unemployed more than 26 weeks or if conditions exist that prevent you from working in your former occupation. Training, both full-time and part-time, and help with job-search skills is available. A typical participant might be a laid-off bank manager taking computer classes.

Support Groups

To provide informal guidance and support for those making job changes, many Puget Sound area groups sponsor support groups. Some have met regularly for years; others are simply made up of people who get together until all of them find new jobs. Some groups are free, others have modest fees. Meeting schedules and formats vary. Such groups are offered by many of the programs described in this chapter and by some of the professional organizations listed in *"Professional Associations: How To Network Even If You Don't Know Anyone."* In addition, the following were at press time offering groups (telephone numbers are for church offices, which may refer you to volunteer group leaders): Eastside Four Square Church, Kirkland, 488-2500; Magnolia Lutheran Church, Seattle, 284-0155; St. John's Episcopal Church, Kirkland, 827-3077; University Presbyterian Church, Seattle, 524-7300; and Westminster Chapel, Bellevue. 747-1461.

2. Your Resume and Cover Letter:
How To Stand Out In The Crowd

Hundreds—even thousands. That's how many unsolicited resumes some Pacific Northwest firms receive every month. And when an employer does advertise an opening, 200 or more responses are not unusual.

With this kind of competition, you need a resume and cover letter that will set you apart. Regardless of your credentials, review these suggestions from managers and recruiters experienced in resume-reading. Recognize that even an Ivy League degree and blue-chip experience cannot compensate for a poorly written resume or unfocused cover letter.

Read the ad carefully. And read it twice: once before you draft your letter and then, when your letter is done, to ensure you're addressing the employer's needs. Cite experience and training that are relevant to the position; if a firm needs an engineer, your application probably doesn't have to mention your past career as an actor. If the ad clearly says this is a temporary position, you shouldn't be asking for a job with advancement opportunity.

Responding to the blind ad. It's always difficult to start the letter that goes to a post office box. Some people use "Dear Sir/Madam." Others try "Dear Sir (or Madam)." Why not skip the salutation? In this context, it's meaningless.

Make your letter visually appealing. Remember, the person reading your application may have already seen 50 or 100...and that's in addition to his or her regular work. So make your letter and resume especially attractive and easy to read. Use wide margins and short sentences. Paragraphs should be short, too; try for six or eight lines for the introductory paragraph and no more than 10 or 12 in each following paragraph.

Getting started. Writing to people you don't know isn't easy. It's especially awkward when you're asking for something. Here are two examples of openings that are straightforward and identify the job you're applying for. (That's important when firms have several openings at the same time or when you're submitting an unsolicited resume.)

"I'd like to know more about your opening for a graphic designer."

"I'm interested in the financial analyst position you advertised in Sunday's paper."

"I'd like to know what opportunities exist in your firm for an accountant."

Avoid the obvious:

"Let me introduce myself. My name is Jane Brown and I am..."

And the cute:

"What will this letter tell you about me? How can it convince you to interview me?"

Watch your ego. Don't underestimate yourself—but don't assume you're the only qualified applicant. Skip openings such as:

"I am an ideal candidate for the position you advertised."

"I am uniquely qualified for..."

Be professional. Would you interview the people whose letters included these comments:

"Why should you interview me? For one thing, I'm fun to have around."

"My husband likes my work and often incorporates my suggestions in his work."

"Words and writing are my gift as well as my passion."

Sell yourself. It's the cover letter where you persuade an employer to interview you. Don't miss the opportunity to emphasize how valuable your experience is.

Make your resume specific. Make it more than a list of jobs. For each position you've held (paid or volunteer), describe your accomplishments—in quantifiable terms. For example:

"Reduced employee turnover 50 per cent in 1989."

"Designed direct mail programs with response rates as high as 5 per cent."

Make your resume concise. The best resume is one page long. If you've had several significant jobs, executive recruiters agree that a page and a half—and *maybe* two pages—might be necessary. A one-page resume with narrow margins is better than one with two pages and wide margins.

Put the "meat" on top. What makes you valuable to a prospective employer? Is it your education? Your internship? Your fluency in foreign languages? Put that first so it can't be missed. (Remember, what's most important to you may not be what an employer values. And what's important to each prospective employer will differ.)

Avoid irrelevant information. The five years you spent as a dental assistant before going into computer sales is not relevant if you're applying for a sales management position. The employer looking for a paralegal doesn't really care that you like cats and gardening.

Don't make yourself sound old. It may be illegal, but age discrimination still exists, say recruiters. Avoid use of the word "retired" and consider eliminating the dates of your degrees.

Use good stationery. Plain white or ivory paper and envelopes are available at any stationer's or at paper mills' retail outlets. (For example, the Paper Pickup at 1911 First Ave. S.) You can buy a ream (500 sheets) of paper for about $15 and a box of 500 matching envelopes for about $25. To make sure your resume and stationery match, have a copy shop duplicate your resume on paper you provide.

Use a good typewriter or printer ribbon. Today, with word processing, desktop publishing and laser printing, everyone's letter and resume can have typeset quality. Make sure yours look perfect. A secretarial service will charge about $20 to type your resume. If you're typing your own resume and your letters, guarantee yourself clear, black type with a carbon ribbon or a new fabric ribbon. If necessary, clean your typewriter keys so every "e" and "d" aren't filled in with ink.

Consider desktop publishing. Brevity is the key to good resumes, but if you have several jobs to list, the smaller typefaces available with desktop publishing software will help you get all the information on a page or two. You can rent computers equipped with desktop publishing software and laser printers at shops like Kinko's and AlphaGraphics. Rental charges vary between $12 and $20 per hour; each laser print is extra.

Include all materials requested. If the ad asks you to submit samples or list specific assignments in a particular function or industry, do so. If you can't, avoid excuses such as "I have no samples; my belongings are in storage" or "I'd send you samples, but I just moved and I can't find anything."

Proofread all your materials—at least twice. It's hard to impress someone if you can't spell his or her name correctly. When a job requires accuracy or good written skills, some managers routinely discard every letter or resume with typing or spelling errors. If possible, have someone else proofread your materials.

Sample Resume, Paid and Volunteer Experience

Kelly Monsen
123 Ballard Ave. N.W.
Seattle WA 98107
(206) 789-0000

Experience:

Big & Better Computer Sales, Seattle WA, 1985-91.
    Sales manager, 1987-91. Managed 20 corporate and retail salespeople for locally-owned computer retailer (now merged into Bigger, Better & Best). Responsibilities: recruiting, training, evaluating, firing, territory assignment, key account sales. Accomplishments: reduced turnover of sales staff by 25 per cent; largest sale in company's 10-year history.

    Sales representative, 1984-86. Handled both retail and corporate accounts; consistently outsold other salespeople by as much as 150 per cent.

Sales trainee, A-to-Z Advertising, Kirkland WA, 1982-83.
Through telemarketing and cold calls, sold advertising specialty items (for example, imprinted pens, calendars, T-shirts) to small businesses. Exceeded quota by at least 20 per cent in each sales period.

Other Relevant Experience:

Development Chair, Bright Eyes Preschool, Seattle WA, 1990-present. Created fundraising program that now provides 30 per cent of budget for 50-pupil cooperative preschool. Developed fundraising concepts, including special events and corporate solicitation. Organized volunteer committees to manage fundraisers, including auction, stroll-a-thon and 35-family garage sale. Created corporate matching program through cold calls on corporate personnel directors.

Education:

Washington State University, Pullman, B.A., Communications (Advertising), 1982.

Sample Cover Letter

123 Ballard Ave. N.W.
Seattle WA 98107
Jan. 15, 1993

Lee Smith
Northwest Helping Hands
P. O. Box 9067
Seattle WA 98111

Dear Ms. Smith:

I'd appreciate an opportunity to learn more about your opening for a development director.

If you're looking for someone who can plan and implement a fundraising program, you may be interested in my experience. As you can see from the enclosed resume, I have several years of sales and development work. I have the ability to organize a campaign, solicit volunteer help and actually make both cold calls and formal presentations.

If you believe my experience would be of value to your organization, I can be reached at 789-0000.

Sincerely,

Kelly Monsen

3. Selling Yourself in the Interview: Advice from Seattle Recruiters

What are the most common errors people make when job-hunting? Here's what Seattle recruiters, personnel managers and career counselors say:

Terrible resumes. Said one executive recruiter: "I see too many bright people with terrific credentials—and absolutely lousy resumes!"

Terrible cover letters. A cover letter is a sales tool; its goal is to get you an interview. Write it the same way you'd write an advertisement about yourself.

No focus. None of us can do everything. Nor do we *want* to do everything. But too often that's what our resumes and cover letters say. "Experienced in marketing, sales, finance, personnel administration and operations," claim some resumes. "Seeking a challenging position in accounting, customer service or market research," say others. Don't make your prospective employer guess where you might fit in best; specify the position you want.

If you've worked in a variety of functions and want to apply that experience in a general management position, make that clear by stating an objective in your resume or letter. Be prepared to explain how your different assignments have prepared you to run an operation.

Making a career change? Your resume should highlight what you've accomplished in your former career and why you're qualified for this new job. When you interview, focus on the value of these combined skills and experience.

No research. To explain how your experience can benefit a potential employer, you need to know something about that organization. Start with the directories and periodicals mentioned in "*Job Bulletins and Valuable Publications.*" Ask your librarian for help, too.

Bad body language. Even if you're desperate for a job, don't let your posture and tone of voice communicate your anxiety.

If you're having difficulty maintaining your self-esteem during the job search and your composure during interviews, look into support groups. Executive recruiters mention that a rigorous exercise program often helps, too.

Poor appearance. Take a long, critical look at yourself in the mirror. Like it or not, you're a "product" on the job market; the better you're "packaged," the easier your sales job. Exercise will help your morale and trim off those extra pounds. When you interview, dress appropriately for the position you seek. (If you know nothing about an employer's dress code—formal or implicit— check its publications. How are the people in the pictures dressed? You may also want to do a little sleuthing in the office parking lot or company cafeteria.)

No enthusiasm. Communicate enthusiasm for the organization. This is as important over the telephone as it is in person. Many employers and recruiters make their first cuts after quick telephone conversations; if you're lukewarm, you may never have the chance to present yourself in person.

Waiting for the job to find you. You've heard it over and over again: make it your business to find a new job. Work at your job search the same way you'll work at the new job. That means using all of your contacts; don't be embarrassed about letting your friends and acquaintances know you're in the job market. Make new contacts, too, with professional associations. Networking is probably the single best way to find a position. Your job search may also mean "cold" calls; you can't be afraid to pick up the telephone and ask employers if they have openings.

4. Job Bulletins and Valuable Publications

Whether you're looking for "who's who" in your industry or "help wanted" advertising, you'll find a variety of directories and periodicals available free, by subscription or in libraries. In general, the most valuable are those published locally. Besides the publications listed here, check *"Professional Associations: How To Network Even If You Know No One"* for information on organizations' newsletters. And ask the staff in your library or college placement center about other directories and industry publications. (Editor's Note: unless otherwise noted, all area codes for telephone numbers are 206.)

Job Bulletins

University of Washington Placement Bulletins
Although use of the placement center is restricted to degree-pursuing UW students, the public can subscribe to any of the three weekly job listings published by the center. The cost is $40 per academic quarter per list (with lower rates for UW alumni subscribing for at least two quarters). The lists, which are ordered by number, include: 1. Nonadministrative positions in K-12 educational programs (most positions require a valid Washington teaching certificate); 2. Administrative positions in K-12 educational programs (for example, business and transportation managers as well as principals) and higher education; and 3. Other public and private sector positions. Most of the listings are for jobs in Washington; however, you may find some in California, Idaho, Oregon or Wyoming. The placement center publishes only the job announcements it is sent; companies, agencies and school districts may have additional openings. To subscribe, contact:

Placement Center
301 Loew Hall FH-30
University of Washington
Seattle WA 98195
543-9104

Seattle Pacific University Educational Vacancy Bulletin

This publication lists only openings for certified staff. At press time
the cost was $25 per three-month subscription (with lower rates for
SPU students and alumni). For information, contact:

Educational Vacancy Bulletin
Career Development Center
Seattle Pacific University
Seattle WA 98109
281-2018

Washington Education Association Position Listing Service

Current job openings for administrators, teachers and support staff in
many schools and colleges in the Northwest are listed in the bulletins
available from the WEA Position Listing Service. A three-month
subscription is $10 for WEA members and $35 for nonmembers. To
subscribe, contact:

Washington Education Association
33434 8th S.
Federal Way WA 98003
941-6700
Toll-free within Washington: (800) 622-3393.

The Employment Paper

Issued by a for-profit publisher, this tabloid includes some job search
columns as well as help wanted ads. Pick it up in your neighborhood
or, if out-of-state, request a free subscription by contacting:

The Employment Paper
329 2nd Ave. W.
Seattle WA 98119
285-6900

Sound Opportunities
Started in 1989 by two graduate students to advertise openings in regional nonprofit organizations, this publication and its parent, Nonprofit Community Network, have applied for nonprofit status. Distributed free to placement offices, libraries, nonprofits and government agencies, it's won many compliments from nonprofit employers. The publication is mailed to individuals by subscription (approximately $10 for a four-month subscription to out-of-state addresses). Contact:

Sound Opportunities
501 N. 36th St., #177
Seattle WA 98103
548-0254

Directories
Access, approximately 550 Washington arts organizations, with contact names and addresses but no information on size. Available for $10 (including postage) from Allied Arts of Seattle, 107 S. Main, #201, Seattle WA 98104. Also in some library reference sections.

Advanced Technology in Washington State 1993 Directory, which lists 1,500 high tech firms statewide. Almost 60 per cent of the listings are for firms along the Interstate 405 belt. Available for $34 in Seattle bookstores or for $36.79 (including tax and postage) from Glenn Avery, Commerce Publishing Corp., P.O. Box 9805, Seattle WA 98109. A DOS-based diskette version is $48. Available in many libraries.

Where to Turn PLUS, published by the Crisis Clinic. A 250-page directory describing social service agencies in King County. Updated biannually. Price: $15 in bookstores or from the Crisis Clinic, 1515 Dexter Ave. N., #300, Seattle WA 98109.

Washington Education Association Directory, which lists all state-approved public and private schools, colleges and universities and many professional associations for educators. Available from Barbara Krohn and Associates, 835 Securities Building, Seattle WA 98101-1162, 622-3538. Approximate cost (including tax and postage): $15.

Washington State Media Directory, issued by the McConnell Co., lists newspapers, magazines and broadcast stations. Updated monthly. Available for $85 (call 285-0140) and in many libraries.

Directory of Lawyers for King County, which lists 6,000 attorneys and law firms as well as King County courts and bar associations. Compiled by the *Seattle Daily Journal of Commerce* staff, it's $12 if you pick it up at the newspaper office, 83 Columbia, or $13 if mailed. Contact: Seattle Daily Journal of Commerce, P.O. Box 11050, Seattle WA 98111.

Northwest Fisheries Association Directory of Members, available in libraries, provides contact information for those interested in fishing and seafood processing.

Contacts Influential, which includes most King, Snohomish, Pierce and Thurston county firms, public and private. Revised each year, it lists top management, size and SIC (industry) codes. The King-Snohomish version lists 64,000 firms. The Pierce-Thurston version lists 17,000 firms. Available in most Seattle-area public libraries in the reference section or at the check-out counter. Subsets are available in mailing list form. Contact: Contacts Influential/Trinet, 1001 Fourth Ave., #3200, Seattle WA 98154-1075, 587-6014.

Washington State Forest Products Directory, a publication of the University of Washington College of Forest Resources, describes forest products firms. Products, number of employees, subsidiaries and markets are noted. Available at local libraries.

Guide to Business-Related Organizations in Puget Sound, a 40-page list of business, professional, alumni and civic groups. Available for $24 from TLS Marketing Consultants, 1321 Queen Anne Ave. N., #209, Seattle WA 98109.

"Greater Seattle Club and Organization Directory," a looseleaf binder at the Seattle Public Library, lists social, civic and professional groups. Usually incomplete and outdated, but a valuable starting point.

R. L. Polk & Co. City Directories. If you pass a store or firm and want to know who owns it, you may find the answer in the appropriate city directory. Participation is voluntary; listings are incomplete.

Libraries across the country may also have these national directories:

The Municipal Year Book, published by the International City Management Association, Washington, D.C.; lists city and county officials.

National Data Book of Foundations: A Comprehensive Guide to

Grantmaking Foundations, published by the Foundation Center of New York. The listing for the Puget Sound area includes several foundations which provide more than $1 million in grants annually.

Directory of the Forest Products Industry, issued by Miller-Freeman Publications, San Francisco. Lists logging, milling and wholesaling operations. Field offices and subsidiaries are also listed by state and city.

Periodicals
For industry information and occasional "help wanted" ads, check:

Puget Sound Business Journal
101 Yesler Way, #200
Seattle WA 98104
583-0701
Annual subscription: $48. A weekly, this publication in each issue spotlights several businesses ranging from the very small to the well-established.

Seattle Daily Journal of Commerce
P.O. Box 11050
Seattle WA 98111
622-8272
Subscription rate: $60 per quarter. This Monday-Saturday publication provides a different industry focus each day.

Marple's Business Newsletter
911 Western Ave., #509
Seattle WA 98104
622-0155
A six-month subscription for this biweekly, which includes no advertising, is $39. It provides valuable background on Northwest firms and industries.

Washington CEO
2505 Second Ave., #602
Seattle WA 98121-1426
441-8415
A new monthly designed to reach top executives, this magazine has company and industry features and earnings reports of locally-headquartered public companies. Annual subscription: $19.95.

Professional Agenda
2314 Third Ave.
Seattle WA 98121
448-5629
A monthly list of professional association events. Annual cost: $24.

Marketing
2314 Third Ave.
Seattle WA 98121
461-1336
Mailed free within the Seattle area, this monthly lists staff promotions, awards and the newsletter of the local American Marketing Association chapter. No telephone requests accepted.

Media Inc.
Media Index Publishing, Inc.
P.O. Box 24365
Seattle WA 98124
382-9220
Annual subscription: $20. A monthly focusing on the advertising and entertainment industries.

Artist Trust
1331 Third Ave., #512
Seattle WA 98101
467-8734
Published by the group Artist Trust, this quarterly advertises internships, grants, awards and shows and galleries where artworks are sold. Available for a $15 contribution.

Seattle Arts
305 Harrison
Seattle WA 98109
684-7171
Published by the Seattle Arts Commission, a City of Seattle agency, this newsletter is mailed free within the Seattle area upon request. Includes "Arts Exchange," free ads for arts organizations. A recent issue listed more than 15 job ads ranging from volunteers to teaching, development and executive director positions.

And don't forget the daily and weekly newspapers:

Seattle Times/Seattle Post-Intelligencer
P.O. Box 84647
Seattle WA 98124
Circulation: 464-2121
A one-month trial subscription to the Sunday issue (a combined Times-P-I publication) is $12 for papers mailed anywhere in the U.S.

Seattle Weekly
1931 Second Ave.
Seattle WA 98101
441-6262
A six-month subscription was at press time $15.95 within Washington state, $21 out-of-state.

There's also the *Journal American,* Everett *Herald, Morning News Tribune, Olympian, Valley Daily News* and Bremerton *Sun.*

Chamber of Commerce Publications

Greater Seattle Chamber of Commerce
600 University St., #1200
Seattle WA 98191
389-7256
The chamber sells both publications it produces and those published by others. Call for a catalog. The relocation packet, which includes state and city maps and an information guide to the economy, housing, schools and recreation, is $9; the packet with a video, "Step One to Seattle," is $25.

Tacoma-Pierce County Chamber of Commerce
P.O. Box 1933
950 Pacific Ave., #300
Tacoma WA 98402
627-2175
A variety of materials, some free, some for sale. Most are also available for a quick review if you walk in.

Bellevue Chamber of Commerce
10500 N.E. 8th, #750
Bellevue WA 98004
454-2464
Offers relocation materials (fees vary). There's also a guide to major employers (scheduled to be updated in 1993). The receptionist can

also refer you to other sources of information in the community.

Everett Chamber of Commerce
P.O. Box 1086
Everett WA 98206
252-5181
Ask for the checklist of materials currently available and any fees.

5. Professional Associations:
How To Network Even If You Know No One

When you know no one—or nothing about an industry or function—a good starting point is professional associations.

Go to the meetings and work at talking to as many members as possible; read the newsletters and use the job banks. Don't hesitate to volunteer; if you work in the association office, you'll be one of the first to see the openings posted in the job bank. If you help on a project, you'll get to know members and you may find yourself on a committee headed by an industry veteran.

Considering career change? Professional associations often allow you to talk to people at a variety of levels within a profession or industry. You'll be able to ask such questions as "How hard is it to break into this field?" and "What's an entry-level job like?" For those who are self-employed or considering starting your own businesses, this chapter ends with a list of organizations you may find helpful.

A few reminders: when you call association officers, it's usually during their workday. Respect their schedules and keep your calls short. When you attend a meeting, it's your responsibility to introduce yourself and clarify your interest. (Passing out resumes over luncheon is not recommended, but you can collect business cards and write follow-up notes to those who mention openings.)

The contacts below were verified at press time, but changes often occur. You may find more recent information in the meeting announcements published in the *Puget Sound Business Journal*, *Professional Agenda* and the daily papers.

Administrative Management Society, Seattle Chapter
Contact: Nancy Andersen, 623-8901
This chapter of an international serves about 80 Seattle and Eastside

middle managers. The society's goal is to provide networking opportunities for those in any function and industry. Nonmembers are welcome at the monthly meetings and can request the newsletter.

Advertising Production Association
P.O. Box 21407
Seattle WA 98111
448-1501
This organization includes 100 who work in traffic and production in advertising agencies, design studios and in-house agencies. The job bank includes entry-level to senior positions. Nonmembers can use the job bank for a $15 fee. Educational meetings are held most months and nonmembers are welcome.

AEPUG
P.O. Box 15902
Seattle WA 98115
If you're an architect, engineer or planner using computer-aided design, consider this group. It meets for CAD roundtables (novices and students are welcome) and pizza feed/discussions. Nonmembers are welcome; the CAD roundtable is free, the pizza session $5. Membership is about 45. Call Paul Wilhelm at 623-1774 or Bill Holt at 726-1806.

AIDS Services and Prevention Coalition
P.O. Box C-2016
Edmonds WA 98020-0999
778-6162
Representatives of government agencies, health care organizations and church groups belong to this group, which meets quarterly to discuss AIDS-related issues and programs. Nonmembers are welcome.

American Association of Cost Engineers, Seattle Section
P.O. Box 4325
Seattle WA 98104
Contact: Phil Larson, NBBJ, 223-5205
Scheduling, estimating, computer applications and claims are examples of the topics discussed by this group, which serves those who determine how much an architectural or engineering project should cost. Most of the 100 members have a background in construction management, architecture or business; most work for architects or independent cost estimating firms. Nonmembers are welcome. The local newsletter lists both "Positions Wanted" and "Positions Available."

American Association of Museums,
Western Museums Conference

Contact: Kathryn Sibley, executive director, (213) 749-0119
Information on paid positions and internships is available at the "job marketplace" at meetings of this group. Although the conference meets only annually, the professional subgroups (for example, the registrars) meet more frequently. Members receive bimonthly job announcements and a quarterly newsletter from the regional conference.

American Electronics Association, Washington Council

11812 North Creek Parkway N., #205
Bothell WA 98011
486-5720
People interested in the software or electronics industry are welcome to attend many AEA meetings; a technical degree is not a requirement. Membership benefits include networking committees (similar to SIGs), some of which meet monthly. Organized by job function (for example, finance, marketing, software engineering), the committees are excellent places to meet people. They are not, however, appropriate places to pass out resumes. The AEA has no job bank, but if you send a resume to the council office, it will be filed for three months; copies will be available to AEA member firms with openings.

American Guild of Patient Account Management,
Evergreen Chapter

Contact: Sharon Thomas, 543-6425
If you work in a health care business office in billing, insurance verification or collections, you may be interested in this group, which has about 220 members. The frequent workshops cover such topics as new Medicare regulations. The quarterly newsletter lists both "Positions Available" and "Positions Wanted." Nonmembers are welcome.

American Institute of Architects, Seattle Chapter

1911 First Ave.
Seattle WA 98101
448-4938
If you're an architect, one of the most valuable tools the Seattle chapter offers is its 400-firm directory, ProFile. The current edition is $50. A number of educational sessions are offered, including programs on job-seeking techniques and the variety of jobs available to architecture graduates. Each spring the chapter usually organizes a job fair, where architectural and engineering firms can explain their specialties and interview job-seekers. As a nonmember, you're

welcome to attend meetings and use the job and resume files. You're also welcome to use the Resource Center for Architecture, where member firms provide illustrations of their work. Designed for people planning to hire architects, the Center will also let you preview the work of a firm.

American Institute of Architects, Southwest Washington Chapter
502 S. 11th
Tacoma WA 98402
627-4006
Nonmembers are also welcome at meetings of this chapter, which serves the area south of Seattle and north of Vancouver. The resume file includes information on people interested in building design, regardless of position. However, most firms checking the file have openings for architects or draftspeople. To contact the 200 members, you can buy a copy of the directory for $15.

American Institute of Graphic Artists, Seattle Chapter
2129 Second Ave.
Seattle WA 98121
448-4940
This organization includes 300 professional graphic designers. Besides meetings, which include speakers or studio tours, there are seminars, some on business management, others on creative topics. Nonmembers are welcome at most events. The newsletter is sent only to members.

American Marketing Association, Puget Sound Chapter
217 Ninth Ave. N.
Seattle WA 98109
623-8632
One of nearly 100 AMA chapters, this group has more than 425 members. Luncheon meetings are second Wednesdays. Nonmembers are welcome.

American Mathematical Association, Pacific Northwest Section
Contact: Larry Curnutt, Bellevue Community College, 641-2412
College teaching is the emphasis of this group, but you need not be a teacher to participate in its annual meeting each spring. The only event for the general membership, the annual meeting is open to nonmembers and graduate students are especially encouraged to attend and present papers. Members receive the national's bimonthly newsletter, "Focus," which includes job listings.

Washington Mathematical Association of Two-Year Colleges
Contact: Phil Hess, Green River Community College
An affiliate of the American Mathematical Association of Two-Year
Colleges, this group includes those who teach math in the state's
community colleges. Membership is $5.

American Planning Association, Washington State Chapter
Contact: 283-2901
Urban planners may be interested in this chapter of the national
association as well as its subgroup, the Puget Sound Section. Members include urban planners who work in government agencies,
planning consultants, planning commissioners, architects, land use
attorneys, planning professors and students. Both groups issue
bimonthly newsletters with listings for "Positions Available" and
"Positions Wanted." For more information, ask for Robin McClelland,
state chapter president, or Roger Wagoner, section president.

**American Production and Inventory Control Society,
Seattle Chapter**
Contact: Katie McGrath, 867-1147
Chartered to provide education about the manufacturing function, this
group has some 70,000 members nationally. The Seattle chapter has
about 1,000, including plant managers, systems analysts, materials
managers, purchasing agents and those who work in inventory control. Nonmembers are welcome at monthly meetings and can request
copies of the newsletter. The job bank is open to members only.

**American Production and Inventory Control Society,
Commencement Bay Chapter**
P.O. Box 112124
Tacoma WA 98411
About 100 belong to this chapter, which draws members from as far
south as Chehalis and Westport. Contact Bill Latham, 863-1097.

**American Society for Training and Development,
Seattle Chapter**
217 Ninth N.
Seattle WA 98109
623-8632
If you work in human resources or training, either on staff or as a
consultant, you may be interested in this group, which boasts 625
members in the chapter serving Seattle, Everett and the Eastside.
Nonmembers can also attend the institutes and some meetings of the
SIGs. If you're a member, you can use the employment referral
service and the membership and resources directories.

**American Society for Training and Development,
Nisqually Chapter**
2020 S. 320th Ave., #A-C-5
Federal Way WA 98023
582-0233
This ASTD chapter announces job openings both in the monthly newsletter and at the meetings. Although passing out resumes during meetings is discouraged, there's a table where you can leave your resume for review and pickup by interested employers. When you're introducing yourself, you can also mention you're in the job market. The chapter primarily serves Pierce, Kitsap and Thurston counties.

American Society of Civil Engineers, Seattle Section
Contact: Sandra Gardner, Newsletter Editor
PEI/Barrett Consulting Group
10800 N.E. 8th St., Seventh Floor
Bellevue WA 98004
If you're a civil engineer, you may want this section's newsletter. It occasionally lists job openings. For a fee, members can also run "Positions Wanted" notices. The section has about 2,000 members, with meetings attracting 70-100. For more information, contact Mark Killgore, 451-4596 or Rick Gilmore, 941-2288.

**American Society of Interior Designers,
Washington State Chapter**
5701 6th Ave. S.
Seattle WA 98108
762-4313
If you're an interior designer or interested in the field, you're welcome at the chapter's general meetings. The chapter directory is available for purchase; it includes more than 375 professional members across the state and some 60 associate (supplier) members.

**American Society of Landscape Architects,
Washington State Chapter**
P.O. Box 95500
Seattle WA 98145
443-9484
This chapter has approximately 280 members. The nonmember fee for the quarterly newsletter is $12. "Positions Wanted" ads are free, even for nonmembers. As a nonmember, you're welcome at chapter and executive board meetings and special events. A valuable resource is a members' handbook issued by the national headquarters. It lists all members and their employers, which include private practices and government agencies. For information: (202) 686-ASLA.

**American Society of Magazine Photographers,
Seattle-Northwest Chapter**
c/o Karl Bischoff
1201 First Ave. S.
Seattle WA 98134
Hotline: 527-0632
This group serves photographers, free-lance and corporate, photographers' assistants, students and corporate affiliates (for example, marketing professionals who commission photography). The chapter holds meetings monthly; nonmembers are welcome and can subscribe to the newsletter. If you're interested in photography as a profession, consider attending programs for the photographers' assistants.

American Society of Women Accountants, Seattle Chapter
314 Lloyd Building
Seattle WA 98101
467-8645
Open to both men and women, this group of 250 is the largest ASWA chapter. It meets monthly for dinner and also conducts educational seminars. The job bank is open to members of any chapter and information about job openings is often distributed at meetings.

American Society of Women Accountants, Tacoma Chapter
Contact: Bev Patterson
1301 Highlands Parkway N.
Tacoma WA 98406
756-7553
ASWA members from across the country attend the annual seminar at Fort Worden sponsored by this chapter, which has 120 members. Both men and women are welcome at the meetings and educational programs. If you're in the job market, there's a job bank and a resume file.

American Society of Women Accountants, Everett Chapter
Contact: Judy Brosius, 653-4454
This chapter has 35 members who meet monthly. Nonmembers are welcome. There's no job bank, but networking is encouraged.

Appraisal Institute, Seattle Chapter
Contact: Colleen Price, Executive Secretary, 622-8425
Interested in real estate? If you've worked in appraising or would like to know more about the field, you're welcome at the monthly meetings of "candidates," people working on their credentials as appraisers. "Positions Wanted" ads are printed in the monthly newsletter, which goes to all members and candidates.

Appraisal Institute, South Puget Sound Chapter
Contact: Carolann Guilford, 564-5676
This growing chapter had 125 members at press time; about 60 per cent work in residential appraising, about 40 per cent in commercial. Nonmembers are welcome at the meetings and can receive the newsletter, which often includes notices of job openings.

Asian Bar Association of Washington
Contact: Dean Lum, 622-3790
Legal issues facing Asian and Pacific-American communities and the concerns of Asian and Pacific-American attorneys are the focus of this group, the local affiliate of the National Asian-Pacific American Bar Association. To be eligible for membership, you must have been admitted to the bar. Nonmembers are welcome at meetings.

Associated General Contractors of America, Inc. of Washington
1200 Westlake Ave. N., #301
Seattle WA 98109
284-0061
Looking for a job in commercial construction? The AGC's monthly "Personnel Mart" publication goes to 800 members in western and central Washington; it includes free resume summaries from people with industry experience. Write your own four-sentence description of your credentials and the job you want; it'll be published without your name. AGC members interested in seeing your complete resume will then contact the AGC office. Contact: Gracia Macy.

Associated Women Contractors
217 Ninth N.
Seattle WA 98109
623-8632
Contactors, suppliers and designers are among the 30 members (men and women) of this group, which provides informal referrals to those seeking jobs. Nonmembers can receive the quarterly newsletter.

Association for Computing Machinery
Contact: Pete Fox, 670-4641, or Woody Pang, 547-0829
If you're a programmer, a systems analyst or a data programming manager, you're welcome at meetings of this chapter of a national. Membership is about 300. You can be added to the newsletter mailing list upon request.

Association for Systems Management, Seattle Chapter

P.O. Box 673

Seattle WA 98111

This group for MIS professionals has about 70 members in the local chapter, which serves the entire Puget Sound area, and 6,000 nationally. Most members are systems analysts or managers at smaller companies. Nonmembers are welcome at the meetings; for a schedule, call Jerry Hillis at 296-0892.

Association for the Care of Children's Health, Puget Sound Affiliate

Contact: Children's Hospital Nursing Staff Development Department, 526-2096, or Kristi Klee, immediate past president, 526-2524

Doctors, nurses, social workers, recreational therapists, child life specialists and parents are among the 65 members of this group, which focuses on the psychosocial issues in pediatric health care. There's a job bank through the national.

Association for Women in Computing, Puget Sound Chapter

P.O. Box 179

Seattle WA 98111

781-7315

Nonmembers are welcome at meetings of this group of 125, part of a national that furthers communication and growth among women in data processing. Meetings attract about 50. If you like, skip the dinner and attend only the speaker's presentation for a reduced fee.

Association for Women Geoscientists, Puget Sound Chapter

P.O. Box 405

Issaquah WA 98027

Formed in 1985, this chapter has about 35 members. Members include hydrologists; seismologists; engineering geologists; academics; and students. Many work in consulting firms or for government agencies. Nonmembers are welcome. The newsletter occasionally lists job openings; you can also receive informal help from members. Contact Marsha Knadle, 553-1641.

Association for Women in Landscaping

P.O. Box 22562

Seattle WA 98122

Formed in the mid-1980s, this local organization includes about 150 who work in landscaping. Some are students, instructors and researchers; others are writers, arborists, designers, contractors, consultants and wholesale and retail salespeople. The meetings and annual conference are open to nonmembers; the job board is for

members only. Contact Susan Hanley at Evergreen Services, 641-
1905.

Association for Women in Science, Seattle Area Chapter
Contact: Reitha Weeks
2410 Dexter Ave. N., #102
Seattle WA 98109
286-8787
Part of the Association for Women in Science, this is the only chapter
in Washington state. Membership is open to men and women,
regardless of education or profession, who support the association's
goals of furthering science education for women and careers in
science for women. The 110 local members include graduate
students, chemists, engineers and those who work in environmental
science (e.g., toxicologists), biotechnology and computer science.
Nonmembers are welcome. The local newsletter includes job
openings; it and the national bimonthly are sent to members.

Association of Northwest Environmental Professionals
2033 Sixth Ave., #804
Seattle WA 98121
441-6020
A new chapter of the National Association of Environmental Professionals, this group requires that a full member have a college degree
and employment "principally concerned with environmental issues."
Membership exceeds 250. Nonmembers are welcome.

Association of Professional Mortgage Women, National Office
P.O. Box C-2016
Edmonds WA 98020-0999
778-6162
If you work in mortgage banking or a related field, you may be
interested in this group, which has several chapters in the Puget
Sound area. Members include men and women who process and
originate loans, whether in banks, mortgage companies, title insurance and escrow firms. Most chapters have employment chairs who
provide informal job-search help.

Seattle Association of Professional Mortgage Women
P.O. Box 2415
Seattle WA 98101
Contact: Karen Weaver, 628-5637
Membership: 75.

Puget Sound Association of Professional Mortgage Women
Contact: Connie Reed, 821-7096 or Patricia Wright, 637-0008
Membership: about 25.

Eastside Association of Professional Mortgage Women
Contact: Ann Wheeler, Chicago Title, 628-5646
Membership: 50.

Everett Association of Professional Mortgage Women
Contact: Susan Langager, 659-3739
Membership: 35.

Olympic Peninsula Association of Professional Mortgage Women
Contact: Ann Galla, 692-3790
Membership: 30.

Tacoma Association of Professional Mortgage Women
Contact: Mary Sheehan, 582-9560
Membership: about 30.

Association of Records Managers and Administrators
Most members of this international work in records or forms management, handling the paper and electronic files that follow us "from birth to death." Typical employers are government agencies, bar associations, law firms, educational institutions, insurance companies and major corporations with archives.

Association of Records Managers and Administrators, Greater Seattle Chapter
Contact: Cheryl Lieberman, 386-2986
Membership: 200. Job openings are announced at meetings and listed in the job bank. Nonmembers can receive copies of the newsletter.

Association of Records Managers and Administrators, Greater Puget Sound Chapter
Contact: Carole Blowers, (800) 624-1234, Ext. 5580
Membership: about 75. Serves Pierce, Thurston, Kitsap and Grays Harbor counties. The newsletter is sent to nonmembers upon request.

Business and Professional Women's Association
361-5048
BPW has approximately 18 chapters or "local associations" in the Puget Sound area. All working women are eligible for membership. The group's purpose is to further the advancement of women. Nonmembers are welcome at meetings. For information, call the BPW

number and ask to be referred to Milly Alspach.

Business Marketing Communications Association
217 Ninth N.
Seattle WA 98109
623-8632
Founded in 1989, this group for senior executives in marketing communications focuses on continuing education, with two morning seminars each quarter. Nonmembers are welcome, but business development is strictly prohibited and no job bank exists.

Cartoonists Northwest
P.O. Box 31122
Seattle WA 98103
Contact: Maureen Gibbs, 226-7623
If you're interested in cartooning or humorous illustration, whether as an amateur or professional, you're welcome at the meetings of this worldwide group. As many as 40 turn out for the meetings, which cover such topics as syndication, gag writing and children's books. The $20 dues pay for the monthly newsletter, which sometimes includes job openings. Nonmembers can receive three issues. The meeting fee is $1.

Child Care Resources
2915 E. Madison, #305
Seattle WA 98112
461-3708
Interested in child care? This agency, formerly Child and Family Resource and Referral, offers a job board and informal referrals to those with experience in early childhood education. If you'd like to teach in a child care center, you can apply for the center's Substitute Teacher Bank. For information, contact Debbie Lee at 461-3719. If you'd like to run a day care center, you can obtain technical assistance and training. And if you're job-hunting and need information on child care, use the information and referral lines.

Child Care Directors Association of Greater Seattle
Contact: Lynn Wirta, 782-2611
About 80 staff members of child care centers belong to this group. Nonmembers are welcome. Openings are announced at meetings and resumes are circulated by the president.

Coalition of Labor Union Women, Puget Sound Chapter
133 Queen Anne Ave. N.
Seattle WA 98109
Contact: Patricia Agostino, 441-7816

Part of a national that promotes unionism, this group of 100 men and women includes business agents and representatives, the people who negotiate contracts, as well as those who work in industries that are organized. Openings are announced at meetings.

Commercial and Investment Brokers Association
414 Pontius N., #A
Seattle WA 98109
621-7603
If you're an experienced commercial real estate broker, you'll benefit from the educational programs and networking provided by this group of 850. If you're considering commercial real estate as a career, plan to attend the "Commercial Connections" conference held every spring. The workshops always include an orientation to commercial real estate and information on how to get started in the field.

Commercial Real Estate Brokers' Association
Contact: T.J. Woosley, 455-5730 or Scott Evans, 454-8211
Exploring commercial real estate as a career? This Eastside organization includes about 70 representatives of smaller commercial brokerages who gather regularly for morning networking sessions. Perhaps best described as a "leads" group, the association's members are happy to help you evaluate commercial real estate as a career option...but you're unlikely to hear of job opportunities.

Commercial Real Estate Women Northwest
2217 Ninth Ave. N.
Seattle WA 98109
623-8632
An affiliate of the National Network of Commercial Real Estate Women, this chapter serves more than 125 members between Everett and Tacoma. Full membership requires two and one-half years professional experience in commercial real estate and full-time employment. Nonmembers are welcome at luncheons.

Computer and Automated Systems Association, Society of Manufacturing Engineers
P.O. Box 7372-P
Seattle WA 98133
Contact: Rich Murrish, 742-8113
Now meeting jointing with Robotics International, this chapter has about 130 members. Many programs are tours of manufacturing facilities, so members can see computer-aided design and manufacturing operations. There's a jobs bulletin available from the Society of Manufacturing Engineers' western regional office.

**Construction Financial Management Association,
Puget Sound Chapter**
Contact: Rick Bellin, 392-1231
If you work in financial management for a builder or developer, you may be interested in this group. Part of a national organization chartered in 1981, this chapter includes more than 130. Most members are financial executives in the construction industry—for example, controllers, treasurers and vice presidents of finance. Nonmembers are welcome. The directory and newsletter are distributed to members.

**Construction Management Association of America,
Pacific Northwest Chapter**
11911 N.E. 1st, #308
Bellevue WA 98005
646-8000
This new chapter of a national organization had about 50 members at press time. Members include project managers and others who work at the management level in commercial, industrial and residential construction. Nonmembers are welcome at the monthly meetings.

Construction Specifications Institute, Puget Sound Chapter
610 Lloyd Building
Seattle WA 98101
382-3393
This affiliate of the national group for architects and specifications writers has approximately 400 members. There are monthly meetings and a newsletter. Nonmembers are welcome.

Construction Specifications Institute, Mount Rainier Chapter
Contact: Dennis Rousey, 922-9299
Founded to serve CSI members in Tacoma, Gig Harbor, Olympia and Federal Way, this group now has about 65 members. The newsletter is sent to prospective members upon request.

Consulting Engineers Council of Washington
1809 Seventh Ave., #508
Seattle WA 98101
623-5936
Submit a copy of your resume (indicate discipline) and the council will file it for three months for review by member firms that have openings. You can also purchase a copy of the council directory (membership is more than 140) for about $10. The newsletter is sent only to members.

Credit Professionals International

If you work in credit, you may be interested in this organization. The 15 chapters in western Washington include collection agencies, credit bureaus and representatives of retailers, banks, credit unions and real estate firms. Any firm with a credit or collections department is eligible for membership. The president of the 55-chapter district has initiated "Positions Wanted" and "Positions Available" in her newsletter, distributed through club presidents. Nonmembers are welcome at meetings.

Credit Professionals International, Seattle
Contact: Delores Stearns, 684-6319
Membership: 30.

Credit Professionals International, Bellevue
Contact: Dawn Llorente, 454-1909
Membership: 20.

Credit Professionals International, North Suburbia
Contact: Kathy McKee, 486-9523
A small chapter serving north King and south Snohomish counties.

Credit Professionals International, South King County
Contact: Lila Cronyn, 588-1858
A small chapter serving Kent, Renton and Auburn.

Credit Professionals International, Everett
Contact: Tina Cochran, 259-5563
Membership: about 16.

Credit Professionals International, Bremerton-Kitsap
Contact: Mary Lou Addy, 377-1100
Membership: 30.

Credit Professionals International, Tacoma
Contact: Carol Owens, 367-4498
Membership: about 35.

Credit Professionals International, Thurston County
Contact: Patt Ekendal, 581-8180
Membership: about 16.

Data Processing Management Association, Puget Sound Chapter
P.O. Box 249
Seattle WA 98111
587-3762

If you work in or with data processing, you're welcome at meetings of this group. There's a variety of positions represented in the membership, from those who run a single PC in a small office to MIS directors. Managers who have taken new responsibilities for data processing—but have no data processing background—will find the meetings helpful.

Data Processing Management Association,
Mount Rainier Chapter
Contact: Tedd Christ, 591-2054
Membership: about 35. Serves Kitsap, Pierce and Thurston counties.

Data Processing Management Association, Evergreen Chapter
Contact: Bill Burkett, 652-0424
Serves Lynnwood area.

Employee Assistance Professionals Association, Pacific
Northwest Chapter
217 Ninth N.
Seattle WA 98109
623-8632
If you work with employee problems (for example, chemical dependencies, mental health, career transitions or financial difficulties), you're welcome at EAP meetings.

The Engineers Club
217 Ninth N.
Seattle WA 98109
623-8632
Engineers of any discipline—including electrical, civil, structural, mining and marine—are welcome at the weekly meetings of this group.

Estate Planning Council of Seattle
Contact: Marjorie Pedersen, Administrative Secretary
3215 N.E. 98th St.
Seattle WA 98115
522-2830
If you work in estate planning, you may be interested in this group, which includes attorneys, CPAs, chartered life underwriters, bank trust officers and planned giving directors. Nonmembers can attend as guests of members. Although there is a national estate planning council, this organization is not affiliated with it or the other Puget Sound councils.

Eastside Estate Planning Council
Contact: Phil Egger, 462-4700
Membership: 115 members.

Snohomish Estate Planning Council
Contact: Mike Doyle, 338-0884
Membership: 60.

Southwest Washington Estate Planning Council
Contact: Al Werner, 352-5774
Membership: about 50. Serves Olympia area.

Estate Planning Council of Tacoma
Contact: Brian Foley, First Interstate Bank, 593-5619
Membership: 100.

Fashion Group of Seattle
314 Lloyd Building
Seattle WA 98101
Hotline: 624-3136
The regional affiliate of an international, Fashion Group is open to
women with at least three years executive experience in retail,
wholesale, apparel design, manufacturing and interior design. This
chapter has about 120 members, with meetings attracting between 30
and 40. Nonmembers are welcome at the meetings, where job
openings are occasionally announced.

Financial Managers Society, Puget Sound Chapter
Contact: Jean Van Court, EDS, 641-4463
Part of a national that was once affiliated with the Savings and Loan
League, this association today draws many of its members from
banks, especially thrifts. Many members serve as controllers or in
other financial management positions; affiliate members include
CPAs and representatives of servicing organizations. Nonmembers
are welcome.

Financial Women International, Seattle Metropolitan Group
Contact: Charlotte Bachman
Federal Reserve Bank
P.O. Box 3567
Seattle WA 98124
343-3706
Formerly the National Association of Bank Women, this group of 65
focuses on education for those in middle and upper management.
Members include chief financial officers, business development

officers, attorneys specializing in business law and related vendors. There are quarterly newsletters from the national and local for members; the national also provides a job bank and guidebooks on resumes.

Focus

509 10th Ave. E.
Seattle WA 98102
329-7918

Job-sharing, flex-time and part-time work is the emphasis of this group, founded in 1974. Monthly workshops are held on resumes and interviewing techniques; members ($10 per month or $30 per year) attend free, nonmembers pay nominal fees.

Forty Plus of Puget Sound

300 120th Ave. N.E., Bldg. 7, #200
Bellevue WA 98005
450-0040

Like Focus, this is a group organized to help job-seekers. Forty Plus of Puget Sound is part of a national oriented to those who are 40 or older. To be eligible for membership, you should have made at least $35,000 and be professional, managerial, executive or administrative in your job level. There are initiation fees, monthly dues and a volunteer commitment. Services include a class using the national Forty Plus curriculum on marketing yourself. Members can use offices equipped with computers, telephones, fax and copy machines, and an answering service. Free orientation sessions.

French-American Chamber of Commerce, Seattle Chapter

400 E. Pine
Seattle WA 98122
860-4915

Organized in the 1980s, this group facilitates trade and development between France and the U.S. If you're interested in international business, attend the luncheons or social events that encourage networking. Nonmembers can attend two luncheons prior to joining. The chamber also offers members a monthly newsletter and a resource library. Membership is about 100.

Home Care Association of Washington

P.O. Box C-2016
Edmonds WA 98020-0999
775-8120

Education for professionals in home health care (including the managers of hospice and rehabilitation organizations) is one of the purposes of this group. The newsletter is available by subscription for nonmembers.

Home Economists in Business
Contact: Susan Maza
3342 56th Ave. S. W.
Seattle WA 98116
Affiliated with the American Home Economics Association, which has a national jobline for members, this group serves about 70 home economists who work in business. Full membership requires a bachelor's degree in home economics and employment in the field. Nonmembers are welcome at meetings. For members, there's a jobs committee chairperson who receives notices of job openings.

Institute of Business Designers
1808 8th Ave.
Seattle WA 98101
622-2015
This group for commercial interior designers serves more than 200 in western Washington. Nonmembers are welcome at the meetings and can receive mailings. The newsletter occasionally lists job openings and people seeking positions.

Institute of Environmental Science, Northwest Chapter
Contact: Ken Beleu
2815 106th Pl. S.E.
Bellevue WA 98004
773-5494
The only chapter in Washington state, this group has about 90 members. Most are involved with tests and measurements of con-taminates. Many are engineers and "techs," those with associate degrees in related fields; several work for Boeing. Others are chemists, physicists, vendors and students—even high school stu-dents. Open to nonmembers.

Institute of Industrial Engineers, Puget Sound Chapter 20
P.O. Box 55475
Seattle WA 98155
Most of this group's 350 members have degrees in industrial engi-neering, but that's not a requirement. Nonmembers are welcome. The newsletter lists the job bank number, available to members and nonmembers alike. Contact Robin Stebbins, 822-6700.

Institute of Management Accountants

Established as an organization for cost accountants, this group now serves management accountants. Most members come from industry rather than public accounting firms. Membership criteria includes a B.A. in accounting or a related field; a C.P.A. is not required.

Institute of Management Accountants, Seattle Chapter

Contact: Wayne Hays, 224-2122 or Beth Reiman, 345-4503
Membership: 400 members. Nonmembers are welcome. There's an informal job referral service available to both members and nonmembers. Newsletters can be picked up by nonmembers at meetings.

Institute of Management Accountants, Bellevue/Eastside Chapter

P.O. Box 93
Bellevue WA 98009
Membership: 200. A board member serves as an informal referral service for both job-seekers (members and nonmembers) and firms with openings. Contact Claudia Campbell, 246-7611.

Institute of Management Accountants, Mt. Rainier Chapter

Contact: Mary Minish, 924-7100 or Lois DeNatale, 924-4374
Membership: more than 350. Serves Federal Way south. Nonmembers are welcome to use the job referral service and to attend the meetings. There's a monthly newsletter for members.

Institute of Management Consultants, Inc., Pacific Northwest Chapter

Contact: Randy Benson, 527-5343
The certifying body for management consulting, this organization includes representatives of large consulting firms (for example, Deloitte + Touche) as well as sole practitioners. Dinner meetings are held quarterly; nonmembers are welcome.

Institute of Real Estate Management, Western Washington Chapter

Contact: Nancy LeMay, Executive Administrator, 462-0635
If you're interested in managing multi-family or commercial real estate, you can arrange to attend a meeting of this group, which includes about 200 representatives of large and small firms.

National Association of Insurance Women International

If you work in insurance—in almost any setting, in almost any function—you're welcome at meetings of this association, which has several chapters statewide. Functions are open to men as well as women.

Insurance Women's Association of Seattle
Contact: Chris Kelly Storbeck, 822-5722
Membership: 90. Nonmembers are welcome at meetings and can receive three complimentary issues of the newsletter. The employment chair discusses openings at meetings.

Insurance Women of Puget Sound
Contact: Marion Alber, 670-9418 or Darla Richards, 485-9552
Membership: nearly 50. Serves Snohomish County and north to the border. The newsletter is available to nonmembers for a nominal fee; both members and nonmembers benefit from the employment chair, who tracks "Positions Available" and "Positions Wanted."

Eastside Insurance Women
Contact: Donna Unger, 455-3933
Membership: about 25. Nonmembers can submit resumes to the employment chair.

Insurance Women of South King County
Contact: Janis Williamson, 852-1680
Membership: about 35. Serves Kent, Renton, Auburn and Federal Way.

Insurance Women of Kitsap County
Contact: Dagmar Boldt-Lacey, 871-4512
Membership: 19. The job bank occasionally has listings.

Insurance Women of Tacoma-Pierce County
Contact: Elaine Stewart, 565-5454
Membership: more than 45. The employment chair announces job openings at the meetings. A sample newsletter is available upon request.

Insurance Women of Thurston County
Contact: Terry Bushnell, 352-7691
Membership: 24. The newsletter is sent upon request to nonmembers, who are also welcome at the monthly meetings. The employment chair provides informal job search help.

International Association of Business Communicators,
Seattle Chapter
217 Ninth N.
Seattle WA 98109
623-8632
Public relations, corporate communications, advertising, marketing

and technical writing are among the functions represented in this 150-member chapter of an international. To join IABC, you must be employed in the field; others are eligible for a $25 per year limited membership. This allows you to access the jobline, a 24-hour taped listing of job openings operated with the Washington Press Association, the Seattle Advertising Federation and the local chapter of the Public Relations Society of America. Your limited membership also includes attendance at monthly job bank meetings, where speakers often make "career discovery" presentations, describing the variety of career paths possible in their industries and how to get started. Nonmembers are welcome at the meetings.

International Association of Business Communicators, Eastside Chapter
Hotline: 392-6915
Contact: Helvi Paterson, 544-1112
The 25 members of the new Eastside chapter meet bimonthly; nonmembers are welcome. The chapter cooperates in the jobline with IABC Seattle.

International Credit Association
An international with U.S. headquarters in St. Louis, this organization provides education for those who work in credit, including credit managers, credit counselors and sales reps for collection agencies and credit reporting bureaus.

Seattle-King County International Credit Association
Reservations: 483-0522
Membership: more than 100. Nonmembers are welcome. Projects include speaking to civic groups and students regarding the use of credit.

Pierce County International Credit Association
P.O. Box 977
Tacoma WA 98401
Contact: (Ms.) George Battle-Wilson, 589-5652
Membership: 130 firms. Nonmembers are welcome at meetings; the job bank is open to everyone.

International Television and Video Association, Seattle Chapter
217 Ninth N.
Seattle WA 98109
623-8632
ITVA has 235 members in Seattle. They include people who work in nonbroadcast television—managers, free-lancers, camera and make-

up people, producers, writers, directors and suppliers. The meetings focus on professional development, but there are opportunities for networking. Nonmembers can attend and the newsletter is available by subscription. There is a national job bank for members; at the local level, members use the Washington State Film and Video Office's hotline, 464-6074, which lists projects in the Puget Sound area that need staff.

Japan-America Society of the State of Washington
600 University, #2420
Seattle WA 98101-3163
623-7900

Interested in U.S.-Japan relations? Consider this group, an affiliate of the National Association of Japan-America Societies. It has 1,300 members, about a third of them Japanese nationals. At least three programs are held each month: one usually focuses on public affairs (for example, a presentation by a Japanese politician), another on cultural affairs and a third on education. In addition, the "5:31 Club" meets for informal networking.

King County Nurses Association
9500 Roosevelt Way N.E., #301
Seattle WA 98115
523-0997

An affiliate of the Washington State Nurses Association, this group of 1,900 registered nurses has no job bank. However, openings are posted in the office and announced at special interest group (SIG) meetings. Nonmembers are welcome at the SIG meetings, which are organized by such functions as staff development nurses, gerontologists and nurse practitioners. The association also offers a nurse legal consultant clearinghouse, referring nurses to attorneys who need medical advice. Two newsletters are issued: one by the general group and one by the nurse practitioner SIG. Sample copies are available to nonmembers.

Lawyers in Transition
Founded by Deborah Arron, the author of *Running From the Law*, to help attorneys looking for jobs outside law and those seeking different positions within the profession, this program is now run by the Washington State Bar Association's Lawyers' Assistance Program. For current information, call Joyce Elvin, 727-8268. (Also see the Washington State Bar Association listing later in this chapter.)

Macintosh Downtown Business Users Group

P.O. Box 3463
Seattle WA 98114
Hotline: 624-9329
Nonmembers are welcome at the general meetings of this group, which has some 1,100 members from Everett to Tacoma. There are also more than 20 SIGs covering topics such as accounting, animation and desktop publishing. The computer bulletin board occasionally lists job openings.

Medical Marketing Association, Puget Sound Chapter

Contact: Kate Larsen, (800) 551-2173
This group of 50 was established in 1990. Members include those who work in the marketing of health care services and medical equipment as well as representatives of biotechnology and communications firms.

Meeting Planners International, Washington State Chapter

Contact: Lillian Sugahara, Greendale Associates
18008 110th Pl. S.E.
Renton WA 98055
226-9338
More than 180 belong to this organization, which was established to serve those who plan and manage conventions, trade shows, seminars, sales and other meetings. Nonmembers can attend two monthly breakfasts prior to joining and can also receive free copies of any job postings.

MIT Enterprise Forum

217 Ninth N.
Seattle WA 98109
623-8632
If you're interested in high technology, you're welcome to attend the meetings of this group. At each, presentations are made by start-up firms. Meetings typically attract 200 to 250. Subscriptions to the newsletter are available upon request.

National Academy of Television Arts and Sciences, Seattle Chapter

217 Ninth N.
Seattle WA 98109
623-8632
If you have experience in television, you're welcome to attend many of the meetings of this group, one of 17 NATAS chapters in the U.S. Membership is about 300. The newsletter is sent only to members.

National Association of Corporate Real Estate Executives, Northwest Chapter

Contact: Robert DeWald, Port of Tacoma
P.O. Box 1837
Tacoma WA 98401
383-9463

If you develop or manage commercial, industrial, retail or restaurant real estate, you may be interested in this group. The local chapter has more than 50 members. Nonmembers are welcome as guests of members. Members include developers, attorneys, architects, brokers and representatives of title insurance firms.

National Association of Credit Management, Western Washington and Alaska

2122 Third Ave.
Seattle WA 98121
728-6333

This group has some 1,420 members in the Northwest and Hawaii. It maintains a resume file (to which nonmembers can contribute) for review by members with job openings. For members, there are nearly 40 meetings each month organized by industry (for example, wholesaling and advertising media) and location. For a schedule, ask for the account executive who covers your geographic area.

National Society of Fund Raising Executives

2033 Sixth Ave., #804
Seattle WA 98121
441-6020

Nonmembers are welcome at this group, which attracts between 50 and 75 to most meetings. Most of those attending are development officers and executive directors of nonprofits.

National Association of Office Parks, Washington State Chapter

P.O. Box C-2016
Edmonds WA 98020-0999
382-9121

Nonmembers are welcome at this real estate group, which has more than 200 corporate members. The quarterly newsletter goes only to members, but the directory can be purchased.

National Association of Professional Organizers

Contact: Ellen Langen, 284-1482

Chartered in late 1990, this affiliate has about 10 members. Although most local members are self-employed, all hire assistants on a contract basis. If you're considering moving into professional organizing, this group also gives you the opportunity to talk with experts.

National Association of Social Workers,
Washington State Chapter
2366 Eastlake Ave. E.
Seattle WA 948102
325-9791
If you have a B.S.W. or M.S.W., you may find job openings posted at
the state office or published in the newsletter. The 2,400 members
statewide are divided into seven geographic units, some of which
meet monthly.

National Association of Women in Construction
Women employed in construction—from pipelayer and secretary to
company owner and controller—are eligible for membership in this
group, formed more than 50 years ago. Its members across the country
include women who work in construction-related fields; for example,
architects, engineers, attorneys and insurance brokers. The national
has just initiated a jobs bulletin. Chapters in the Puget Sound area
include:

National Association of Women in Construction, Seattle Chapter
P.O. Box C-81435
Seattle WA 98108
Contact: Tricia Manning, 762-4211
Membership: about 50. Established 30 years ago. The occupational
research and referral chair receives job announcements from employ-
ers and provides referrals to job-seeking members and others in the
industry.

National Association of Women in Construction,
Greater Bellevue Chapter
Contact: Rita Morris, 836-0373
Membership: fewer than 25.

National Association of Women in Construction,
Greater Everett Chapter
Contact: Diane Ferguson, Group Four, Inc., 775-4581
Membership: about 25. Has an occupational research and referral
chair.

National Association of Women in Construction,
Tacoma Chapter
Contact: Donna Jones
3508 Pacific Highway E.
Tacoma WA 98424
922-1990

Membership: about 30. Has an occupational research and referral chair.

National Investor Relations Institute, Seattle Chapter

Contact: Joe LePla, Floathe Johnson Associates, 822-8400

If you work in investor relations, including finance or communications, you're welcome at this group. There are about 35 members, many from newly public companies. An informal job referral service exists through the national for members. Some local members also offer information interviews and referrals.

National Lawyers Guild, Seattle Chapter

2005 Smith Tower
Seattle WA 98104
622-5144

Law students and paralegals interested in public interest law can apply for internships through the guild's "Summer Project." Positions are available in locations across the U.S. Applications are available in December and due Feb. 1; write Sandra Kurjiaka, Project director.

Netherlands Business Organization

Contact: Mark Roeland, 643-2673

This local organization includes both Dutch natives in business in the Northwest and Washingtonians in business in the Netherlands and other countries. If you're interested in work in the ports or in export-import, you're welcome at meetings. Speakers include ambassadors and members of foreign trade councils.

Network of Editors and Writers

Contact: Donna Mirkes, 543-3660 or Rebecca Deardorff, 543-9199

This group of 100 is open to University of Washington employees and free-lancers doing work for the UW. Members include writers and editors. Because programs often focus on concerns specific to UW employees, meetings may provide valuable background for someone considering the university as an employer. Although job openings are sometimes announced at meetings, remember that all permanent UW positions are filled through the campus personnel office.

Nonprofit Direct Marketing Association

Contact: Susan Howlett, 545-8509

An affiliate of the National Development Officers Association, this group of 120 meets monthly to consider the challenges of raising funds with direct mail. Meetings are free and open to guests.

Northwest Area Music Association
611 E. Howell
Seattle WA 98122
322-5045
This local organization represents the greater Seattle music business: musicians, record-label owners, concert promoters, agents, attorneys and the media. As well as annual meetings, the group of 450 organizes several awards programs and conferences. Working on these projects is an excellent way to get experience in the industry and make contacts.

Northwest Development Officers Association
2033 Sixth Ave., #804
Seattle WA 98121
441-6020
People at all levels in nonprofits—from volunteers and board members to executive directors—attend the meetings of this local organization. Nonmembers are welcome at the meetings, which attract as many as 140, and can also receive a three-month subscription to the job bulletin.

Northwest Ethics Institute
Contact: Ray Cole, 623-1572
Organized about five years ago, this local group offers monthly programs on such topics as government, the environment and business and medical ethics. The 100 members include educators, attorneys and accountants as well as those who work in business and health care. There is no job bank and the group does not focus on jobs in any particular industry. Nonmembers can request copies of the newsletter.

Northwest Florists' Association
P.O. Box C-2016
Edmonds WA 98020-0999
778-6162
Retail and wholesale florists and nursery owners from five western states and two provinces are represented in this group, which holds an annual convention and issues a quarterly magazine. The chapter office can advise you on networking opportunities.

Pacific Northwest Association of Church Librarians
P.O. Box 12379
Seattle WA 98111
Contact: 365-4131
If you work in a church or religious school's library, whether on a

volunteer or paid basis, you're welcome at meetings of this group, which has more than 100 members in Washington, Oregon and Idaho.

Pacific Northwest Historians Guild
Contact: Dan Peterson, 587-2916
Historians, archivists and librarians are among the 100 members of this group. Speakers occasionally address job opportunities in the field; informal networking is also encouraged. Nonmembers are welcome.

Pacific Northwest Library Association
Jobline: 543-2890
This regional group's jobline at the University of Washington Graduate School of Library and Information Science lists opportunities for professionals and paraprofessionals in public, academic and corporate libraries in the western U.S. and Canada.

Pacific Northwest Newspaper Association
P.O. Box 11128
Tacoma WA 98411
272-3611
This trade association represents 60 daily papers in six western states. Its bulletins to publishers include free extracts of resumes from those seeking jobs or internships. Simply send your resume to the association and its staff will summarize your qualifications and objective.

Pacific Northwest PC Users Group
P.O. Box 3363
Bellevue WA 98004
728-7075
Some 1,000—from Everett to Tacoma—belong to this group. Nonmembers are welcome. There are also 30 SIGs, most of which meet at least monthly. You'll find both "Positions Wanted" and "Positions Available" on the club's electronic bulletin board; "Positions Available" are also mentioned in the club newsletter.

Pacific Northwest Personnel Management Association, Seattle Chapter
3247 20th W.
Seattle WA 98199-2301
283-0395
Part of the national Society for Human Resource Management, this group includes attorneys and consultants as well as those who work in recruiting, organizational development and corporate personnel in

general. There's a job bank and newsletter for members. There are other chapters in south King County, Olympia and on the Eastside.

Planning Forum

This group of 80 is affiliated with the International Society for Strategic Management and Planning. Members include consultants and managers with primary responsibility for strategic planning. Topics for the meetings range from environmental risk management to new product development. Nonmembers are welcome. Contact David Hunter, Children's Hospital, 526-2002.

Professional Geographers of Puget Sound

401 E. Mercer, #22
Seattle WA 98102
Established about two years, this local organization serves geographers from Everett to Olympia who work in government (about half of the membership), research, consulting and such related fields as banking. Although you don't need a geography degree to join, most members have studied the field either as undergraduates or graduate students. The quarterly newsletter has a jobs column where current openings are posted. The association also offers a resume service, allowing members to have their resumes inserted with newsletters. Nonmembers can receive one complimentary copy. Dues are $12. Call Eric Friedli, 684-8369 or Carlyn Orians, newsletter editor, 528-3320.

Professional Secretaries International, Seattle
Sacajawea Chapter

Contact: Doris Heistuman-Box, 764-5371
If you work as a secretary or in a similar support role, you're welcome at PSI, which provides education and networking for those making careers as secretaries. The downtown Seattle chapter, which has about 70 members, includes men and women. Services include a job bank.

Professional Secretaries International, Lake Washington
East Chapter

23326 75th Ave. S.E.
Woodinville WA 98072
Membership: 80 members. There is an informal job bank. Call Annette Tomkins, 940-6413.

Professional Secretaries International, Mount Rainier Chapter
Contact: Ann Piraino
7022 190th St. Ct. E.
Puyallup WA 98373-1892
846-0231
Membership: 35. Also sponsors student chapters. Information about job openings is published in the newsletter and announced at meetings.

Professional Secretaries International, Washington Evergreen Chapter
Contact: Lorna Rubenaker, 237-8600
Membership: 30, many of them Boeing employees. There's an informal job referral service.

Project Management Institute, Puget Sound Chapter
Contact: Fred Ostman, Group Health
521 Wall St., Mailstop ACC1, Facilities
Seattle WA 98121
448-4994
Project managers in pharmaceuticals, aerospace, health care and construction are among the 200 members. Organized about 10 years ago, this chapter serves project managers from Bellingham to Olympia. The newsletter lists both "Positions Available" and "Positions Wanted."

Propeller Club of the United States, Port of Seattle Chapter
217 Ninth N.
Seattle WA 98109
623-8632
This chapter of an international for the maritime industry has about 350 members. The meetings attract everyone from accountants and insurance underwriters to those who manufacture nuts and bolts for ships. The group sponsors Seattle's annual Maritime Week festivities each May. Nonmembers are welcome.

Public Relations Society of America
217 Ninth N.
Seattle WA 98109
623-8632
The Puget Sound chapter has more than 350 members. To join, you must be employed in a professional position in the public relations field. However, nonmembers are welcome at the luncheons and at professional development workshops. The day-long "PR Primer" is especially appropriate for people at the entry level. For a $25 fee,

nonmembers can use the jobline cosponsored by the IABC chapters, the Seattle Advertising Federation and the Washington Press Association.

Puget Sound Career Development Association
1750 112th Ave. N.E., #C-224
Bellevue WA 98004
Started in the 1980s, this local group of about 100 includes career counselors, job placement specialists and those who work in vocational rehabilitation. Many members are self-employed; others work in Ys, social service agencies and in educational placement centers. There are no eligibility requirements. The meetings attract about 40. A newsletter is published regularly. Dues are $20. Contact Larry Gaffin, 325-9093.

Puget Sound Engineering Council
Composed of representatives from 14 engineering and mathematics societies, this group organizes events like the annual Engineering Fair to promote engineering and math to schoolchildren. It's also active in legislative affairs. Of particular interest to job-seekers is the council's newsletter, "Puget Sound Engineering," which announces the activities of many engineering societies and occasionally runs a "Position Available" ad. This publication is available by subscription for $12 a year: write P.O. Box 7372-P, Seattle WA 98133.

Puget Sound Radio Broadcasters Association
Contact: David Ellenhorn
1601 Fifth Ave., #2100
Seattle WA 98101
447-7000
This local organization includes 30 Puget Sound area radio stations, representing more than 300 radio industry professionals. Nonmembers are welcome at meetings. The newsletter and directory are distributed to members.

Puget Sound Research Forum
P.O. Box 12796
Seattle WA 98111
Contact: Rob Coughlin, Gilmore Research, 726-5555
Started by market researchers, this group now represents both the public and private sectors. Membership: about 150. Besides education, its purpose is networking. At each meeting, those attending can introduce themselves. There's also a job bank for members and nonmembers. Student memberships are $12.50 and full memberships $25.

Robotics International, Society of Manufacturing Engineers
Contact: Mary Lynch
P.O. Box 872
Issaquah WA 98027
391-5379
This group, which has more than 40 members, recently began joint meetings with CASA. Members include engineers and engineering managers, manufacturing supervisors and designers; employers represented include the underwater warfare station at Keyport, Hanford, Boeing and PACCAR. Nonmembers and students are welcome.

Sales and Marketing Executives
2033 Sixth Ave., #804
Seattle WA 98121
441-6020
The local affiliate of an international, SME is open to everyone with a supervisory position in sales or marketing. A three-month trial subscription to the newsletter is sent free to nonmembers who meet membership eligibility requirements.

Seattle Advertising Federation
2033 Sixth Ave., #804
Seattle WA 98121
448-4481
The Seattle chapter of the American Advertising Federation offers seminars, a monthly newsletter and regular meetings. Nonmembers can receive one complimentary newsletter issue. Ad 2, the affiliate organization for those younger than 31, sponsors a job bank for members and nonmembers.

Tacoma Ad Club
Contact: Nancy Knutsen, 572-6042
The Tacoma chapter, which also draws from Olympia and Bremerton, has about 115 members. Nonmembers can receive the newsletter and attend the monthly luncheons. There's a job bank for members.

Seattle Art Directors & Copywriters Club
Contact: Dory Toft, Livingston & Co., 382-5500
This informal group, which exists primarily to bring advertising industry leaders to Seattle to speak, has in the past attracted as many as 200 to its presentations. At press time the group was inactive; if you're interested in helping revitalize it (and, in doing so, networking in the advertising community), contact Ms. Toft.

Seattle Association of Women Economists
Contact: Suzanne Shwetz
8911 Ravenna Ave. N.E.
Seattle WA 98115
464-2339
If you're interested in economics, you're welcome at the meetings of this locally-chartered group, which has about 40 members. Job openings are announced at meetings and in the monthly newsletter. The newsletter and directory are sent only to members; annual dues are $10.

Seattle Club of Printing House Craftsmen
Contact: Bayless Bindery
501 S.W. 7th
Renton WA 98055
226-6395
If you'd like to work in printing or for a printing supplier, you can network through this group. Affiliated with an international organization, it has 200 members in the Seattle area. Nonmembers are welcome.

Seattle Design Association
P.O. Box 1097 Main Branch
Seattle WA 98111
328-2725
Graphic designers, illustrators, photographers, copywriters, printers, production managers, architects, interior designers and fine artists are welcome to join this group of 200. Newsletters are sent to members.

Seattle Direct Marketing Association
217 Ninth N.
Seattle WA 98109
623-8632
Direct response marketing and telemarketing are the focus of this group of 125, which meets monthly and conducts an annual seminar. Meetings are announced in *Marketing*. There's also a monthly newsletter.

Seattle Economists Club
467-8404
Economists from business, utilities and government join economic consultants and academics in this group, which has about 150 members. Nonmembers are welcome at meetings. Members can have their resumes inserted with the monthly meeting notices. Openings are occasionally announced at meetings. Dues: $20.

Seattle Mortgage Bankers Association
1425 Fourth Ave., #914
Seattle WA 98101
622-8425
A chapter of the National Mortgage Bankers Association of America, SMBA has about 100 corporate members. Participants include underwriters, loan processors and loan officers as well as people who work in secondary marketing and income properties.

Seattle Retail Financial Executives
Contact: Kristy Gibson, Ernst & Young, 621-1800
Affiliated with the National Retail Federation, this group includes people who work for retailers in such functions as personnel, finance and internal audit. There are also several representatives of public accounting firms who have retail clients. The meetings usually attract about 45.

Seattle Storytellers' Guild
P.O. Box 45532
Seattle WA 98145-0532
Professional and amateur storytellers as well as those interested in the art are among the 400-plus members of this locally chartered group, which draws most of its membership from King, Snohomish and Pierce counties. If you'd like to promote yourself as a storyteller, the group also compiles a directory for distribution to schools and libraries. Open to nonmembers. Dues are about $15. Call Naomi Baltuck, 621-8646.

School Health Association of Washington
22323 Pacific Highway S.
Seattle WA 98198
An affiliate of the American School Health Association, this chapter has about 350 members statewide. Members include school health educators, nurses and counselors as well as representatives of nonprofits and social service agencies. Two conferences are held each year; nonmembers are welcome and there's ample opportunity to network. A newsletter, in which job openings may be announced, is published bimonthly. Dues are $15. Call Karen Dalton, executive director, 824-2907.

Society for Intercultural Education, Training and Research, Pacific Northwest Chapter
217 Ninth N.
Seattle WA 98109
623-8632

As many as 70 attend the bimonthly meetings of this new chapter, which is open to anyone with an interest in the Pacific Rim. Many of the founding members were teachers of English As A Second Language. The SIETAR newsletter is available to nonmembers by subscription.

Society for Marketing Professional Services, Seattle Chapter
Contact: Katherine Hitchcock, David Evans & Associates, Inc.
415 118th Ave. S.E.
Bellevue WA 98005
455-3571
If you'd like to market professional services, especially for architectural, engineering or interior design firms, attend the meetings of this group. The only SMPS chapter in Washington, it includes nearly 200.

Society for Public Health Education, Pacific Northwest Chapter
P.O. Box 24973
Seattle WA 98124-0973
One of 20 U.S. chapters, this group welcomes you to its meetings if you're pursuing or have received a degree in health education or a related field (for example, nursing or dietetics), or if you work in health education or promotion. The 120 members work in hospitals, nonprofits, corporations and universities. Dues are $20. Members of the local chapter can use the jobline for an additional $10 fee per year; the job bank has typically averaged 125 openings annually. The fee includes a copy of the 75-page "Employment Resources Guide for Health Educators in the Pacific Northwest." Job search workshops are offered occasionally; they are free and open to nonmembers. Call Penny O'Leary, 236-1242.

Society for Technical Communications, Puget Sound Chapter
217 Ninth N.
Seattle WA 98109
623-8632
If you work in technical communications—writing, editing, graphic design or illustration—you can ask that your resume be included in the STC chapter's resume book, which is available for review by firms with openings. Or, for $25, you can access the STC jobline. There's also an electronic bulletin board with job postings. One reminder: most jobs in technical communications require some computer knowledge and a background in at least one technical field (for example, computer science, engineering or medicine). Nonmembers can receive a complimentary three-month subscription to the newsletter. You're also welcome at the monthly meetings. Chapter membership: about 500.

Society of Architectural Administrators
Contact: Linda Benny, NBBJ
111 S. Jackson
Seattle WA 98104
223-5555

If you're interested in working in the design profession in a support role, consider this group. The largest SAA chapter in the U.S., it has about 60 members representing architectural, engineering, interior design and cost estimating firms in western Washington. Nonmembers are welcome at the dinner meetings. There's also a jobline; the nonmember cost per month is $10. Call Ms. Benny, the 1992-93 president, or Sandy Tobkin, Zimmer Gunsul Frasca, 623-9414, who handles the jobline.

Society of Chartered Property Casualty Underwriters, Pacific Northwest Chapter
Contact: Harvey Bush, 525-9032

Insurance brokers, claims adjustors and representatives of insurance companies are examples of those who belong to this group, which is only for those who have passed property casualty underwriting certification exams and earned the CPCU designation.

Society of Industrial and Office Realtors, Washington State Chapter
Contact: Terry Wirth, 454-4545

About 30 belong to this group for commercial real estate. The organization, which has experience and sales volume eligibility requirements, provides continuing education and a college scholarship. Nonmembers are welcome at monthly meetings as guests of members.

Society of Plastic Engineers, Pacific Northwest Chapter
P.O. Box 88929
Seattle WA 98188

About 500 in western Washington belong to this group, which welcomes nonmembers. Most members work in manufacturing; some hold jobs in distribution or design. About half are engineers.

Society of Professional Journalists, Western Washington Chapter
217 Ninth N.
Seattle WA 98109
623-8632

Nonmembers are welcome at meetings of this chapter of 200. The only job bank is through the national office in Chicago. The newsletter and directory are distributed to members.

Society of Women Engineers, Pacific Northwest Section
P.O. Box 31910
Seattle WA 98103
Contact: Sandra Schaffer, 644-4010
Such educational programs as "Math Counts" and "Expanding Your Horizons" are two projects of this organization, which serves 145 women who work in engineering. All engineering disciplines are represented in the group, which also offers a speakers bureau for elementary through high school classes. For those making job changes, there's a job bank.

Structural Engineers Association of Washington
P.O. Box 4250
Seattle WA 98104
682-6026
Providing education and promoting the engineering profession are two of the missions of this organization, which has 650 members and three chapters in the state. In the Puget Sound area, the Seattle chapter serves King County and north; the Southwest chapter serves Tacoma and south. Most members are in private practice. Nonmembers can attend the monthly meetings. They can also subscribe to the newsletter, which occasionally lists positions.

Tax Executives Institute, Seattle Chapter
Contact: Wayne Lundberg, Univar, 889-3686
About 60 belong to this organization, part of a national of in-house tax directors. To join, you must meet certain experience and responsibility requirements and be sponsored by a current member. Individual practitioners (attorneys, accountants and financial consultants) are not eligible. You can attend a meeting as a guest of a member. The president accepts resumes and routes them to interested companies.

Washington Association for the Education of Young Children
841 N. Central Ave., #126
Kent WA 98032
854-2565
Part of the National Association for the Education of Young Children, this group provides support for those who educate and care for children from birth to age 8. Members include day care providers and directors and those who teach in preschools and elementary schools. There are 18 "affiliates" or chapters in the state; they range in size

from 175 to 300 members. For information on your affiliate, call the state office. It organizes an annual conference and publishes a monthly newsletter which occasionally lists openings.

Washington Association for Financial Planning
217 Ninth N.
Seattle WA 98109
623-8632
This group emphasizes education for financial planners. Instead of monthly meetings, the group offers four symposiums each year; nonmembers are welcome. Membership: about 200.

Washington Association of Health Underwriters
If you work in insurance, especially in individual or group health insurance or disability, you'll find this association of interest. It has three chapters in the Puget Sound area.

King County Health Underwriters
Contact: Sandra Hartman, 454-9870
Membership: about 250. You must be a member to use the job bank and receive the newsletter.

Southwest Washington Association of Health Underwriters
P.O. Box 196
Tacoma WA 98401-0196
Contact: Nancy Giacolone, 272-2228.
Membership: about 85. Serves those south of King County.

Northwest Washington Association of Health Underwriters
Contact: Terry Beebe, Harmon & Associates
P.O. Box 1179
Stanwood WA 98292
629-4536
Membership: 35. Serves those who work north of King County.

Washington Association of Landscape Professionals
P.O. Box 729
Mercer Island WA 98040
236-1707
Informal referrals are offered by this group, which includes about 100 landscape contractors, designers and suppliers. Nonmembers are welcome. The magazine is available to nonmembers, too.

Washington Association of Marriage and Family Therapy
217 Ninth N.
Seattle WA 98109
623-1820
Education is the primary goal of this group, which has 450 members. Most are self-employed, although a few work for institutes. A chapter of the American Association of Marriage and Family Therapy, the organization offers a newsletter and networking luncheons.

Washington Association of Personnel Services
P.O. Box 129
Bellevue WA 98009
If you work in personnel placement, either permanent or temporary, or as an executive recruiter, you may be interested in this affiliate of the National Association of Personnel Services. For more information about membership, call C.C. Salzberg, 453-5767; for general information, check with Sue Lundin, 583-2711.

Washington Community College Mathematics Conference
An event, rather than a group, this conference has been held annually since the 1960s. There are no officers and no mailing address; the community college math departments rotate the responsibility for organizing the meeting. It's an excellent place to network with college math teachers and learn of job openings. There are no eligibility requirements. For information, contact your community college math department.

Washington Council on International Trade
2515 Fourth Ave.
Seattle WA 98121
443-3826
If you work with international trade policies (perhaps as an executive in governmental affairs or international sales and marketing), you may be interested in this group, which has about 200 corporate members and about the same number of individual members, including students and academics.

Washington Film and Video Association
217 Ninth N.
Seattle WA 98109
623-8632
A locally-chartered organization of 200, this group serves free-lancers in film and video production. Nonmembers are welcome; the directory is distributed only to members. The bimonthly newsletter is available upon request. There's no job bank; the group uses the state hotline, 464-6074.

Washington Home Economics Association
Contact: Diane Grossenbacher
6911 189th Pl. S. W.
Lynnwood WA 98036
778-7147
Affiliated with the American Home Economics Association, this group has 420 members. They include cooperative extension agents, teachers, fabric store owners and day care center operators as well as people who work in commodity commissions, communications and other businesses. Active membership requires a degree in home economics and employment in the field; other membership categories are open to students, graduates of other college programs, graduates of associate programs and home ec graduates who work part-time.

King County Home Economics Association
Contact: Chrish Lind, 448-4473
The 44 members of this chapter have four meetings a year; "Positions Available" are announced and members seeking work can describe the positions they'd like. Nonmembers may attend one meeting.

Puget Sound Home Economics Association
Contact: Gail Cowan, 589-7830 or 876-9139
This chapter has about 30 members who meet five times a year.

Washington Legal Assistants Association
2033 Sixth Ave., #804
Seattle WA 98121
441-6020
If you're interested in working as a paralegal (also called a legal assistant), you're welcome to join this group. Statewide, there are four chapters: Seattle, Tacoma, Spokane and Yakima. For information on chapter meetings in your area, ask the state office to forward your message to the appropriate local contact. Members can access a jobline and they receive a newsletter.

Washington Museum Association
Contact: Ellen Ferguson, 543-5115
The 250 members of this group include volunteers and representatives of both small and large museums across the state. You must be a member (dues are $20) to attend the two annual functions. A resource available from the WMA is its "Directory of Museums of Washington State," with more than 400 entries; the cost is $13.95 to nonmembers.

Washington Newspaper Publishers Association
3838 Stone Way N.
Seattle WA 98103
634-3838
Want to work on a newspaper? WNPA, which represents 136 community newspapers (most of them weeklies), includes brief summaries of resumes from job-seekers in its newsletter, which is issued to newspaper publishers every two weeks. To have your qualifications and career objective listed, contact WNPA for its resume form. There's no charge.

Washington Organization of Nurse Executives
190 Queen Anne Ave. N., Third Floor
Seattle WA 98109
285-0102
This statewide group of 400 serves nurses who are executives, managers and other administrators in hospitals, long-term care facilities, public health, universities and risk management. For specifics on the council serving your area, call Karen Herrik. Nonmembers are welcome at most programs. The office staff provides an informal job referral service.

Washington Press Association
217 Ninth N.
Seattle WA 98109
623-8632
A statewide group with about 150 members, WPA primarily serves writers: journalists, publicists and free-lancers. It participates with the IABC chapters, the Seattle Ad Club and PRSA to produce a jobline, open to nonmembers for $25. The jobline fee also entitles you to attend the monthly job bank meetings.

Washington Society of Association Executives
778-6162
If you are—or have been—head of a trade or professional association or a chamber of commerce, you may be interested in this group. The 320 members include suppliers to associations. The monthly newsletter goes only to members; the directory is available for purchase.

Washington Society of Certified Public Accountants
902 140th Ave. N.E.
Bellevue WA 98005
644-4800
An affiliate of the American Institute of Certified Public Accountants, this group has 15 chapters and about 7,100 members. About half the

members work in public accounting, 38 per cent in private accounting, and the balance in government or education. There are also about
300 associate members. Members are assigned to chapters by
address. Puget Sound chapters include Olympia, Peninsula, Tacoma,
South King County, Seattle (downtown), and North Seattle. There's
also the Bellevue Area, Sammamish Valley, and Snohomish County
chapters. For more information, contact John Mix, chapter relations
director. The society office offers a job services program for job-
seekers at any level in accounting. You can have your resume on file
for three months, available for review by firms with openings. You
can also review and photocopy announcements of openings posted at
the society office. Job openings are also listed in the monthly
newsletter sent to members.

Washington Software Association
18804 North Creek Parkway, #112
Bothell WA 98011
483-3323
Jobline: 487-6250
The WSA has more than 250 corporate industry members in addition
to supplier, individual and student members. Many of the members
list open positions on the jobline. In late 1992, an electronic bulletin
board will also be introduced. To learn more about the software
industry in this area, you can attend meetings and any of the 13 SIGs:
topics range from technical support and object-oriented programming
to human resources and finance and operations. For information
about SIGs, call Sally J. Gadd, the WSA's programs manager.
Students can ask about the chapter at the University of Washington.

Washington Speech and Hearing Association
2033 Sixth Ave.
Seattle WA 98121
441-6020
If you're a speech pathologist or audiologist, consider this group,
which has several hundred members statewide. Members are divided
into six regions; meeting schedules vary by location.

Washington State Association of Broadcasters
1200 Westlake Ave. N., #414
Seattle WA 98109
286-2056
An organization for broadcast stations, this group provides such
station services as help with broadcast license renewals and lobbying.
It also maintains a list of job openings at stations across the state.

Washington State Bar Association
2001 Sixth Ave., Fifth Floor
Seattle WA 98121-2599
727-8200
Both resumes and notices of openings for attorneys are kept in
notebooks in the foyer of the bar association office. You can consult
the book weekdays between 8 and 4:30. To submit your resume, mail
it to "Resume Service," Public Affairs Department.

Washington State Biotechnology Association
623-8632
Organized to promote the continued growth of the biotechnology
industry in this state, the WSBA includes about 75 members, some
corporate, some individual. Student memberships are also available.
You need not be active in biotechnology to join.

Washington State Chefs' Association
Hotline: 725-1545
Nonmembers are welcome at most meetings of this group.

Washington State Dental Hygienists Association
P.O. Box 389
Lynnwood WA 98046
771-3201
There's no formal job bank in this organization of 900, but informal
referrals are available from the office and networking takes place at
the local level. There are 13 component societies in the state,
including groups in Seattle, Tacoma, South King County, Kitsap
County, Olympia and the Olympic peninsula. Call the state office for
information.

Washington State Tax Consultants, State Support Office
Contact: Roy Scruggs
P.O. Box 4097
Bremerton WA 98312
674-2552
If you're a tax preparer, whether self-employed or employed by a
firm, you're welcome at this group, which has about 200 members in
11 chapters across the state. Chapters do not have job banks, but
informal networking is encouraged. Most chapters publish newsletters; all offer meetings that help you meet continuing education
requirements.

Washington State Veterinary Medicine Association
2050 112th N.E.
Bellevue WA 98009
454-8381
Veterinarians new to the Northwest can receive a sample copy of the association newsletter, which includes listings of both openings and people seeking work. New graduates of Northwest vet schools can request a complimentary six-month subscription.

Washington Women in International Trade
P.O. Box 9243
Seattle WA 98109
Contact: Christine Parker, 441-3622
Affiliated with the Organization of Women in International Trade, this group has about 150 members. Nonmembers are welcome at the monthly meetings.

Washington Women in Timber
P.O. Box 21785
Seattle WA 98111
Contact: Jill Mackie, 682-7262
One of 12 groups affiliated with Federated Women in Timber, this organization was formed about 1980. Members include natural resource attorneys, governmental affairs specialists, foresters and those who work in family-owned forest products companies. Its purpose is education—especially public education about forest management. Statewide, there are about 200 members.

Washington Women Lawyers
705 Second Ave., #816
Seattle WA 98104
622-5585
Chartered to further the integration of women in the legal profession and to promote equal opportunities for women, this statewide group has eight chapters. Some have several hundred members. All meet monthly. Members include attorneys and those working in related fields, legislators, bar association officials and law students. Both men and women are eligible for membership. There is a statewide directory and quarterly newsletter; each chapter also has a newsletter; some publish job openings. The King County chapter also has a job bank. For the contact person in your area, call Tiffanie Kilmer, state executive director.

Women and Mathematics
Contact: Sarah Selfe, 543-7835

Affiliated with the Mathematical Association of America, WAM has about 15 chapters across the U.S. Its members strive to help children recognize the importance of math. WAM has no regular meetings; instead, men and women who work in math, science, computer science and engineering volunteer as mentors and speakers. The local group, organized in the 1980s, had about 15 participants at press time.

Women Construction Owners and Executives, Washington
Contact: Melissa Thompson, 285-9197
Part of the 400-member national, Women Construction Owners and Executives, this group has about 15 members in Washington state. Recent meeting topics have included collections, legal aspects of hiring and firing and risk management. You're welcome at the bimonthly meetings if you meet membership criteria.

Women In Communications, Inc.
610 Lloyd Building
Seattle WA 98101
682-9424
This group is for women in all areas of communications—journalism, advertising, public relations and marketing. Meetings are open to everyone, although the job bank is reserved for members.

Women in Graphic Arts
Contact: Carla Perry, Northwest Multi Forms
20133 42nd N.E.
Seattle WA 98155
361-0773
Open to men and women who work in design, printing, the paper industry and related businesses, this local organization is in its sixth year. Today it has about 130 members; about 40 per cent are self-employed. There's a job bank and newsletter.

Women in Trades
6543 Seward Park Ave. S.
Seattle WA 98188
A regional support and networking organization for women in nontraditional jobs, especially the building trades, WIT meets monthly. Nonmembers are welcome. Call Patricia Coley, 723-0229.

Women + Business
441-6020
This organization's primary project is the annual Women + Business conference. All planning is done by the W + B board; volunteers are used only during the conference.

Women's Business Exchange
382-1234
This organization of business people encourages business and personal growth through networking, professional education, leadership training and mentoring. Nonmembers are welcome. Membership services include a career support group and directory.

Women's Fisheries Network
Contact: Christy Suelzle, Administrator
2442 N.W. Market, #199
Seattle WA 98107
742-2810
Established in 1983 in Seattle to support women in the fishing industry, this group prompted the organization of a national that now has three chapters: one here, one in the Northeast and a third in Alaska. About 200 men and women belong to this chapter; members work in fishing, processing, cold storage and equipment as well as in financial services, insurance, government and education. Nonmembers are welcome at the meetings. The career development committee posts "Positions Available" and "Positions Wanted" at meetings and maintains the same information in a notebook.

Women's Math Network
An informal group with no official name, this includes women who teach math or computer science at the college level in the Puget Sound area. Through it women new to the area may learn of part-time teaching jobs. Responsibility for organizing meetings is rotated; for information, call a community college math department and ask for a woman instructor.

Women's Transportation Seminar
Contact: Pat Levine, 553-4210 or Sharon Parker, 684-1008
One of 22 chapters of a national, this group of 200 men and women includes transportation professionals and others concerned about transportation. The local chapter's focus is on "people moving," with many members working in transit engineering and transportation planning. The monthly meetings are open to nonmembers and the monthly newsletter occasionally lists "Positions Available." The national has a jobline and a job bank is being developed here.

World Affairs Council
Stouffer Madison Hotel, #501
515 Madison St.
Seattle WA 98104
682-6986

Affiliated with the National Council of International Visitors, this group of 1,000 provides opportunities for international education. It regularly sponsors lectures by well-known policy-makers. You can network at the council's many special events and by volunteering in the council offices; many students and recent graduates find jobs through such volunteer work. There's a special $15 student membership.

World Trade Club
P.O. Box 21488
Seattle WA 98111
448-8803
Nonmembers are welcome at this group, which allows networking and provides information about international business. There's a newsletter and directory for members. Club members organize "country forums." Some meet irregularly, others as often as monthly. These free programs, which may feature bankers, consultants and businesspeople working in import-export, are often mentioned in the club newsletter. Or call the club secretary for information.

Professional Associations for the Self-Employed

Several Northwest professional groups emphasize the needs of the self-employed. These groups do not have job banks and may require that you be self-employed prior to membership. They provide valuable continuing education and support for entrepreneurs.

Associated Builders and Contractors of Western Washington
111911 N.E. 1st, #308
Bellevue WA 98005
646-8000
The Puget Sound economy, partnering in construction and safety are examples of recent meeting topics at this group of 200, part of a national. To belong, you must have a contractor's license or, in the case of those qualifying for "supplier" or "industry professional" membership, a business license.

Home-Based Business Association
P.O. Box 111132
Tacoma WA 98411
If your business is operated from your home, you're eligible for membership in this group, which serves about 40 of the self-employed in the Seattle-Tacoma area. Nonmembers are welcome at meetings. Contact Ralph Fly, 848-1354.

Independent Computer Consultants Association, Seattle Chapter
869-1199

A consultant referral service is one of the membership benefits of this group of about 50, part of a national. Most members represent one or two-person firms, so the monthly meetings focus on the needs of small businesspeople.

Independent Insurance Agents and Brokers of King County
778-6162

If you work in insurance, you may find this group's meetings and educational seminars helpful. Nonmembers are welcome.

National Speakers Association, Puget Sound Chapter
Contact: Helen Hesketh, Executive Secretary, 562-0302

If speaking and training are an important part of your business, you may find this group's monthly meetings and special workshops helpful. Speaking techniques and marketing yourself are examples of the topics covered. Nonmembers are welcome. Sample copies of the newsletter are available; a one-year subscription is $25. There are about 100 members. If you join, you can participate in "Showcase," an annual event that helps speakers market themselves.

Northwest Marine Trade Association
1900 N. Northlake Way, #233
Seattle 98103
634-0911

If you work in boating, you may be interested in this nonprofit, which was founded nearly 50 years ago and now has about 1,000 members. Some are large—for example, boatbuilders Bayliner and Tollycraft—but many are small. You must be affiliated with the marine industry to belong.

Society of Professional Graphic Artists
P.O. Box 31258
Seattle WA 98103-1258
Contact: Dan Ballard, 634-0084

If you're self-employed as a graphic designer or illustrator or in production, you can attend two meetings of this group prior to joining. Focuses on the business of design.

Washington State Association of Life Underwriters
4201 Roosevelt Way, #206
Seattle WA 98105
632-4330

If you're a life insurance agent, consider this group, part of the National Association of Life Underwriters. It has 2,200 members across the state in 18 chapters; the Puget Sound area has six chapters. The Seattle chapter (see below) has its own office. Information on these following chapters is available from the state office: Snohomish (serving Snohomish County), Cascade (serving Bellevue, Redmond and Kirkland), Tacoma, Olympic Peninsula and Southwest (serving Thurston County).

Seattle Life Underwriters Association
P.O. Box 99266
Seattle WA 98199
623-9265
This group has some 550 members. Most are life and health insurance brokers and agents. About 40 per cent are self-employed. Nonmembers are welcome.

Washington State Electrical Contractors Association
11911 N.E. 1st, #308
Bellevue WA 98005
646-8000
If you have a contractor's license, you're eligible for membership in this statewide group of about 60. Its primary purposes are education and training in the industry and governmental affairs.

Washington State Hispanic Chamber of Commerce
P.O. Box 24623
Seattle WA 98124
340-1556
Part of the U.S. Hispanic Chamber of Commerce, this group was founded in 1983. It now includes 85 firms, both small businesses and large corporations. You need not be Hispanic to join.

Women Business Owners
2113 E. Olive
Seattle WA 98122
236-3131
Established in 1979, this group of about 120 is an affiliate of the National Association of Women Business Owners. Nonmembers are welcome to attend meetings and functions; full membership requires that you own your own business.

Women Entrepreneurs Network, East Sound Chapter
P.O. Box 3522
Bellevue WA 98009
340-1679
This group is for women who have—or want—their own businesses. This chapter serves about 40 from Arlington to Tacoma. The meetings are designed to provide support and information, especially for the many one-person firms represented. Nonmembers are welcome.

6. Joblines
230 Round-the-Clock
Job Listings

To provide application information and updated lists of job openings, many Seattle-area firms and agencies offer 24-hour taped messages on special telephone lines. Usually revised weekly, most taped messages are brief; often only job titles are included. Some joblines allow you to request application forms or other messages. A few firms have lines staffed with personnel specialists who can discuss openings with you.

Today most messages require the use of a Touchtone telephone. A few must be accessed through main switchboards. The joblines are typically easier to reach before and after regular working hours. Calling before 8 a.m. or on weekends will also reduce your toll charges if you must call long distance. All area codes are 206 unless otherwise indicated.

Businesses and Organizations

Advanced Technology Laboratories: 487-7799

Alaska Airlines: 433-3230

Alaskan Copper: 623-5801, Ext. 639

Alliant Techsystems: 356-3024

Alpac Corp.: 326-7436

Applied Voice Technology: 820-6000, Ext. 3980

Architectural Office Support Positions
See Society of Architectural Administrators in *"Professional Associations: How To Network Even If You Know No One."*

Associated Grocers Inc.: 767-8788

AT&T
Management: (800) 348-4313
Nonmanagement: (800) 423-6992

Auburn General Hospital: 833-7711, Ext. 429

Bailey-Boushay House: 223-6770

Battelle: 528-3090

Blue Cross of Washington and Alaska: 670-4773

Boeing: 394-3111 (Toll-free within Washington: 800-525-2236)

Budget Rent-A-Car: 243-3951

Cascade Savings Bank: 339-5500, Ext. 814

Chateau Ste. Michelle: 488-1133

Children's Hospital and Medical Center: 526-2230

City Credit Union: 340-4500, #7

Costco: 828-8100, Ext. 416

Darigold: 286-6730

Data I/O: 867-6963

Drug Emporium: (800) 745-JOBS

Eddie Bauer: 861-4851

Eldec Corp.: 743-8215

Ernst: 621-6880

Everett Clinic: 339-5400 (800-533-7035, Ext. 5400)

Evergreen Hospital Medical Center: 899-2502

Film Industry (Washington State Film and Video Office): 464-6074

First Interstate Bank of Washington: 292-3551

Fisher Broadcasting Co.: 443-6444

Frank Russell: 596-5454

Fred Hutchinson Cancer Research Center: 667-2977

Fred Meyer: 439-5667

Genetic Systems/Sanofi: 861-5045

Good Samaritan Hospital: 848-6661, Ext. 1905

Group Health Cooperative of Puget Sound
Administrative and support positions in Seattle, Bellevue and Everett:
448-2745
Group Health nursing positions in Seattle, Bellevue and Everett:
 448-2743
Medical assistants, LPNs, medical clerical and technical positions in
Seattle, Bellevue and Everett: 448-2744
All positions in Tacoma, Federal Way, Olympia and Kitsap County:
383-7832

GTE Northwest
Management positions: 261-5667
Hourly positions: 261-5777

Harborview Medical Center: 223-8409

Heath Tecna: 395-HIRE

The Herald: 339-3009

Hewlett-Packard Co.: 335-2930

Highline Community Hospital: 431-5325

Holland America Line-Westours: 286-3496

IBM: 587-3192

Industrial Engineering
See Institute of Industrial Engineers in *"Professional Associations:
How To Network Even If You Know No One."*

Intermec: 348-2820

InterWest Savings Bank: 679-4181 (Toll-free within Washington,
800-422-0235), through operator

John Fluke Manufacturing Co. Inc.: 356-5205

Kaiser Aluminum: 591-0425

KCTS/9: 443-4800

KeyBank of Puget Sound: 684-6189

King Broadcasting Co.: 443-6444

King County Medical Blue Shield: 464-5588

KIRO, Inc.: 728-5205

Kits Cameras: 872-5144

Manpower Temporary Services: 447-5627

McCaw Cellular Communications Inc.: 828-8484

The Morning News Tribune: 597-8590

Mount St. Vincent: 938-8998

MultiCare Medical Center: 594-1256

Nintendo of America: 861-2170

Northwest Hospital: 361-1791

Northwest Kidney Center: 292-3924

Overlake Hospital Medical Center: 462-5150

Pacific First Savings Bank: 224-3330

Pacific Medical Center: 326-4120

PEMCO Financial Center: 628-8740

Pioneer Bank: 771-2525

Precor: 486-9292, Ext. 444

Providence Hospital, Everett: 258-7562

Providence Medical Center: 320-2020

PTI Communications: 851-1376

Public Relations/Publications
See International Association of Business Communicators, PRSA
and WPA in *"Professional Associations: How To Network Even If
You Know No One."*

Puget Sound Bancorp.
From Seattle: 447-2017, Ext. 5307
From Tacoma: 593-5307

Puget Sound Blood Center: 292-2302

Puget Sound Hospital
From Tacoma: 474-0561, Ext. 103
From Seattle: 623-1417, Ext. 103

Puget Sound Power & Light Co. (Puget Power): 454-6363, Ext. 2692

Recreational Equipment Inc.
Corporate positions: 395-4694
Distribution center: 891-2562

Red Lion Hotel: 433-1893

Restaurants Unlimited: 634-0550, through operator

Safeco: 545-3233

Safeway: 455-6501

St. Claire Hospital: 581-6419

St. Francis Community Hospital
From Seattle: 838-9700, Ext. 7930
From Tacoma: 952-7930

St. Joseph Hospital and Health Care Center: 591-6623

Schwartz Bros. Restaurants: 647-4864, #6

Seafirst Corp.: 358-7523

Sea-Land Service Inc.: 593-8042

Seattle Sheraton Hotel and Towers: 287-5505

The Seattle Times: 464-2118

Siemens Quantum: 391-1231, #6

Software Industry (A service of the Washington Software Association): 487-6249

Starbucks Coffee Co.: 447-4123, Ext. 2

Stevens Memorial Hospital: 744-4194

Stouffer Madison Hotel: 583-0300, through operator

Swedish Hospital Medical Center: 386-2888

TRAMCO: 347-6969, Ext. 2600

Trident Seafoods Corp. (Hourly positions): 783-3818, through operator

Unigard: 644-5326

UniSea Inc. (Hourly positions): 883-0884

United Airlines: (708) 952-7077

University of Washington Medical Center
Nursing positions: 548-4470
General positions: 543-6969

U.S. Bank: 344-5656

U S West Communications: 345-6126

Valley Medical Center: 251-5190

Virginia Mason Clinic: 223-6496

Virginia Mason Hospital: 223-6798

Washington Energy Co.: 622-6767, Ext. 2800

Washington Mutual Savings Bank: 461-8787

West Coast Grocery: 593-5876

Westin Hotel: 728-1000, Ext. 5766

Weyerhaeuser Co.: 924-5347

ZymoGenetics: 547-8080

General

Senior 55+ Hotline (A service of the Mayor's Office, City of Seattle): 684-0477

Government Agencies

City of Auburn: 931-3077

City of Bellevue: 455-7822

City of Bothell: 486-9473

City of Bremerton: 478-5241

Community Transit: 348-2333

City of Edmonds: 771-0243, #1

City of Everett: 259-8768

City of Federal Way: 661-4089

City of Kent: 859-3375

King County: 296-5209

City of Kirkland: 828-1161

Kitsap County: 876-7169

City of Lacey: 491-3213

Libraries (a service of the Pacific Northwest Library Association): 543-2890

METRO: 684-1313

Pierce County: 591-7466

Pierce Transit: 581-8097

City of Puyallup: 841-5596

City of Redmond: 556-2121

City of Renton: 235-2514

City of Seattle: 684-7999

Seattle Center: 684-7218

Seattle City Light: 233-2181

Seattle Housing Authority: 443-4376

Port of Seattle: 728-3290

Seattle Public Library: 386-4120

Snohomish County: 388-3686

Snohomish County PUD: 347-5599, Ext. 9151

City of Tacoma: 591-5795

Port of Tacoma: 383-5841, Ext. 244

Thurston County: 786-5499

City of Tukwila: 433-1828

Federal Employment

McChord Air Force Base: 984-2277

Army Corps of Engineers: 764-3739

Fort Lewis Army Base: 967-5377

Central Intelligence Agency: (800) JOBS-CIA

Department of Commerce: 526-6294

NOAA: 526-6051

Environmental Protection Agency: 553-1240

Federal Aviation Administration
General: 227-2014
Air traffic controllers: 227-1012

Federal Emergency Management Agency: 487-4600, #4

General Services Administration: (415) 744-5056

Housing and Urban Development: 553-8184

Internal Revenue Service: 553-2639

National Park Service: 553-4409

Office of Personnel Management (General Federal Openings): 442-4365

Postal Service
Seattle and Everett positions: 442-6240
Tacoma, Bremerton and Olympia positions: 756-6148

Puget Sound Naval Shipyard: (800) 562-5972

State Employment

Washington State Convention and Trade Center: 447-5039

State of Washington: 586-0545
From Seattle: 464-7378

Western State Hospital: 756-3933

Schools, Colleges and Universities

Antioch University-Seattle: 441-5352, using automated telephone system

Bates Technical College: 596-1652

Bellevue Community College: 641-2082

Edmonds Community College: 771-1510

Everett Community College: 388-9229 (Live voice)

The Evergreen State College: 866-6000, Ext. 6361

Pacific Lutheran University: 535-8598

Renton Technical College: 227-5312

Seattle Community Colleges (All campuses): 587-5454

Seattle Pacific University: 281-2065

University of Puget Sound: 756-3368

University of Washington and University of Washington Medical Center: 543-6969

Auburn School District: 931-4916 (Live voice)

Bainbridge Island School District: 842-2920

Bellevue School District: 455-6009

Bethel School District: 536-7270

Central Kitsap School District: 698-3470

Clover Park School District: 589-7436

Edmonds School District: 670-7021

Everett School District: 259-2935

Federal Way School District
Certified positions: 941-2058
Classified positions: 941-2273

Fircrest School: 364-0300, Ext. 244

Franklin Pierce School District: 535-8829

Highline School District: 433-6339

Issaquah School District: 392-0707

Kent School District (Classified positions): 859-7508

Lake Washington School District: 828-3243

Mercer Island School District: 236-3302

Mukilteo School District: 356-1237

Northshore School District: 489-6381

Peninsula School District: 857-3565

Puyallup School District: 841-8666

Renton School District: 235-5826

Seattle Public Schools: 298-7382

Shoreline School District: 361-4367

South Central School District: 244-2100 (Live voice)

South Kitsap School District: 876-7389

Sumner School District: 863-2232

Tacoma School District
Certified positions: 596-1300
Classified positions: 596-1265

Catholic Schools
See Catholic Archdiocese of Seattle, below

King's Schools: 546-7533 (Live voice)

Nonprofits

Catholic Archdiocese of Seattle: 382-4564

The Defender Association: 447-3900, Ext. 513

Fremont Public Association: 548-8331

Planned Parenthood of Seattle-King County: 328-7721

7. Employers: Businesses and Organizations

When we say "jobs," many of us think first of business. And with good reason, because that's where many of the best jobs are. In the Seattle area, businesses give you the opportunity to be a cashier, carpenter, computer programmer—and corporate executive. You can work in graphic design or employee relocation or conference planning. You can build or sell or finance airplanes, trucks or boats, plant trees or create computer games, deliver babies or publish books.

Whatever your choice, you'll find that most jobs are hands-on. Because few Puget Sound businesses are very large (today Washington state boasts the headquarters of just five Fortune 500 companies), even executive positions require "shirt sleeves" management.

This chapter lists businesses and many nonprofits that provide business-like services (for example, medical care, publishing and recreation). The emphasis is on organizations that offer managerial, professional and technical opportunities; unless otherwise noted, employers have at least 20 such positions. There is no one list of all Puget Sound businesses; to supplement the listings here, check the directories referenced in "*Job Bulletins and Valuable Publications.*"

A & H Stores
1420 Maple Ave. S.W., #201
Renton WA 98055
255-7083
This retail drug and Hallmark store chain employs about 150. Personnel is handled by Shirley Prothero.

Accel/Exchange
15395 S.E. 30th Pl.
Bellevue WA 98007
644-7000

This electronic banking network, headed by Tom Bass, operates automated cash machines in the Northwest and western Canada. It's also a data processing service bureau.

Ackerley Communications of the Northwest
800 Fifth Ave., #3700
Seattle WA 98104
624-2888
Airport advertising displays, billboards, radio station KJR and the SuperSonics basketball team are among the local operations of this firm. Senior management and its support staff are located in this office; for information about openings elsewhere, contact the units directly.

Ackerley Airport Advertising
2001 Sixth Ave., #1702
Seattle WA 98101
728-0100
Direct resumes to Patti Davies, controller.

Ackerley Communications of the Northwest, Inc.
Outdoor Division
3601 Sixth Ave. S.
Seattle WA 98134
682-3833
Direct resumes to Bill Barber.

KJR/KLTX
See Broadcast Stations later in this chapter.

Seattle SuperSonics
190 Queen Anne N.
Seattle WA 98109
281-5800
Direct inquiries to Bob Whitsett, the general manager.

Adams News Co., Inc.
1555 W. Galer
Seattle WA 98119
284-7617
This distributor of magazines and books employs about 100 in such departments as accounting, sales, distribution and warehouse. Limited turnover, but if you'd like to apply, call for the name of the department head who should receive your resume.

Advanced Technology Laboratories
22100 Bothell Highway S.E.
P.O. Box 3003
Bothell WA 98041
487-7000
Jobline: 487-7799 (Touchtone telephones only)
This manufacturer of medical diagnostic ultrasound equipment (used by obstetricians, cardiologists and other specialists) has been a subsidiary of Westmark International Inc. In spring, 1992, however, shareholders approved ATL's spin-off as a separate public company with Dennis Fill as chairman and CEO.

Aetna Life & Casualty Co.
1501 Fourth Ave., #1100
Seattle WA 98101
467-2640
Shelley Jacobson handles personnel for this insurance company, which employs about 270 locally.

Agena Corp.
9709 Third Ave. N.E.
Seattle WA 98115
525-0005
Nancy Kittrick is the personnel manager for this software developer, which develops products for property and casualty insurance agents.

Airborne Freight Corp.
P.O. Box 662
Seattle WA 98111
285-4600
Jobline: 281-4815
In the Puget Sound area, Airborne employs more than 1,100. Job openings are posted in the personnel office at corporate headquarters, 3101 Western Ave., second floor. Just ask the receptionist for help.

Alaska Airlines
P.O. Box 68900
Seattle WA 98168
433-3200
Jobline: 433-3230
This airline's jobline lists job titles, qualifications and, in the case of group interviews, where interviews will be held.

Albertsons Food Centers Inc.
11000 N.E. 33rd Pl., #102
Bellevue WA 98004
827-8070
Most hiring for this Boise-based supermarket chain is done in the stores, where openings are often posted. Some administrative staff is hired by this regional office.

Aldus Corp.
411 First Ave. S., #200
Seattle WA 98104
622-5500
Jobline: through operator
Carrie Cole is the personnel director for this desktop publishing and graphics software firm, which employs more than 700. Established in 1984, Aldus is today one of the largest U.S. software developers.

Allenmore Hospital
South 19th and Union
Tacoma WA 98405
572-2323
This 105-bed facility is now owned by MultiCare Health System, but recruiting is handled by the Allenmore staff. Job openings are posted in a glass case outside the personnel office and advertised in the *Morning News Tribune.*

Alliant Techsystems Inc.
Marine Systems West
6500 Harbor Heights Parkway
Everett WA 98204-8899
356-3000
Jobline: 356-3024
Formerly Honeywell's Marine Systems Division, Alliant specializes in undersea warfare technologies. According to the *Puget Sound Business Journal,* there are about 900 employees, mostly engineers and technical staff. Applications are available in the lobby.

Allied Telesis Inc.
11410 N.E. 122nd Way
Kirkland WA 98034
820-9007
Described by the *Puget Sound Business Journal* as a "large-scale, low-cost producer of 'building blocks' for Ethernet, a networking standard used to connect a wide variety of software," Allied moved its corporate offices from California in mid-1992. President is Tony Russo.

Almac/Arrow Electronics Corp.
14360 S.E. Eastgate Way
Bellevue WA 98007
643-9992
Lynn Marshall handles human resources for this wholesaler of electronic equipment, which employs about 60.

Allstate Insurance Co.
19015 North Creek Parkway
Bothell WA 98011
489-9000
Jobline: 489-5111
Allstate's regional operations center employs about 1,000, mostly in customer service and insurance processing.

Alpac Corp.
P.O. Box C-14117
Seattle WA 98114
323-2932
Jobline: 326-7436
Barbara Creveling handles personnel for this soft drink bottler and distributor, a subsidiary of the Skinner Corp., which has several offices.

Altair Research
1515 Dexter Ave. N., #200
Seattle WA 98109
282-0725
This firm specializes in telephone surveys. Its full-time staff is very small, but it often employs part-timers to field surveys. Contact: Ruth Sparks.

Amaze
11810 115th Ave. N.E.
Kirkland WA 98034-6923
820-7007
This new company, which provides "The Far Side" calendar and "Cathy" daily planner for personal computers, employed about 30 at press time. Dan Elenbaas is president.

American Airlines

Seattle-Tacoma International Airport
Seattle WA 98158
433-3951
Personnel inquiries should go to L.W. Cooper, the general manager of
AA's regional operations. The airline employs about 550 here.

American Plywood Association

P.O. Box 11700
Tacoma WA 98411
565-6600
The testing and promotion of panel products such as plywood is the
function of this trade association, which employs engineers with
backgrounds in wood science as well as publicity writers and publications editors. Local employment is about 100. Personnel is handled
by William H. Allen, vice president and director, Financial and
Administrative Services.

American States Insurance Company

P.O. Box 12316
Seattle WA 98111
670-9200
Linda Bertucci is the personnel manager for this 185-employee firm.

Andrew Corp.

19021 120th N.E.
Bothell WA 98011
485-8200
Amy Wilson is the personnel manager for this firm (formerly Emerald
Technology), which develops communications software for mini-
computers.

Applied Microsystems Corp.

P.O. Box 97002
Redmond WA 98073-9702
882-2000
Jobline: 882-5668
Gale Mowrer is the human resources manager for this high tech
electronics manufacturer. The firm, which employs more than 200
locally, has few entry-level opportunities. A B.S.E.E. and experience
are required for most engineering positions and a B.S.E.E. and an
M.B.A. are preferred for product management positions. Recent
openings were for design and test engineers and a key accounts
manager.

Applied Voice Technology Inc.
P.O. Box 97025
Kirkland WA 98083
820-6000
Jobline: 820-6000, Ext. 3980
This software firm develops voice and telephone call processing systems, including voice messaging products. Established more than 10 years ago, it employs about 85. Recent openings were for a product marketing manager, technical writer and software engineer.

Arima Marine
47 37th St. N.E.
Auburn WA 98002
939-7980
Established in 1980, Arima makes small Fiberglas power boats for sport fishing. According to a recent Seattle *Times* article, annual sales are about $3 million. Juichi Arima is the designer, founder and company owner. Personnel is handled by Don Gross, vice president.

Arthur Andersen & Co.
801 Second Ave., #900
Seattle WA 98104
623-8023
This "Big 6" accounting and consulting firm employs about 300 locally. Preston Prudente is the personnel contact.

Arctic Alaska Fisheries Corp.
P.O. Box 79021
Seattle WA 98119
282-3445
This bottom fishing firm employs more than 200 in its Seattle office. If you'd like to work on one of the fishing boats, applications are accepted year around. For more information, contact the personnel office. (At press time, acquisition of Arctic by Tyson Foods Inc. was pending.)

Associated General Contractors of Washington
1200 Westlake N., #301
Seattle WA 98109
284-0061
With a staff of about 25, this trade association provides the building industry with publications, educational programs, insurance and pension plans, labor and legal assistance. It also lobbies. For information on its job bulletin, see *"Professional Associations: How To Network Even If You Know No One."*

Associated General Contractors of Washington
Southern District Office
P.O. Box 11105
Tacoma WA 98411-0105
472-4476

Associated Grocers Inc.
P.O. Box 3763
Seattle WA 98124
762-2100
Jobline: 767-8788
Joan Baily is the personnel director for this grocery co-op, which employs more than 1,000. AG provides a variety of services to its members, including merchandising help, market research and insurance. The jobline lists job titles, requirements, locations, hours and some salary information. Openings are also posted in the human resources office. Applications are available in the lobby of the AG building at 3301 S. Norfolk, at the south end of Boeing Field.

Associated Press
P.O. Box 2144
Seattle WA 98111
682-1812
Interested in writing for the AP? You'll need at least two years of journalism experience. The Seattle bureau has 14 news employees and the Olympia bureau four; the Seattle staff also includes 11 employees without newswriting responsibilities. Contact: Dan Day, bureau chief.

AT&T
700 Fifth Ave.
Seattle WA 98104
Joblines:
Management: (800) 348-4313
Nonmanagement: (800) 423-6992
In this area, AT&T employs about 2,000, but personnel is centralized in Oakland, Calif. Recent openings on the jobline were for account executives, telemarketing sales reps and operators.

Attachmate Corp.
13231 S.E. 36th
Bellevue WA 98006
644-4010
John Williams is the human resources administrator for this high tech firm, which develops hardware and software to connect IBM PCs and mainframes.

Auburn General Hospital
20 Second St. N.E.
Auburn WA 98002
833-7711
Jobline: 833-7711, Ext. 429
At this 100-bed hospital, applications are available from the switchboard operator until 9 p.m.

The Austin Co.
800 S.W. 16th
Renton WA 98055
226-8800
Engineers in all disciplines are the most likely to find openings at
Austin, a 200-employee subsidiary of National Gypsum. Laura
Schauer is the personnel services administrator for this facilities
design firm.

Autodesk Retail Products
11911 North Creek Parkway S.
Bothell WA 98011
487-2233
(Ms.) Cloyse Bianchi is personnel director for this 100-employee
firm, which develops software for computer-aided design. Formerly
Generic Software.

Automobile Club of Washington
330 Sixth N.
Seattle WA 98109
448-5353
This affiliate of the national auto club employs about 360 statewide
and 175 in its office in Seattle. Other Puget Sound offices are in
Bellevue, Tacoma, Lynnwood, Everett, Bremerton, Renton and Olympia. If you're interested in a summer job, call Human Resources about
the temporary counter positions.

AVTECH Corp.
3400 Wallingford Ave. N.
Seattle WA 98103
634-2540
More than 300 work for this manufacturer of electronic components
for aircraft. Stan Hiraoka is personnel manager.

AWD Technologies
10940 N.E. 33rd Pl.
Bellevue WA 98004
889-4522
The environmental remediation subsidiary of Dow Chemical Co., AWD is headed locally by Barbara Trenary. The *Puget Sound Business Journal* recently quoted her as describing AWD as a full-service environmental firm which identifies and defines environmental problems and then designs and implements the solutions.

Bader Martin Ross & Smith, P.S.
1000 Second Ave., #3400
Seattle WA 98104-1022
621-1900
Alvin Martin is the managing partner of this accounting firm, formed by six former partners in the local office of the now dissolved firm of Laventhol & Horwath. Established in late 1990, the firm employs about 40.

Ball-Incon Glass Packaging Corp.
5801 E. Marginal Way S.
Seattle WA 98134
762-0660
Jaime Navarro handles personnel for this manufacturer of glass containers. Employment: about 650.

Bank and Office Interiors
5601 6th Ave. S.
Seattle WA 98108
768-0253
This firm offers both commercial interior design and manufacture of office furniture. The 112 local employees include sales reps, designers and accountants as well as manufacturing, installation and warehouse crews. Human resources director: Cindy Libowsky.

Bank of California
910 Fourth Ave.
Seattle WA 98164
587-6100
Karen Markus is vice president, human resources, for this bank, which employs about 130 in Seattle. Other small offices are in Bellevue and Tacoma.

Bank of Sumner
801 Alder
P.O. Box 1650
Sumner WA 98390
863-6301
Linda Dryden is president of this small, multi-branch local bank.

Bardahl Manufacturing Corp.
P.O. Box 70607
Seattle WA 98107
783-4851
This manufacturer of engine additives and lubricants has a small staff.
Inquiries can be directed to Sharon Robinson, controller.

Bartell Drug Co.
4727 Denver S.
Seattle WA 98134
763-2626
Karl Wilkinson handles personnel for this family-owned chain of
nearly 40 neighborhood drug stores. There are limited openings for
pharmacists and such administrative staff as buyers.

Battelle Seattle Research Center
P.O. Box C-5395
Seattle WA 98105
525-3130
Jobline: 528-3090
Battelle Memorial Institute is a nonprofit research organization that
employs 8,200 worldwide. Its goal is to generate, apply and commer-
cialize technology. One of the four largest Battelle facilities is in
Richland, Wash., which employs 3,300. Satellites of the Richland
operation include the Seattle program, which employs 200, and the
Marine Research Laboratory on the Olympic peninsula.

In Seattle are the Human Affairs Research Center, which analyzes the
complex social problems related to the application and development
of technology; Battelle Seminars Program, which offers short continuing education programs for professionals; and Seattle Conference
Center, which provides conference facilities and services, including
audio-visual, clerical and transportation.

B & V Waste Science and Technology Corp.
1201 Pacific Ave., #1100
Tacoma WA 98402-4301
383-1436

This multi-disciplined engineering firm with expertise in the management of hazardous waste liabilities has about 35 in its local office. Resumes can go to Bernice Kammers.

Baxter Healthcare Corp.
Bartels Diagnostic Division
P.O. Box 3093
Bellevue WA 98007
392-2992
Nancy More is the personnel manager for this manufacturer of medical diagnostic kits. The administrative staff is small.

Baxter Healthcare Corp.
Hospital Supply Division
3650 148th N.E.
Redmond WA 98052
885-4166
If you're interested in work at this wholesale distributor of hospital supplies, you must submit a company application form with your resume. Due to consolidation, the combined staff in the office, warehouse and sales departments was less than 20 at press time.

BDM International Inc.
163000 Christensen Rd.
Building 2, #300
Seattle WA 98188
246-2100
This subsidiary of the Ford Aerospace Company employs about 40. Many positions require an engineering background. Resumes can be directed to "Personnel."

Bell Industries
Illuminated Display Division
P.O. Box 97056
Redmond WA 98073-9756
885-4353
Shelly Rasmussen is the human resources administrator for this 130-person aerospace subcontracting division.

Bellevue Square Managers
P.O. Box 908
Bellevue WA 98009
454-2431
A division of Kemper Development, this is the management firm for Bellevue Square's 1.3 million-square-foot shopping center. When

openings occur in the staff of six, the department managers handle their own hiring. Some management functions are handled by Kemper Development (see later in this chapter).

Ben Bridge Jewelers, Inc.
P.O. Box 1908
Seattle WA 98111
628-6870
Jon and Ed Bridge head this firm, recently described by *Washington CEO* as the largest privately-owned Northwest jeweler. More than 80 years old, the company operates in 42 states. Resumes can be sent to Cathy Hall, vice president.

Benson & McLaughlin, P.S.
2201 Sixth Ave., #1400
Seattle WA 98121
441-3500
This accounting and consulting firm employs about 75.

Berger/ABAM Engineers, Inc.
33301 9th Ave. S.
Federal Way WA 98003
241-2040
Ann Kennedy is the personnel director for this 55-employee structural engineering firm.

BioControl Systems Inc.
19805 North Creek Parkway, #101
Bothell WA 98011
487-2055
This small firm (about 20 employees at press time) manufactures a diagnostic kit for detecting salmonella.

Biomembrane Research Institute
210 Elliott Ave. W., #305
Seattle WA 98119
285-1309
Jeff Werther handles personnel for this organization, spun off from Oncomembrane to do studies relating to cancer. Employs about 50.

Blue Cross of Washington and Alaska
7001 220th St. S.W.
Mountlake Terrace WA 98043
670-4000
Jobline: 670-4773

This provider of group and individual insurance plans employs about 1,700. Positions include attorneys, underwriters, actuaries, programmers, systems analysts and accountants.

Boeing

Ranked No. 12 on the 1992 "Fortune 500" list, Boeing provides hundreds of opportunities, both permanent and free-lance. The largest divisions are: Commercial Airplane; Defense and Space; and Computer Services. Unlike the first two groups, Computer Services has both external and internal operations. Besides supporting all Boeing divisions with computing and telecommunications services, it also functions as a profit center, providing information services to other organizations. For more information about Boeing, you can review the annual report, available by contacting the company's general offices at 7755 E. Marginal Way S., Seattle WA 98108.

Boeing Employment Center
P.O. Box 3707 MS 31-11
Seattle WA 98124
Jobline: 394-3111
Toll-free within Washington: (800) 525-2236
This detailed tape-recorded message, the jobline for all Boeing divisions, describes the positions for which applications are currently being accepted. Applications can be picked up at the employment offices listed below or you can submit a resume to the address above. Boeing offers a wide variety of opportunities, including such "non-aerospace" positions as firefighter, medical technologist and food service worker. Recently applications were being issued to manufacturing engineers, tool and die makers, environmental engineers and industrial hygienists.

SeaTac Employment Center
17930 Pacific Highway S.

Everett Employment Center
3003 W. Casino Rd.

Boeing Employees Credit Union

P.O. Box 97050
Seattle WA 98124-9750
439-5700
The largest Puget Sound area credit union, this thrift organization serves current and former Boeing employees. It employs more than 200. Inquiries can be directed to Lisa Dord in Human Resources.

Bogle & Gates
601 Union St., #4700
Seattle WA 98101
682-5151
Leann Stamper is the personnel director for this law firm, which employs more than 400 in Seattle.

The Bon Marche
Third and Pine
Seattle WA 98181
344-2121
This upscale retail chain has always been a star for its parent company, now emerged from bankruptcy as Federated Department Stores, Inc. The 42-store retailer (with 23 stores in Washington) is headquartered above its flagship store in the heart of Seattle's retail district. Personnel manager is Andrea Hosfild.

Borders Perrin & Norrander
1115 First Ave.
Seattle WA 98101
343-7741
Peter Hatt heads this full-service advertising agency, a branch of the Portland firm of the same name.

Bouillon Christofferson & Schairer, Inc.
1201 Third Ave., #800
Seattle WA 98101
682-3910
Mary Kay Haveman is the human resources contact at this engineering consulting firm, which has offices in Seattle, Portland and Sunnyvale, Calif.

BP Chemicals Inc.
Advanced Materials Division, Aerospace Composites
3016 Auburn Way N.
Auburn WA 98002
854-3000
This aerospace subcontractor employs about 500. Linda Thomas is the human resources director. Builds fiber-composite sub-assemblies.

Brazier Forest Industries, Inc.
701 Fifth Ave., #4500
Seattle WA 98104
386-5800

This forest products firm, with annual sales estimated at $75 million, employs about 30 in its headquarters office. Marcia Corum is the human resources manager.

Bremerton Sun
P.O. Box 259
Bremerton WA 98310
377-3711
From Seattle: 842-5696
Mike Phillips is the executive editor, Tom DeFeo the managing editor, Michael Stevens the advertising director and Tim Lavin the personnel director for this 40,000-circulation daily newspaper. Its job openings are advertised in its own classified pages.

Brems Eastman Glade
3131 Elliott Ave., #280
Seattle WA 98121
284-9400
The principals of this advertising agency are Chris Brems, Sue Eastman and Steve Glade.

Bristol-Myers Squibb Pharmaceutical Research Institute
3005 First Ave.
Seattle WA 98121
728-4800
This research facility employs nearly 300, most in technical positions. Most staff members have degrees (ranging from B.S. to Ph.D) in the sciences. Many openings are advertised. A jobline is to be installed soon. For more information, contact Jan. Sitterley.

Broadcast Stations
Most of the stations listed below have at least 20 staff members; because few have personnel departments, resumes can be directed to the general manager unless otherwise indicated. Openings are infrequent at the smaller stations.

KCIS/KCMS
See Crista Ministries

KCPQ/13
P.O. Box 98828
Tacoma WA 98499
582-8613
From Seattle: 625-1313

Besides full-time jobs, this television station offers internships—and you need not be a student to qualify. Usually 12 weeks in length and often requiring 30 hours of work per week, these unpaid stints are available in a variety of departments, including research, sales, promotion and programming. For more information, write Adele Hauck.

KCTS/9
401 Mercer St.
Seattle WA 98109
728-6463
Jobline: 443-4800 (Touchtone telephones only)
Seattle's public television station employs about 150. Unpaid internships are offered to those with aptitude in broadcast journalism or production (you need not be a student). For details, contact Tamara Burdic, intern coordinator.

KEZX-FM
2615 Fourth Ave., #150
Seattle WA 98121
441-3699

KFOX/KKFX-AM
101 Nickerson, #260
Seattle WA 98109
728-1250

KING 5
See King Broadcasting Co.

KING-AM/KING-FM
Classic Radio, Inc.
333 Dexter Ave. N., #400
Seattle WA 98109
448-3666
Spun off from King Broadcasting when that firm was sold, these radio stations are owned by the Bullitt sisters. Employment is about 40. Don Oylear is the general sales manager and Jennifer Ridewood, the business manager, the personnel contact.

KIRO TV, KIRO-AM/KWMX-FM
See KIRO, Inc.

KISW-FM
712 Aurora N.
Seattle WA 98109
285-7625

KMTT-FM/KTAC-AM
1100 Olive Way, #1650
Seattle WA 98109
233-1037

KZOK-AM/FM
200 W. Mercer
Seattle WA 98119
281-5600

KJR-AM/KLTX-FM
190 Queen Anne Ave. N.
Seattle WA 98109
285-2295

KKNW-FM
1109 First Ave., #300
Seattle WA 98101
292-8600

KPLU-FM
Tacoma WA 98447
535-7758
Toll-free within Washington: (800) 677-5758
Located at Pacific Lutheran University, this public radio station posts
its openings at the campus personnel office. You can also mail a
resume to the station.

KPLZ-FM/KVI-AM
Tower Building, #200
Seventh and Olive
Seattle WA 98101
223-5700

KSTW/11
2320 S. 19th
P.O. Box 11411
Tacoma WA 98411
572-5789
About 125 work for this local television station. For information on
openings, check with the receptionist; she'll have the postings.

KTZZ/22
945 Dexter N.
Seattle WA 98109
282-2202
This local television station employs about 50. There's no news programming. For information on openings, call the receptionist.

KUBE-FM
120 Lakeside, #310
Seattle WA 98122
322-1622

KUOW-FM
A National Public Radio affiliate at the University of Washington. See *"Employers: Schools, Colleges and Universities."*

KXRX-FM
Shamrock Broadcasting
3131 Elliott Ave., Seventh Floor
Seattle WA 98121
283-5979

Brown & Haley
P.O. Box 1596
Tacoma WA 98401
593-3000
If you've tasted Almond Roca, you've sampled one of the many products this pioneer Tacoma firm (still family-owned) manufactures or distributes internationally. Personnel director is Debbie Schrader.

Burlington Environmental, Inc.
2203 Airport Way S.
Seattle WA 98134
223-0500
Owned by Burlington Resources and the Sabey Companies, this firm has been merged with Chemical Processors Inc., which recovers and processes solvents, acids and other hazardous industrial byproducts. Jay Bulson is the human resources manager.

Burlington Resources
999 Third Ave., #4500
Seattle WA 98104
467-3838
A spinoff of Burlington Northern, this firm does natural resource exploration and development. Laurie Hanson handles personnel.

Buttonware
P.O. Box 96058
Bellevue WA 98009
454-0479
This 30-person firm develops software for IBM-compatible personal computers. Christiana Carter coordinates personnel.

The Callison Partnership
1420 Fifth Ave., #2400
Seattle WA 98101
623-4646
David Olson and Gerry Gerron are the co-managing partners of this architectural and interiors firm, one of Seattle's largest with more than 250 employees. Callison's projects include the Nordstrom stores and Kirkland's Carillon Point. Katie Grabow and Chris Englin are the human resources coordinators.

Care Computer Systems Inc.
636 120th Ave. N.E.
Bellevue WA 98005
451-8272
Computer hardware and software for nursing homes is provided by this 100-employee firm. James L. Ingalls is president and Kim Allen, administrative assistant, coordinates personnel.

Care Unit Hospital of Kirkland
10322 N.E. 132nd
Kirkland WA 98034
821-1122
Margaret Howell is the personnel coordinator for this 83-bed chemical dependency care facility.

Cascade Natural Gas Corp.
P.O. Box 24464
Seattle WA 98124
624-3900
This gas distribution company serves several eastern Washington and Oregon communities. Its western Washington service areas include Bellingham, Mt. Vernon and Bremerton. Openings for the Seattle office, which employs about 120, and the Bremerton facility, which employs 30, are posted at state Job Service Centers. Personnel is handled by Fran Dols.

Carver Corp.

P.O. Box 1237
Lynnwood WA 98046
775-1202

Barb Pepin is the human resources manager for this manufacturer of audio components, which employs about 300. Carver's products are considered "top-quality," the *Puget Sound Business Journal* recently noted, and founder Robert Carver "enjoys a reputation as an audio-industry genius."

Cascade Savings Bank

2824 Colby Ave.
Everett WA 98201
339-5500
Jobline: 339-5500, Ext. 814

Jessie White is the personnel manager for this thrift.

Catapult, Inc.

10900 N.E. 4th St., #1350
Bellevue WA 98004
646-6767

Formerly Egghead University, Catapult markets and delivers personal computer software training, usually to corporate clients. Department heads hire their own staff; call for the name of the individual who should receive your resume. Recent openings were for technical writers and PageMaker specialists.

Cedar Shake and Shingle Bureau

515 116th Ave. N.E., #275
Bellevue WA 98004
453-1323

This trade association provides quality control and promotion for the producers of cedar building products. The office staff of 12 includes the marketing employees who create publications and advertising. The 12 field employees inspect shakes and shingles and provide assistance to designers and builders. Mike Westfall is the president.

CellPro

22322 20th Ave. S.E., #100
Bothell WA 98021
486-7644

This biotech company is growing rapidly, with 100 employees expected by the beginning of 1993. Most openings are advertised in the Seattle papers; support positions are also posted at Job Service Centers.

Central Garden & Pet Supply
700 Milwaukee Ave. N.
Algona WA 98001
624-4833
This wholesaler of garden and pet supplies includes a former subsidiary of the Weyerhaeuser Co. Management recruiting is handled by Lori Tasker.

Chateau Ste. Michelle
P.O. Box 1976
Woodinville WA 98072
488-1133
Jobline: through operator
The headquarters for one of Washington's first wineries, now a division of Stimson Lane. Other Stimson Lane subsidiaries in Washington are Columbia Crest Winery and Whidbey's Greenbank Farm. This facility employs about 150 in administrative, bottling, public relations and tour operations. Deborah Milter handles personnel.

Chemical Waste Management, Inc.
19002 72nd Ave. S.
Kent WA 98032
251-6227
A leader in hazardous waste management, Chemical Waste accepts applications locally only for advertised positions. Unsolicited resumes should be sent to its northern California human relations office:

Chemical Waste Management, Inc.
Kathy King
4227 Technology Dr.
Fremont CA 94538

Chicago Title Insurance
701 Fifth Ave., #1800
Seattle WA 98104
628-5666
Jennifer Luce is the human resources administrator for this firm; many managers also hire their own staff.

Children's Hospital and Medical Center
P.O. Box C-5371
Seattle WA 98105
526-2000
Nurse recruiter: 526-2112
Jobline: 526-2230

A 203-bed facility with outpatient clinics, Children's employs approximately 2,200. You'll find a variety of positions described on the jobline. If you cannot apply in person, mail a resume and cover letter to the Human Resources office or call the office at 526-2111 to request an application. If you're a registered nurse, call the nurse recruiter during business hours; you'll be sent an application packet with information about the hospital.

Christensen, O'Connor, Johnson & Kindness
1420 Fifth Ave., #2800
Seattle WA 98101
441-8780
This firm of patent attorneys employs about 90. Personnel is handled by Gary Tomlinson, executive director.

Christiansen & Fritsch Direct Response Advertising
1008 Western Ave., #301
Seattle WA 98104
223-6464
Ron Christiansen and Bill Fritsch are the principals in this 25-person agency, which has both Seattle and Portland offices.

CH2M Hill
P.O. Box 91500
Bellevue WA 98009
453-5000
This engineering consulting firm employs more than 400 in the local branch. The firm hires a variety of professionals, including architects, landscape architects, chemical engineers, electrical engineers, civil engineers and graphic designers. Recruiting is handled by Fran MacPhail, the personnel coordinator, and her assistant, Colleen Lawson.

CityBank
P.O. Box 7028
Lynnwood WA 98046
745-5933
Conrad Hanson is president of this locally-owned bank, which serves north King County and Snohomish County. Resumes can be directed to Belinda Faylona in personnel.

City Credit Union of Seattle
801 Third Ave.
Seattle WA 98101
340-4500
Jobline: 340-4500, #7
This is a three-branch credit union.

Clark, Nuber & Co.
P.O. Box 3844
Bellevue WA 98009
454-4919
This accounting and consulting firm employs about 80. Personnel manager: Ann Rael.

Cole & Weber Inc.
308 Occidental Ave. S.
Seattle WA 98104
447-9595
The local affiliate of New York-based Oligvy & Mather, this advertising agency is one of Seattle's largest. According to *Washington CEO*, 1991 billings reached $83 million. It employs approximately 125. Personnel is handled by Dolly Shale, vice president, administration.

Columbia Winery
P.O. Box 1248
Woodinville WA 98072
488-2776
About 30 (full-time and part-time) work at this winery headquarters. Besides the administrative staff, there's a bottling crew. Columbia has no personnel manager, but inquiries can be directed to the appropriate department head. For part-time banquet work, contact Lori Reeder, banquet/events manager.

Commerce Bank of Washington
1201 Third Ave., #3900
Seattle WA 98101
292-3900
John Kephart, director of administration, handles personnel for this single-branch bank established in 1988. Total employment: about 25. Focus: business customers.

Community Memorial Hospital
P.O. Box 218
Enumclaw WA 98022
825-2505

Dennis Popp is administrator and Dave McLachlan handles personnel for this 28-bed facility.

Comprehensive Health Education Foundation (CHEF)
22323 Pacific Highway S.
Seattle WA 98198
824-2907
Carl Nickerson is president of this small nonprofit, which publishes a variety of health education materials for schoolchildren.

Connelly Skis
P.O. Box 716
Lynnwood WA 98046
775-5416
Dana Sprouse is the human resources manager for this manufacturer of water skis.

Consolidated Freightways
P.O. Box 3585
Seattle WA 98124
763-1517
This motor carrier and air freight forwarder employs about 160 locally. Steve Hillstead, group operations manager, is the personnel contact.

Consolidated Restaurants Inc.
P.O. Box 380
Mercer Island WA 98040
232-9292
This restaurant chain includes the Metropolitan Grill, Hiriam's at the Locks and Elliott's on the Pier. You can apply at the restaurant where you'd like to work or, for management positions, contact Molly Hancock, operations director, at the address above.

Contel
Merged into GTE/Northwest.

Continental, Inc.
720 Third Ave., Eighth Floor
Seattle WA 98104
623-3050
Continental Savings Bank, Continental Mortgage, property management and escrow companies are the divisions of this firm, for which Ann Hedquist is personnel manager. After November, 1992, the firm will be located in Two Union Square.

Coopers & Lybrand
999 Third Ave., #1800
Seattle WA 98104-4098
622-8700
Larry Pihl is personnel director for this "Big 6" accounting and consulting firm, which employs more than 140 in Seattle.

Cornerstone Columbia Development Co.
1011 Western Ave., #500
Seattle WA 98104
623-9374
This real estate development and management firm, which is expected to be disbanded soon, is doing no hiring.

Costco Wholesale Corp.
10809 120th Ave. N.E.
Kirkland WA 98083
828-8100
Jobline: 828-8100, Ext. 416
This warehouse retailer opened in Seattle in 1983 and now has about 90 stores across the U.S. and Canada. Gail Smith is the personnel director.

CPC Fairfax Hospital
10200 N.E. 132nd St.
Kirkland WA 98034
821-2000
Peggy Trachte is director, business services, for this 133-bed acute psychiatric care facility. Each hospital department handles its own hiring; for mental health or nursing positions, contact Janice Wynne-McGuire, nursing services.

Crystal Mountain
P.O. Box 158
Enumclaw WA 98022
825-3865
Nearly 500 work at this ski resort in the winter and there's a 38-person permanent staff; some work on the mountain and others in the Enumclaw office. The five department managers are food and beverage, whose staff includes an executive chef; finance and accounting; base area operations; mountain; and ski school/races. The permanent staff also includes electricians, carpenters, positions in marketing, and personnel.

Custom Software Services Inc.
10900 N.E. 4th St., #900
Bellevue WA 98004
455-3507
Legal and accounting software are created by this 50-member firm.
Beverly Cotton is personnel director.

Dain Bosworth Inc.
Each branch of this brokerage firm handles its own hiring; contact the
manager of the office in which you're interested.

Dain Bosworth Inc.
1201 Third Ave., #2500
Seattle WA 98101
621-3111

Dain Bosworth Inc.
P.O. Box C-96062
Bellevue WA 98009
462-5050

Data I/O Corp.
10525 Willows Rd. N.E.
Redmond WA 98073
881-6444
Jobline: 867-6963
James Russell handles personnel for this electronics firm, which
employs about 500 locally. Recent openings were in software
engineering and database maintenance.

Darigold Inc.
P.O. Box 79007
Seattle WA 98119
284-7220
Jobline: 286-6730
In western Washington, 600 work for this co-op, which manufactures
and wholesales dairy products and animal feed. Thomas Lee is the
personnel director.

Davis Wright Tremaine
1501 Fourth Ave., #2600
Seattle WA 98101
622-3150
Alma Perez handles personnel for this law firm, which employs
approximately 250.

Dean Witter Reynolds Inc.

Each office of this brokerage firm hires its own staff. If you're interested in a broker's position, contact the branch manager. Inquiries regarding support positions (for example, sales assistants, cashiers or new accounts representatives) should go to the operations manager.

Dean Witter Reynolds Inc.
601 Union St., #2900
Seattle WA 98101
464-4000

Dean Witter Reynolds Inc.
3400 188th S.W., #101
Lynnwood WA 98037
771-2405
From Seattle: 464-4040

Dean Witter Reynolds Inc.
P.O. Box 3567
Bellevue WA 98009
455-8000

Deloitte + Touche

700 Fifth Ave., #4500
Seattle WA 98104
292-1800

Martha Tanner, human resources director, is responsible for all recruiting—accountants, consultants and support staff—at this "Big 6" firm's offices in Seattle, Bellevue and Anchorage. The three locations employ an estimated total of 500.

Delta Airlines

Applications for this airline are available at its offices at the Seattle-Tacoma International Airport and at Delta ticket offices. Or call the central personnel office in Atlanta at (404) 715-2600.

Delta Marine Industries Inc.

1608 S. 96th
Seattle WA 98108
763-2383

A manufacturer of molded fiberglass boats, both pleasure and commercial, Delta Marine employs about 250. Ann Powell is personnel director.

Denny's, Inc.
11411 N.E. 124th, #110
Kirkland WA 98034
821-4640
Mark Mueller handles personnel for this restaurant chain.

Digital Equipment Corp.
District Headquarters
P.O. Box 92835
Bellevue WA 98009
637-4000
If you have a B.S. in computer science, mathematics or engineering and you'd like to work in sales, software services or customer service, you can send a resume to Digital's employment department. Bellevue is the district headquarters for the 700 employees in Washington, Oregon, Montana, Idaho, Alaska and Utah.

Digital Systems International Inc.
7659 178th Pl. N.E.
Redmond WA 98052-4953
881-7544
This high-tech firm produces computerized outbound calling equipment. Personnel manager is Tom Shepherd.

Dilettante Inc.
2300 E. Cherry
Seattle WA 98122
328-1530
Brian Davenport manages this family-owned manufacturer of premium chocolates. Pat Burghardt, production manager, hires the chocolate makers, and Mannfried Funk staffs the retail shops. The small administrative staff oversees the wholesale operation.

Dinner + Klein
P.O. Box 3814
Seattle WA 98124-9983
682-2494
Becky Quimby handles personnel for this printing and mailing firm, which employs more than 50.

Drug Emporium Northwest
12515 116th Ave. N.E.
Kirkland WA 98034
820-1616
Jobline: (800) 745-JOBS

This retailer has a small corporate staff and 13 stores in the Puget Sound area. Most openings are advertised or announced in the stores. Adrienne Wigenstein is the personnel director.

Eagle Hardware & Garden Inc.
101 Andover Park E., #200
Tukwila WA 98188
431-5740
David Heerensperger, formerly head of Pay 'N Pak, is establishing a new retail chain, which began 1992 with four stores open and three more on the drawing board for the year. An additional three to five stores are planned for 1993, according to the *Puget Sound Business Journal*. Direct resumes to Bryan Price.

E.A. Nord Co., Inc.
P.O. Box 1187
Everett WA 98206
259-9292
Mike Negrete is the personnel manager and Don Davis the office manager for this door manufacturer, which is now a division of the Klamath Falls, Ore.-based Jeld-Wen.

Eaton Corp./Opcon
720 80th St. S.W.
Everett WA 98203
353-0900
Lisa Hansen is the personnel administrator for this high-tech manufacturer of photo-electric controls. The receptionist has a list of openings.

EBASCO Services Inc.
10900 N.E. 8th St., #500
Bellevue WA 98004-4405
451-4500
Some 300 work for this firm, which includes: EBASCO Environmental, which cleans up hazardous wastes; EBASCO Services, the industrial engineering unit; and EBASCO Constructors, which builds hydroelectric plants. Max Asaf is head of personnel administration.

EC Corp.
520 Pike, #1701
Seattle WA 98101
624-7100
SureFind, the electronic classified ads that can be accessed by telephone, is the first product of this start-up. Conceived by James Lalonde, who is now president.

ECOS
2203 Airport Way S.
Seattle WA
623-3300
This firm, owned by the Sabey Companies and Burlington Resources, is constructing a garbage incinerator in eastern Washington. The staff is very small.

Ecova Corp.
18640 N.E. 67th Ct.
Redmond WA 98052
883-1900
Now a subsidiary of Waste-Tech Services, which itself is part of Amoco Corp., Ecova offers on-site waste remediation. Michael Elkins is president and Andrea Marshall personnel director for the firm, which employs about 35 in the corporate office.

Eddie Bauer Inc.
Human Resources Office
14850 N.E. 36th
Redmond WA 98052
882-6100
Jobline: 861-4851
This specialty retailer employs about 2,000 locally in the corporate headquarters, catalog sales and Seattle-area stores. Founded in Seattle, the chain today is owned by Spiegel Inc. and has more than 125 stores across the U.S. Openings are posted in the lobby of the corporate office. Recent openings included vendor relations manager, inventory analyst, assistant product manager, senior programmer and marketing assistant.

Edmark Corp.
P.O. Box 3218
Redmond WA 98073-3218
746-3900
A growing, publicly-held company, Edmark publishes educational software and printed reading materials. In 1991, sales were $4.3 million. Sally Narodick is the chief executive.

Egghead Discount Software
22011 S.E. 51st St.
Issaquah WA 98027
391-0800
A leading software retailer, Egghead has about 200 outlets across the U.S. Fiscal year 1991 sales were $519 million, according to the

Seattle *Times*. Job openings are available for review in the headquarters reception area.

Eldec Corp.
P.O. Box 100
Lynnwood WA 98046-0100
743-8206
Jobline: 743-8215
Eldec's business is custom design and manufacturing of electronics for aerospace, defense, marine and industrial applications. The firm employs 1,400 locally. Many positions require a B.S.E.E. or a B.S.M.E. and experience in aerospace. The firm anticipates a continuing need for systems design engineers and for software engineers, especially those who have two to three years experience with embedded software.

Elgin Syferd/DDB Needham
1008 Western Ave., #601
Seattle WA 98104
442-9900
Ron Elgin heads this advertising and public relations firm, which now employs about 80.

EMF
15110 N.E. 95th St.
Redmond WA 98052
883-0045
Anna Lee MacPherson handles personnel for this manufacturer of high-volume sorting equipment for the reprographic and printing industry.

Enchanted Parks Inc.
36201 Enchanted Parkway S.
Federal Way WA 98003
838-8676
Austin Ross handles personnel for this amusement park, which can see its winter staff of 25 increase to as many as 800 during the spring and summer. Permanent positions include maintenance (ride and grounds), advertising, accounting, human resources and administrative. Seasonal positions, which can be full-time or part-time, include ride operators, lifeguards, costumed characters, caterers and gift shop clerks.

Encore Publishing Inc.
87 Wall St.
Seattle WA 98121
443-0445
Encore is a small firm that produces—but does not write—the performing arts programs and magazines for such organizations as A Contemporary Theatre, Seattle Opera and Oregon Shakespeare Festival Portland. All writing and editing is done by the arts organizations. For information regarding advertising sales or administrative positions, contact Paul Heppner, publisher.

Enterprise Bank of Bellevue, N.A.
11225 S.E. 6th
Bellevue WA 98004
454-7070
Thomas Cleveland is president of this single-branch bank. Established in 1989, it employs about 25. Focus: niche markets, including small businesses.

The Enterprise
P.O. Box 977
Lynnwood WA 98046
775-7521
Al Hall heads this publishing company, a unit of Lafromboise Newspapers. The Enterprise publications are weekly newspapers serving four areas: Edmonds/Lynnwood/Mountlake Terrace/Mill Creek; Wallingford; North City/Lake Forest Park; and Shoreline Highlands/Lake City.

Enumclaw Courier-Herald
P.O. Box 157
Enumclaw WA 98022
825-2555
A weekly newspaper edited by Jack Darnton, this is published in combination with the Buckley *News-Banner*. Owned by the Longview Daily News, it has a small staff.

Enviros Corp.
5808 Lake Washington Blvd. N.E.
Kirkland WA 98033
827-5525
Jim Quarles is president of this small biotech firm.

Ernst & Young
999 Third Ave., #3300
Seattle WA 98104
621-1800
Rob Goffigon handles professional recruiting and Lynn Howe administrative hiring for this "Big 6" accounting and consulting firm, which employs more than 200.

Ernst Home Centers
1511 Sixth Ave.
Seattle WA 98101
621-6700
Jobline: 621-6880 (Touchtone telephones only)
This chain of hardware stores employs about 250 in the corporate offices. Job openings can be reviewed at the reception desk on the third floor. If you're interested in working in one of the 45 stores in the Puget Sound area, you can check at the corporate office or in a store itself.

ESCA Corp.
11120 N.E. 33rd Pl.
Bellevue WA 98004
822-6800
About 250 are employed by this manufacturer of integrated computer systems for utilities. Technical backgrounds are not necessary for all positions. Jill Boyle is the personnel director.

Esterline Corp.
10800 N.E. 8th
Bellevue WA 98004
453-9400
About 45 work in the corporate office for this aerospace and electronics firm, which owns more than 20 companies around the world, including six former units of Criton Technologies. Local subsidiaries include Korry Electronics and Hytek Finishes. Brian Desautels is the personnel administration manager for the corporate office.

Evans/Kraft Inc.
190 Queen Anne Ave. N.
Seattle WA 98109
285-2222
One of Seattle's oldest and largest advertising agencies, this firm also offers public relations, food publicity and test kitchens. Accounts at press time included Seafirst Bank, Treetop, QFC and Eagle Hardware. A unit of Evans Communications, Inc., Salt Lake City, it

recently acquired Ehrig & Associates. If you're interested in an account executive position, contact John Eastham, head of client services. Mike Mogelgaard is creative director and Dee Munson head of the Evans Food Group.

Everett Mutual Savings Bank
P.O. Box 569
Everett WA 98206
258-3641
Lori Christenson is vice president, human resources, for this Snohomish County thrift.

Everett News Tribune
P.O. Box 499
Snohomish WA 98291
258-9396
A free weekly published in combination with the Snohomish County *Tribune*, this paper has a small staff. The publisher is Dave Mach and the editor Leslie Hynes.

Evergreen Bank
See Pemco Financial Center

Evergreen Hospital Medical Center
12040 N.E. 128th
Kirkland WA 98034
821-1111
Jobline: 823-7581
Cindy Johnson handles personnel for this 130-bed hospital. Recent openings have been for social workers, secretaries, accounting clerks and collections representatives.

Evergreen Services Corp.
12010 S.E. 32nd St.
Bellevue WA 98005
641-1905
Commercial landscaping and landscape management services are offered by this firm, which has seven facilities in western Washington. Rodney Burley is president and Susan Hanley human resources manager. The firm employs a maximum of 75 (including seasonal workers) in such positions as administrative, marketing, horticulturists and field managers. For mid-level and above positions in the field, vocational training is preferred.

Executive Consulting Group
1111 Third Ave., #2700
Seattle WA 98101
689-2200
Andrew MacDonald is the president of this 20-year-old consulting group, which employs about 40. (Ms.) Lee Kowbel handles recruiting.

The Fearey Group Inc.
1809 Seventh Ave., #1111
Seattle WA 98101
343-1543
Pat Fearey heads this public relations firm. At press time, the firm employed 12. Applicants should have a background (either education or experience) in public relations, marketing or journalism.

Federal Home Loan Bank of Seattle
1501 Fourth Ave., #1900
Seattle WA 98101-1693
340-2300
One of 12 Federal Home Loan Banks, the FHLB of Seattle is a federally chartered wholesale bank that serves housing lenders in eight western states. Similar to a "banker's bank," the FHLB has the unique advantage of federal status in the capital markets. It raises funds that are then loaned to member institutions. Besides serving as a credit facility, the FHLB offers such correspondent banking services as overnight and term investments, securities safekeeping and check processing. There's also a financial library and research staff. Contact: Darren Hamby, human resources director.

Federal Reserve Bank of San Francisco, Seattle Branch
1015 Second Ave.
Seattle WA 98104
343-3634
The Federal Reserve, the seller of savings bonds and T-bills, is a government-regulated private corporation which also functions as a banker's bank. Many functions have been centralized in San Francisco, reducing opportunities in Seattle. Most openings here are entry-level , often in check processing. For these jobs, some experience with check processing in a commercial bank is helpful. There are also occasional clerical and building security openings. Openings are posted in the personnel office. Linnea Trier is the personnel manager.

First Choice Health Network, Inc.
1100 Olive Way, #1480
Seattle WA 98101
292-8256
One of the state's largest preferred provider networks, First Choice is headed by Clayton Field.

First Interstate Bank of Washington
P.O. Box 160
Seattle WA 98111
292-3111
Jobline: 292-3551
This subsidiary of First Interstate Bancorp, Los Angeles, employs about 2,200 in Washington. Job openings are posted in the human resources office, located on the ninth floor of the First Interstate Building in downtown Seattle, 999 Third Ave.

First Mutual Bank
P.O. Box 1647
Bellevue WA 98009
455-7300
Robin Carey handles personnel for this thrift, which employs about 100. John Velaas is president.

Fisher Companies Inc.
1525 One Union Square
Seattle WA 98101
624-2752
This privately-owned holding company employs fewer than 10. Most job opportunities are at the units, which include Fisher Broadcasting and Fisher Mills.

Fisher Broadcasting Inc.
100 Fourth Ave. N.
Seattle WA 98109
Jobline: 443-6444
Openings at KOMO radio and television are described on the taped message. You can pick up an application at the station's front desk or request one by sending a postcard to the personnel office.

Fisher Mills Inc.
P.O. Box C-3765
Seattle WA 98124
622-4430
Dave Olson, controller, handles management personnel for this flour milling company.

Floathe-Johnson Associates
P.O. Box 97050
Kirkland WA 98083
822-8400
Maury Floathe heads this advertising and public relations firm, which specializes in high technology clients. Besides Kirkland, where it employs about 68, the firm has offices in Boise and Beaverton. Clients include Hewlett Packard, Tektronix and Intel.

Flow International Corp.
21440 68th Ave. S.
Kent WA 98032
872-4900
This firm develops ultrahigh-pressure waterjets and abrasive-jets for industrial cutting and milling. According to a 1992 *Puget Sound Business Journal* story, Flow is focusing on three market areas: aerospace, automotive and food and forest products industries. Human resources manager is John Hopp.

Fluke Capital Management Co.
11400 S.E. 6th, #230
Bellevue WA 98004
453-4590
Dennis Weston is the chief operating officer for this venture capital firm.

Food Services of America
Corporate Office
P.O. Box 84628
Seattle WA 98124
933-5000
FSA employs about 600 in its branch, which is located at 18430 E. Valley Highway in Kent. Openings are usually listed in a notebook available at the reception desk. Most opportunities are in manufacturing and warehousing.

Foss Maritime Co.
660 W. Ewing St.
Seattle WA 98119
281-3877
One of the Northwest's oldest firms, Foss is today owned by Totem Resources. Employs about 100 in its offices alone. Many openings are advertised. Contact: Ken Carnahan, human resources.

Foster Pepper & Shefelman
1111 Third Ave., #3400
Seattle WA 98101
447-4400
This law firm employs about 300. Inquiries should be directed to the human resources director, (Mr.) Carroll Livingston.

FourGen Software
115 N.E. 100th St.
Seattle WA 98125-8098
522-0055
This firm, which sells modifiable accounting software worldwide, employs about 90 locally. Resumes are accepted at all times.

Frank Russell Co.
909 A St.
Tacoma WA 98402
572-9500
Jobline: 596-5454
International financial consulting and financial management are offered by this firm, which includes Frank Russell Trust Co., Frank Russell Investment Co., Russell Analytical Services and Frank Russell Securities. Local employment: more than 800.

Fratelli's Ice Cream
1824 E. Madison
Seattle WA 98122
324-5939
Personnel inquiries regarding this small premium ice cream company can be directed to the owners, brothers Peter and John Morse.

Frederick & Nelson
Closed in May, 1992.

Fred Hutchinson Cancer Research Center
1124 Columbia
Seattle WA 98104
667-5000
Jobline: 667-2977 (Touchtone telephones only)
About 1,700 are employed by this research center. Job openings are posted in the personnel office at 1730 Minor Ave., ninth floor; inquiries can be mailed to the above address at Mail Stop MP-900.

Fred Meyer Inc.
14300 First S.
Seattle WA 98168
433-6404
Jobline: 439-5667
This discount retailer maintains a small regional office in Seattle, with about 50 people working in personnel, merchandising, groceries and engineering. Turnover is limited. Openings are posted on the jobline. For information about openings in a Fred Meyer store, stop at the customer information desk of the appropriate store.

Fred S. James & Co.
2101 Fourth Ave., #1700
Seattle WA 98121
441-5900
This insurance broker employs about 200. Its Bellevue and Tacoma offices have been consolidated with the Seattle staff. Personnel is handled by David Broadbent, finance director.

French Creek Cellars
17721 132nd Ave. N.E.
Woodinville WA 98072
486-1900
This winery employs fewer than 10.

Frontier Bank
Main Office
6623 Evergreen Way
Everett WA 98203
347-0600
Bob Dickson is president of this bank, which was established in 1978 and had 11 branches by 1992. The personnel coordinator, Becky Bladen, can be reached at 258-0303; her office is at 4201 Rucker, second floor.

General Hospital Medical Center
1321 Colby St.
P.O. Box 1147
Everett WA 98206
258-6300
This 225-bed facility posts its job openings outside the personnel office (enter from Fourteenth Street) and advertises in the Everett *Herald*.

Generra Sportswear Co. Inc.
278 Broad St.
Seattle WA 98121
728-6888
Buzz Williamson is the personnel manager for this fashion sportswear manufacturer, which employs about 200 locally.

Genetic Systems/Sanofi
6565 185th Ave. N.E.
Redmond WA 98052
728-4900
Jobline: 861-5045
About 170 are employed in Seattle and Redmond by this biotech firm, a subsidiary of the New York-based Sanofi. Recent openings: manufacturing technician, quality assurance technician and office specialist.

Genie Industries
P.O. Box 69
Redmond WA 98073
881-1800
Marla Williams is the human resources director for this manufacturer of commercial and industrial lifting equipment. Total Seattle-area employment: 550.

Geosafe Corp.
401 Park Place, #209
Kirkland WA 98033
822-4000
This subsidiary of Battelle currently employs fewer than 20 people, so job openings are infrequent. If you're interested in a sales or marketing position, you can contact Jim Hansen; for engineering, Craig Timmerman; and for finance or administration, Tom Atterbury.

Gerry Sportswear
1051 First Ave. S.
Seattle WA 98134
623-4194
Because most fabrication is done off-shore, this manufacturer of outerwear and Western garments employs fewer than 15 locally. Shirley Zaic, controller, handles personnel.

Gilmore Research Group
2324 Eastlake Ave. E., #300
Seattle WA 98102
726-5555

This market research firm employs approximately 400. Its services include Northwest Certified Surveys (NCS), which provides field audits, telephone surveys and product demonstrations.

Gilmore Temporary Personnel
2722 Colby, #506
Everett WA 98201
252-1195
A subsidiary of the Gilmore Research Group, this firm provides temporary clerical workers.

Glant Pacific Companies
P.O. Box C-3637
Seattle WA 98124
628-6222
Pacific Fabrics, a fabric and craft retailer, Pacific Iron & Metal, a scrap recycler, and Pacific Building Materials are the divisions of this firm, which employs more than 200. Carol Canfield handles personnel.

GMA Research Corp.
11808 Northup Way, #270
Bellevue WA 98005
827-1251
Jamie Baba handles personnel for this market research firm, which employs about 20.

Golden Grain Macaroni Co.
4100 Fourth Ave. S.
Seattle WA 98134
623-2038
This division of Quaker Oats makes rice mixes and pasta. The personnel manager is Vicki Rosellini.

Good Samaritan Hospital
407 14th Ave. S.E.
Puyallup WA 98372
848-6661
Jobline: 848-6661, Ext. 1905
Rehabilitation therapist, social worker, secretary, home health care aide and clerk are examples of recent openings at this 200-bed facility.

Great American Bank FSB
425 S. Franklin
Olympia WA 98501
754-6565

Debbie Kauffman handles human resources for the Washington division of this thrift.

Great Northwest Federal Savings and Loan Association
Merged with Washington Mutual Savings Bank.

Great Western Bank
P.O. Box C-91080
Bellevue WA 98009
Human Resources: 451-2000, Ext. 156
Linda Jennings is the personnel director for this thrift, a subsidiary of a California firm.

Gretag Systems Inc.
11720 North Creek Parkway N.
Bothell WA 98011-8223
483-2121
Joann Spaulding handles personnel for this photo-processing equipment firm. Gretag, which employs about 120, was recently described by the *Puget Sound Business Journal* as "dominating" the U.S. market for mass production photo-packaging equipment.

Group Health Cooperative of Puget Sound
521 Wall St.
Seattle WA 98121
Human Resources: 448-2728
Joblines:
Administrative and support (Seattle, Bellevue and Everett): 448-2745
Nursing (Seattle, Bellevue and Everett): 448-2743
Medical assistants, LPNs, medical clerical and technical (Seattle, Bellevue and Everett): 448-2744
All positions, Tacoma, Federal Way, Olympia and Kitsap County: 383-7832
This health maintenance organization employs thousands in its hospitals and clinics in the Puget Sound area. For more information on the positions listed on the joblines, you can visit the Human Resources offices in Seattle, 521 Wall St., 448-2711, or Tacoma, 1148 Broadway Plaza, #210, 383-7818. If you're a free-lance writer, you can direct inquiries regarding assignments to *View*, the magazine sent to Group Health members. Contact the managing editor, Jan Short, at 448-5999 or the address above.

GTE Northwest
1800 41st St.
Everett WA 98201
261-5321
Joblines:
Management positions: 261-5667
Hourly positions: 261-5777
A unit of the Connecticut-based GTE Corp., GTE Northwest is the second largest telephone company in Washington, employing more than 3,000.

GTE Telecom
22027 17th Ave. S.E.
Bothell WA 98021
487-8300
A unit of GTE, GTE Telecom produces software modules to manage and control communications networks. Contact: Carol Bender, senior human resources administrator.

Hagen, Kurth, Perman & Co.
1111 Third Ave., #500
Seattle WA 98101
682-9200
Norm Hagen is president of this accounting firm, which employs about 70. It offers audit, tax and advisory services and computer hardware and software systems. Jerry Smith heads the computer division.

Harrison Memorial Hospital
2520 Cherry Ave.
Bremerton WA 98310
377-3911
This 297-bed facility posts its openings just outside the personnel office. There is limited turnover in non-nursing positions; inquiries can be directed to Kathy Mork. Vicki Lee-Calvin is the nurse recruiter.

Hart Crowser
1910 Fairview Ave. E.
Seattle WA 98102
324-9530
This engineering consulting firm has a small office in Tacoma, but all hiring and most work is done from Seattle. Paula Houston is the human resources manager for the practice, which recently advertised for hydrogeologists, chemists, environmental engineers, mechanical engineers and chemical engineers.

hDC Computer Corp.
6742 185th Ave. N.E.
Redmond WA 98052
885-5550
This software developer, which offers software utilities for Windows applications, employs fewer than 30.

HDR Engineering, Inc.
Building C, #200
11225 S.E. 6th
Bellevue WA 98004
453-1523
This branch of a national firm employs about 100 locally. The most frequent openings are for civil, structural or environmental engineers. Inquiries should be directed to Gary Bleeker, the local manager.

Heath Tecna Aerospace Co.
19819 84th Ave. S.
Kent WA 98032
872-7500
Jobline: 395-HIRE
This aerospace subcontractor employs more than 1,300. Assembly position openings are usually posted at the Auburn Job Service Center. For professional positions, contact personnel director Karen White.

Health and Hospital Services Corp.
1715 114th S.E.
Bellevue WA 98004
454-8068
This nonprofit owned by the Sisters of St. Joseph of Peace operates hospitals, nursing homes, a health maintenance organization and a chemical dependency treatment firm in the Northwest. Only about 15 work in the corporate headquarters. Resumes can be directed to Scott Houston, director, human resources.

Heart Technology Inc.
2515 140th Ave. N.E.
Bellevue WA 98005
869-6160
Karen Grosz is the human resources administrator for this newly public firm founded by former engineering professor David Auth. His development, a device that unblocks arteries, is a less expensive alternative to bypass surgery. Heart employs about 125. You can learn of most openings by stopping at the main reception desk, where applications are also available.

Hebert Research Inc.
13705 Bellevue-Redmond Road
Bellevue WA 98005
643-1337
If you're interested in a research analyst position at this market
research firm, direct your inquiry to Bryan Johnson, vice president.
For jobs in data collection (often with telephone surveys), contact the
data collection supervisor. At Hebert, most telephone survey jobs are
full-time permanent; a few part-timers are hired.

Helly-Hansen (U.S.) Inc.
P.O. Box 97031
Redmond WA 98052
883-8823
Kelly MacDonald handles personnel for this activewear designer and
manufacturer, a branch of a Norwegian firm. The corporate office is
small and stable, so openings are limited.

The Herald
P.O. Box 930
Everett WA 98206
339-3000
Jobline: 339-3009
This 60,000-circulation daily, which has both Everett and Lynnwood
offices, is owned by the Washington *Post*. Stan Strick is editor.

Herring/Newman Direct Response Advertising
414 Olive Way, #300
Seattle WA 98101
343-9000
This direct response advertising agency now employs about 50. If
you'd like to apply for an account services position, send your resume
to Mary Ward-Smith. If you're an art director, contact Bruce Bulloch.
Copywriters should direct their resumes to Virginia Lawson.

Hewitt/Isley
119 Pine, #400
Seattle WA 98101
624-8154
Tim Spelman handles personnel for this architectural firm, which
employs about 35.

Hewlett-Packard Co.
8600 Soper Hill Rd.
Everett WA 98205
335-2000
Jobline: 334-2244
The Lake Stevens Instrument Division of this national electronics firm employs about 1,100. There are full-time, part-time and student positions.

Hill and Knowlton
520 Pike St., #2929
Seattle WA 98101
682-6944
Art Merrick is senior vice president and general manager of this 15-person branch of the national public relations firm.

Hillhaven
1148 Broadway Plaza
Tacoma WA 98401-2264
572-4901
This public company, which operates convalescent care and retirement housing, employs several hundred locally. The Seattle *Times* recently described it as the nation's second-largest provider of long-term care. Job openings are posted in the fourth floor personnel office.

Highline Community Hospital
P.O. Box 66657
16251 Sylvester Rd. S.W.
Seattle WA 98166
431-5304
Jobline: 431-5325
This 220-bed facility provides a variety of programs, including senior citizen health care, alcohol and drug abuse treatment and eating disorders treatment. Recent openings were for RNs, X-ray and ultrasound technicians, switchboard operator and dietary technician.

Holland America Line-Westours
300 Elliott Ave. W.
Seattle WA 98119
281-3535
Jobline: 286-3496 (Touchtone telephones only)
If you're interested in the cruise and tour industry, you can check this firm's openings by visiting the human resources office. Holland America has full-time, part-time and seasonal positions; some are located in Seattle, some in Alaska and others aboard cruise ships.

Examples of the seasonal positions are ticket agents in Seattle and bus drivers, tour directors and hotel staff in Alaska. Shipboard positions (all requiring experience) include cruise directors, hairdressers, photographers, casino games operators, nurses, doctors and dentists.

Hornall/Anderson Design Works Inc.
1008 Western Ave., #600
Seattle WA 98104
467-5800
If you're a graphic designer, your inquiry should go to John Hornall.

H.O. Sports Inc.
17622 N.E. 67th Ct.
Redmond WA 98052
885-3505
Angela Aronica handles some personnel functions for this water ski manufacturer. Herb O'Brien, president, hires the professional and managerial staff. H.O. currently employs about 100.

Host International, Inc.
Seattle Tacoma International Airport
Seattle WA 98158
433-5611
A unit of Marriott, Host operates restaurants, catering and in-flight kitchens for airlines. Local employment: about 625. Openings are posted in the state Job Service Centers and in the Host office on the ticketing level of the main terminal.

Howard Johnson & Co.
1111 Third Ave., #1700
Seattle WA 98101
625-1040
Katie Krogman and Valerie Hartfield handle personnel for this 150-employee employee benefits consulting firm, which has offices in Washington, California and Nevada.

Howard Needles Tammen & Bergendoff
600 108th Ave. N.E., #405
Bellevue WA 98004
455-3555
Carol Pomeroy is the personnel director for this architectural and engineering firm. Total employment: about 130.

Howard S. Wright Construction
P.O. Box 3764
Seattle WA 98124
447-7654
A division of Wright Schuchart, Inc., this is a general contracting and construction management firm. Direct inquiries to "Human Resources."

Hytek Finishes
8127 S. 216th
Kent WA 98032
872-7160
A unit of Esterline Corp., Hytek provides specialized metal finishing for aerospace. Doug Evans is president. Support staff is hired by Gloria Swanlund, office manager.

IBM
P.O. Box 1830
Seattle WA 98111
587-4400
Jobline: 587-3192
This IBM office is a sales and service center. At press time IBM was accepting resumes only for customer engineering positions.

Icicle Seafoods Inc.
4019 21st Ave. W.
Seattle WA 98199
282-0988
Julie Aydelotte is the human resources manager for this seafood processor. One of Seattle's largest, it maintains operations in the Northwest and Alaska.

I. Magnin
601 Pine St.
Seattle WA 98101
682-6111
This upscale specialty retailer employs about 90 in its one Northwest store. You can apply by mail or in person at the personnel office.

Immunex Corp.
51 University St.
Seattle WA 98101
587-0430
Anita Williamson is the human resources director for this public biotech firm, which focuses on the research, development, marketing and manufacture of immunological therapeutic products. The *Seattle*

Weekly recently described it as Seattle's "largest and most successful biotech firm." Job openings are posted at the reception desk (use the 1201 Western Ave. entrance). Immunex employs more than 350.

Interlinq Software Corp.
10230 N.E. Points Drive, #200
Kirkland WA 98033
827-1112
Robert M. Delf is chief executive and Sandy Scribner personnel manager for this 40-employee developer of software for the mortgage banking industry.

Intermec
P.O. Box 4280
Everett WA 98203-9280
348-2600
Jobline: 348-2820
Intermec, now a subsidiary of Litton Industries, designs, manufactures, markets and services hardware and software bar code printers and readers. Recent openings have been for electrical, manufacturing and software engineers, graphic designers, human resources specialists, and test technicians. Total employment: about 800.

Interpoint Corp.
P.O. Box 97005
Redmond WA 98073-9705
882-3100
About 350 work for this manufacturer of communications and military microelectronics. Founded in 1969, Interpoint is now a leading manufacturer of hybrid electronics parts, according to *Washington CEO*. Fiscal 1991 sales were reported to be $30.4 million. Shannon Dillingham is the human resources manager.

International News
19226 70th Ave. S.
Kent WA 98032
284-6397
About 30 work for this fashion sportswear firm. Valerie Schorn handles personnel.

InterWest Savings Bank
P.O. Box 1649
Oak Harbor WA 98277
679-4181
Toll-free within Washington: (800) 422-0235
Jobline: Through operator

This thrift has several offices in the Seattle area. Resumes should be directed to "Human Resources" at the corporate office or to the branches specified on the jobline.

Jay Jacobs, Inc.
1530 Fifth Ave.
Seattle WA 98101
622-5400

This specialty retailer has expanded across the country; its 282 stores include about 20 in the Seattle area. There's also a distribution center in Kent. Openings aren't posted, but you can pick up an application at the personnel office. For corporate management positions, contact (Ms.) Romnie Callaghan, human resources director.

J.C. Penney Co., Inc.
District Office
P.O. Box 24087
Seattle WA 98124
575-4865

If you'd like to work in sales at Penney's, you can pick up an application in any store, usually at the switchboard. Stores often have sales support, warehouse and alterations positions, too. Many jobs are seasonal or part-time. If you're interested in management in the 13-store district extending from Northgate to Aberdeen, submit a resume to Jerry Ulsond, district personnel manager, at the address above. College students pursuing retailing should inquire about summer internships; many former interns return to Penney's as management trainees or assistant buyers.

John Fluke Manufacturing Co. Inc.
6920 Seaway Blvd.
Everett WA 98206
347-6100
Jobline: 356-5205

A leading manufacturer of electronic test equipment, especially hand-held digital equipment, Fluke is headquartered in Everett, and has both domestic and international operations. Openings are posted in the employment office as well as on the jobline. Recent openings: cost accountant, engineering manager, marketing communications manager and maintenance mechanic.

John Graham Associates
520 Pike St., #1100
Seattle WA 98101
461-6000

James Pearce handles personnel for this architectural, engineering and planning firm, which employs more than 60.

The Johnson Management Group
8250 165th Ave. N.E., #100
Redmond WA 98052
885-9970
Charles Cosby is president of this 18-person firm which provides financial and production software for real estate and building.

Journal American
P.O. Box 90130
Bellevue WA 98009-9230
455-2222
This Eastside daily newspaper, with a circulation of about 28,000, is owned by the Persis Co., Honolulu. The company also owns the Mercer Island *Reporter* and the Bothell-Woodinville *Citizen,* both weeklies. In 1990 it purchased the *Valley Daily News.* John Perry is the managing editor and Nick Chernock the vice president, human resources.

Kaiser Aluminum
3400 Taylor Way
Tacoma WA 98421-4396
591-0484
Jobline: 591-0425
Environmental engineer, electrical supervisor and design drafter are examples of recent openings at this industrial firm's Tacoma operation.

Kemper Development
P.O. Box 4186
Bellevue WA 98009
646-3660
The manager for Bellevue Place, this firm also provides some services (for example, accounting) for Bellevue Square. Cathie Blumenthal handles personnel.

Key Bank of Puget Sound
P.O. Box 90
Seattle WA 98111
684-6180
Jobline: 684-6189
A subsidiary of the New York-based KeyCorp., this bank is merging with Puget Sound Bancorp., the largest independent banking com-

pany in Washington. Shortly after the April, 1992 merger of BankAmerica Corp. and Security Pacific Corp., Key Bank also bought several branches of Security Pacific. The two transactions are expected to give Key Bank the No. 2 market share position in this state, according to *The Wall Street Journal*. Applications can be mailed to the address above or delivered to the human resources office, 36th floor, Gateway Tower, 700 Fifth Ave. After the merger with Puget Sound, the bank headquarters will relocate to Puget Sound's longtime location, 1119 Pacific Ave., Tacoma.

Kidder Peabody & Co. Inc.
1001 Fourth Ave. Plaza, #2600
Seattle WA 98154
628-8511
Cheryl Archer handles personnel inquiries for this stock brokerage and investment banking firm. Seattle employment is about 110.

King Broadcasting Co.
333 Dexter Ave. N.
Seattle WA 98109
Jobline: 448-3915 (Touchtone telephones only)
Recently sold by the founding Bullitt family to the Providence (R.I.) *Journal*, this broadcasting company now includes KING-5 television, the Puget Sound-area NBC affiliate, and several other television stations. The radio stations, KING-AM/FM, are now owned by Classic Broadcasting, headed by the Bullitt sisters. Northwest Mobile Television was sold to former executives. Job applications and notices of personnel openings are available in the King lobby.

King County Medical Blue Shield
P.O. Box 21267
Seattle WA 98111
464-3654
Jobline: 464-5588
Robert Sword is personnel director for this health-care insurance firm, which employs more than 700. A subsidiary is:

Washington Physicians Service
1800 9th Ave.
Seattle WA 98111
382-0414

KIRO, Inc.
2807 Third Ave.
Seattle WA 98121
728-7777
Jobline: 728-5205 (Touchtone telephones only)
Owned by Bonneville Broadcast Corp., Salt Lake City, KIRO operates KIRO-TV, Channel 7 television, the CBS affiliate; KIRO-AM radio, 710: KWMX-FM (formerly KSEA-FM) radio, 101.7; and Third Avenue Productions. You can pick up a job application in the KIRO lobby any day between 8 a.m. and 7:30 p.m. or request one by mail from the human resources office. Examples of recent openings: news assistant, television news director, sales receptionist, radio sales manager, temporary television photojournalist and maintenance person. If you're a college junior or senior or a vocational college student, you may be eligible for a three-month unpaid internship; for details, write Margaret Williams.

Kits Cameras
6051 S. 194th St.
Kent WA 98032
872-3688
Jobline: 872-5144
This photographic gear retailer has 100 locations in six western states plus a photo processing center in the Kent area. If you'd like to work in a store, apply with the store manager.

Kitsap Federal Credit Union
1025 Burwell St.
Bremerton WA 98310
478-2200
Brenda Willenborg is vice president, human resources, for this thrift, one of Puget Sound's largest. Total employment: about 150.

Kitsap Newspaper Group
7689 N.E. Day Rd.
Bainbridge Island WA 98110
842-8305
This firm publishes several small weekly community newspapers, including the Kitsap County *Herald*, Central Kitsap *Reporter* and Port Orchard *Independent*. The Seattle-area publication is the Bainbridge Island *Review*. Sherry Havens is the company human resources director.

Knight Vale & Gregory
1145 Broadway Plaza, #900
Tacoma WA 98402
572-7111
Michelle Chopp handles personnel for this public accounting firm.

KPMG Peat Marwick
601 Union St., #3100
Seattle WA 98101
292-1500
This public accounting and consulting firm's Seattle and Bellevue offices have been consolidated in Seattle, where Mike Van Demark handles administrative recruiting. An affiliated firm, Regis McKenna (see later in this chapter), is now also located in Seattle.

Korry Electronics Co.
901 Dexter N.
Seattle WA 98109
281-1300
A designer and manufacturer of illuminated aviation control panels, this firm is a division of the Esterline Corp. Direct inquiries to Marlene Winter, the personnel manager.

Kramer, Chin & Mayo, Inc.
1917 First Ave.
Seattle WA 98101
443-5300
Sharon Webb is the personnel manager for this engineering firm, which employs more than 100.

K2 Corp.
19215 Vashon Highway S.W.
Vashon WA 98070
463-3631
This alpine ski manufacturer employs about 425 locally. For information on openings, you can contact Charlie Jenkins or the personnel office, which is open Monday through Thursday.

Laidlaw Transit Inc.
P.O. Box 81127 Georgetown Station
Seattle WA 98108
767-4130
The yellow buses that criss-cross Seattle daily with schoolchildren are from Laidlaw, which today is North America's largest school bus operator. The firm also operates a charter department. Most openings are for bus-driving, a part-time position. Other positions at the two

Seattle terminals include accounting clerks, dispatchers and mechanics. You must apply in person for many positions; visit the Laidlaw offices at 7739 First Ave. S. or 13525 Lake City Way N.E.

Lamonts Apparel Inc.
3650 131st Ave. S.E.
Bellevue WA 98006
644-5700
This chain of more than 50 "family department stores" employs about 200 in the corporate office and more than 1,000 in the stores. Openings are advertised. You can also call or visit the human resources office.

Landau Associates, Inc.
P.O. Box 1029
Edmonds WA 98020
778-0907
This environmental and geotechnical engineering consulting firm has about 75 employees. Resumes can be directed to "Human Resources."

Learning World
500 Westlake Ave. N.
Seattle WA 98109
464-1600
Rich Ockwell, the general manager, and Beth Lyden, the accounting manager, handle personnel for this small chain of educational toy stores.

Leviton Manufacturing, Inc.
Telcom Division
2222 222nd St. S.E.
Bothell WA 98021-4416
486-2222
About 100 work in the Canyon Park operation of this data and voice communications firm. Professional recruiting is the responsibility of Lori Steusser. Leviton American, another division of the parent firm Leviton, runs a distribution facility in the Southcenter area.

Lindal Cedar Homes, Inc.
P.O. Box 24426
Seattle WA 98124
725-0900
Barbara Thompson handles personnel for this manufacturer of precut homes. It employs about 150 locally.

Livingston & Co.
800 Fifth Ave., #3800
Seattle WA 98104
382-5500
Roger Livingston heads this advertising agency, one of Seattle's largest. Billings in 1991 were $35 million, according to *Washington CEO*. Personnel manager: Linda Lester.

Longacres Race Course, Inc.
Although the thoroughbreds continued to race here through the 1992 season, Boeing has purchased the site and is beginning construction of an office campus. The current operator of the track, the Emerald Racing Association, is seeking another location.

Lumberman's
3773 Martin Way E., Bldg. A
Olympia WA 98506
456-1880
Bob Stewart is the personnel director for this building supply firm, the only Puget Sound-area division of Lanoga Corp. Lumberman's operates six stores and a warehouse in this area. Each store hires its own staff. The Olympia headquarters staff has 50 employees; turnover there is limited. When openings do occur, they're often advertised in the *Olympian*.

MacDonald-Miller Co.
P.O. Box C-47983
Seattle WA 98106
763-9400
At this mechanical contracting firm, department managers do their own hiring.

Magnolia Hi-Fi & Video
3701 Seventh S.
Seattle WA 98134
623-7872
Alice Chong handles personnel for this retailer of mobile electronics and home audio and video equipment.

Mahlum & Nordfors
2505 Third Ave., #219
Seattle WA 98121
441-4151
John Mahlum and Vince Nordfors head this architectural firm, which employs about 55.

Manson Construction and Engineering Company

P.O. Box 24067
Seattle WA 98124
762-0850

Turnover is limited at this marine construction firm, but when openings do occur, they're often listed in job banks for the National Women in Construction and Associated General Contractors. The firm, which does most of its work for the Port of Seattle, employs professionals in positions such as accountant, civil engineer, estimator, contract administrator and systems analyst. The field work force is unionized. If you're an engineer, contact Robert Stevens, chief estimator.

Manus Services Corp.

1130 Rainier Ave. S.
Seattle WA 98144
325-2200

This firm has two divisions, Manus Direct Response Marketing and Manus Temporary Services. The marketing division is one of Seattle's larger marketing communications firms. Aimee Des Champs handles personnel for both.

Marco Seattle

2300 W. Commodore Way
Seattle WA 98199
285-3200

Hank Schlapp handles personnel for this shipyard, which employs about 150.

Marine Digest

P.O. Box 3905
Seattle WA 98124
682-3607

This monthly magazine focuses on the marine industry. Editor Theresa Morrow welcomes inquiries regarding free-lance pieces.

Mariposa/Savannah

P.O. Box 40
Woodinville WA 98072
483-6556

These firms, divisions of Charles O. Berg Inc., retail women's junior fashions in 10 stores in the Puget Sound area. Local employment is about 120. Karen Wallgast is the personnel director.

Market Trends Research Group
3633 136th Pl. S.E., #110
Bellevue WA 98006
562-4900
This market research firm employs about 30 in its Puget Sound area office. It also has an office in Portland. Contact: Bill Young.

Marvin Stein & Associates
2221 Fifth Ave.
Seattle WA 98121
441-1449
Yolanda Stein handles personnel for this commercial interior design firm.

McCann-Erickson
1011 Western Ave., #600
Seattle WA 98104
682-6360
Amanda Dwyer handles personnel for this large advertising agency, a unit of the Interpublic Group of Companies, New York. Billings in 1991 reached $49 million, according to *Washington CEO*.

McCaw Cellular Communications Inc.
5400 Carillon Point
Kirkland WA 98033
827-4500
Jobline: 828-8484 (Touchtone telephones only)
This cellular telephone company employs an estimated 700 in the Puget Sound area. The jobline is organized by region; if you're interested in a specific position, you can leave an inquiry on the tape.

McChord Credit Union
P.O. Box 4207
Tacoma WA 98438
584-6413
Jobline: 589-8012
This credit union accepts applications only for open positions. You can pick up an application form at the personnel office on the second floor of the Lakewood branch. Recent opportunities: marketing coordinator and teller.

McHugh Restaurants
419 Occidental S., #501
Seattle WA 98104
223-9353
This upscale restaurant chain, which runs New Jake's, the Leschi

Lake Cafe, F. X. McRory's and the Roost, has a very small corporate staff, but resumes are always welcome. If you're interested in a restaurant position, contact Katie Berg.

Media Index Publishing, Inc.
P.O. Box 24365
Seattle WA 98124
382-9220
This firm publishes *Media Inc.*, a monthly tabloid for the Washington and Oregon advertising, entertainment and production industries. There are staff writing positions and free-lance material is also purchased. Contact Richard K. Woltjer. (Submission of unsolicited manuscripts is not recommended.) The firm also publishes an annual index to regional film, video and audio production and a media buying guide.

Mercer Island Reporter
P.O. Box 38
Mercer Island WA 98040
232-1215
Owned by the Persis Corp., which also owns the *Journal American*, this weekly has an editorial staff of six headed by Virginia Smyth.

Merrill Lynch & Co.
The Puget Sound branch offices of this brokerage firm are divided into three groups, with each group handling its own hiring. Besides brokers (called financial consultants by Merrill Lynch), there are support positions in sales and operations.

Merrill Lynch & Co.
1215 Fourth Ave.
Seattle WA 98161
464-3500
In the larger of the Seattle offices, Marilyn Brown, the sales manager's assistant, coordinates hiring for financial consultants. Sales assistants are hired by Margo Lindberg and operations assistants by Lona McAlister.

Merrill Lynch & Co.
10900 N.E. 4th St., #2130
Bellevue WA 98004
462-8140
Hiring for the smaller Seattle office and the Bellevue, Bellingham, Lynnwood, Everett and Richland offices is done in this office. Resumes can be directed to Charles Weaver.

Merrill Lynch & Co.
820 S. A St., #700
Tacoma WA 98401
597-8311
Hiring for the Tacoma and Federal Way offices is done here. Resumes
can be directed to Rod Hagenbuch.

Metropolitan Federal Savings and Loan Association
1520 Fourth Ave.
Seattle WA 98101-1648
625-1818
Cathy McAlhaney handles personnel for this thrift.

Microcomputer Electronics Corp.
12421 Willows Rd. N.E., Second Floor
Kirkland WA 98034
821-2800
Inquiries regarding this firm, which designs and develops integrated
flight management systems, can be directed to "Human Resources."

Microrim Inc.
15395 S.E. 30th Pl.
Bellevue WA 98007
649-9500
R:Base is the best-known product of this software firm. Seattle-area
employment: about 60. You can direct a resume to Carol Cissell, the
corporate administrator.

Microsoft Corp.
One Microsoft Way
Redmond WA 98052-6399
882-8080
This large software firm does not have a jobline, but openings are
posted in its recruiting office, Building 21. Postings are updated each
Monday afternoon. You'll also find openings, both permanent and
contract, advertised in the Seattle papers. Resumes are always
accepted; address yours to "Recruiting."

Milgard Manufacturing
P.O. Box 11368
Tacoma WA 98411-0368
922-6030
Gary Buchanan is the human resources director for this privately-
owned manufacturer of windows and doors.

Milliman & Robertson, Inc.
1301 Fifth Ave., #3800
Seattle WA 98101
624-7940
Sharon Barker handles personnel for this firm of consulting actuaries.

Millstone Coffee Inc.
729 100th S.E.
Everett WA 98208
347-3995
From Seattle: 827-2109
Phil Johnson heads this firm, which wholesales some 70 varieties of coffee across the U.S. The corporate staff includes about 50. Human resources director: Calene Jensen.

Molbak's Greenhouse & Nursery
13625 N.E. 175th
Woodinville WA 98072
483-5000
Kathy Kemper handles personnel for this large nursery and retail operation. Molbak's also owns a Pike Place Market retail store:

Seattle Garden Center
1600 Pike Place
Seattle WA 98101
448-0431

Momentum Distribution Inc.
500 108th N.E., #1900
Bellevue WA 98004-5536
646-6550
This distributor of graphics products and industrial textiles employs several hundred across the U.S., but the corporate staff is only about 30. Richard Engebrecht is chairman and CEO.

The Morning News Tribune
P.O. Box 11000
Tacoma WA 98411
597-8511
From Seattle: 447-0541
Jobline: 597-8590
This Tacoma daily, with a weekday circulation of about 116,000, is owned by McClatchy Newspapers of Sacramento. If you are applying in person, you must complete your application at the Tribune office at 1950 State St. Another McClatchy subsidiary:

Pierce County Herald
P.O. Box 517
Puyallup WA 98371-0170
841-2481

Moss Adams
1001 Fourth Ave., #2900
Seattle WA 98154
223-1820
Sue Carpenter is the personnel contact for this public accounting and consulting firm.

The Mountaineers
300 3rd W.
Seattle WA 948119
284-6318
Steve Kostie, member services manager, handles most personnel inquiries for this nonprofit, which has 13,200 members and four volunteer-run branches (in Olympia, Bellingham, Everett and Tacoma). The main office employs about 15, mostly in member services (which takes reservations for Mountaineers outings). There's also a small deli and room rental staff. Internships may be available in the conservation department; for information, contact Maryann Mann, conservation division manager. The Mountaineers publishing operation has its own location:

Mountaineers Books
1011 S.W. Klickitat, #107
Seattle WA 98134
223-6303
Donna DeShazo heads this division, which issues approximately 30 titles a year. There's a staff of about 15 and free-lance opportunities.

MultiCare Medical Center
409 S. J St.
P.O. Box 5299
Tacoma WA 98405
594-1250
Jobline: 594-1256
Tacoma General and Mary Bridge Children's hospitals are the major units of this medical center. Recent openings have been in accounting, computer programming, marketing, social work and building security.

Murray Pacific Corp.
1201 Pacific Ave., #1750
Tacoma WA 98402
383-4911
From Seattle: 838-9913
This is the corporate headquarters. Unsolicited resumes are discouraged. The timber division, which hires its own staff, is located at:

Murray Pacific
Timber Products Division
3502 Lincoln Ave. E.
Tacoma WA 98421
383-5871
The office staff here is small; most employees work in purchasing, exporting or sales.

Musak Limited Partnership
400 N. 34th, #200
Seattle WA 98103
633-3000
This background music company employs about 200 in its two corporate offices. Turnover is limited and the few openings are usually advertised in the daily papers. Matthew McTee is head of human resources.

Nalley's Fine Foods
P.O. Box 11046
Tacoma WA 98411
383-1621
Potato chips, pickles, salad dressings and canned beef stew are examples of the products of this division of Curtice-Burns. A subsidiary of Nalley's is Adams Peanut Butter, also of Tacoma. Jacqueline Bateman, personnel manager, handles inquiries regarding professional and administrative positions. In Tacoma alone, the firm employs about 1,000.

The NBBJ Group
111 S. Jackson
Seattle WA 98104
223-5555
Scott Johnson handles personnel for this firm, one of the area's largest architects. An interior design subsidiary handles its own hiring:

Business Space Design
111 S. Jackson
Seattle WA 98104
223-5000
Personnel director: Michael Kreis.

NC Machinery
P.O. Box 88786
Seattle WA 98138-2786
251-5800
A subsidiary of the Skinner Corp., this is a Caterpillar equipment dealership. Mike Omalev is the personnel director.

Neopath, Inc.
1750 112th Ave. N.E., B-101
Bellevue WA 98004
455-5932
This biotech firm is developing an automated Pap smear screening system. Mike Lorenz is president and chief executive officer.

NeoRx Corp.
410 W. Harrison
Seattle WA 98119
281-7001
Paul Abrams is president and Wanda Applebaum the personnel contact for this cancer research firm, which currently employs about 125.

Nintendo of America
P.O. Box 957
Redmond WA 98073
882-2040
Jobline: 861-2170 (Touchtone telephones only)
Helping customers play games is one of the jobs available at this video-game developer, a subsidiary of the Kyoto-based Nintendo Co. Ltd. that dominates the U.S. home video game market. Other recent openings: material planner, paralegal and assistant general counsel.

Nordstrom
628-2111
If you're interested in working in one of this specialty retailer's stores, apply at the appropriate store's personnel office. If you're interested in a corporate position, your application should be submitted as indicated:

For advertising, merchandising, benefits, data processing and store planning:

Nordstrom Personnel
Seaboard Building
1501 Fifth Ave.
Seattle WA 98101

For finance and credit:

Nordstrom Personnel
Arcade Building
1321 Second Ave.
Seattle WA 98101

North Pacific Bank
P.O. Box 9188
Tacoma WA 98409
472-3333
Ronda Ross is the human resources director for this community bank.

Northwest Administrators Inc.
2323 Eastlake Ave. E.
Seattle WA 98102
329-4900
If you're interested in administration of employee benefits plans, you can direct your resume to Debbie Skaare, human resources. Openings are usually advertised in the Seattle *Times*.

Northwest Airlines
Employment Department
Minneapolis-St. Paul International Airport
St. Paul MN 55111
(612) 726-2111
If you're interested in Northwest's openings here or elsewhere in the country, contact the central employment office.

Northwest Hospital
1550 N. 115th St.
Seattle WA 98133
364-0500
Jobline: 361-1791
This 281-bed hospital and its affiliated clinics offers a variety of opportunities. Job announcements are posted near the personnel office and cafeteria.

Northwest Kidney Center
700 Broadway
Seattle WA 98122
292-2946
Jobline: 292-3924
This outpatient dialysis center has several satellite operations. Job openings are posted in the personnel office; applications are accepted between 1 and 4 p.m. weekdays. Recent openings were for pharmacists, nurses and dialysis technicians.

Northwest Mobile Television
12698 Gateway Dr.
Seattle WA 98168
242-0642
Purchased by three former King executives as part of the sale of King Broadcasting assets in 1992, NMT is now headed by Steven Clifford, chairman and CEO, and Tim Abhold, president. According to the *Puget Sound Business Journal*, NMT is the largest mobile television company in the industry with annual revenues estimated at $15 million.

Northwest Parent Publishing
2107 Elliott Ave., #303
Seattle WA 98121
441-0191
Ann Bergman heads this firm, which publishes *Seattle's Child, Eastside Parent* and *Pierce County Parent* for educators and families with small children. The staff is small; many employees are part-timers. If you're a free-lance writer or photographer, query before sending material.

Norwest Venture Capital
777 108th N.E.
Bellevue WA 9800
646-3444
One of the partners in Northwest Mobile Television (see above), this venture capital firm is headed locally by George Still Jr.

Oberto Sausage Co., Inc.
P.O. Box 429
Kent WA 98035
623-3470
Sausage and specialty meats are manufactured at three Puget Sound area plants by this firm. Sydney Johnson handles personnel.

O'Brien International Inc.
P.O. Box 97020
Redmond WA 98073-9720
881-5900
Sharon Black handles personnel for this manufacturer of water skis, sailboards and other water recreational equipment. A subsidiary of the Coleman Co., O'Brien employs about 145.

Ocean Beauty Seafoods Inc.
P.O. Box C-70739
Seattle WA 98107
285-6800
One of the largest fish processors based in Seattle, Ocean Beauty includes a subsidiary, Washington Fish. Contact: Ed Adele.

Odom Corp.
P.O. Box 24627
Seattle WA 98124
623-3256
This privately-held holding company is headed by John Odom, who handles management recruiting. Subsidiaries include Alaska Beverage and Coca Cola Northwest Bottling.

The Olympian
P.O. Box 407
Olympia WA 98507
754-5490
Toll-free within Washington: (800) 869-7080
James H. Stevenson is managing editor of this 31,000-circulation daily, a Gannett publication. Dan Walker is advertising director and Carol Achatx personnel director. Openings are posted in the personnel office.

Olympic Savings Bank
P.O. Box 1950
Seattle WA 98111-1950
382-4900
Contact: Faith Collins in human resources.

Olympic Venture Partners
2420 Carillon Point
Kirkland WA 98033
889-9192
George Clute is one of the managing partners at this venture capital firm.

Oncomembrane
1201 Third Ave., #5100
Seattle WA 98101
285-1808
Established in 1986 by Otsuka, this biotech is developing cancer diagnostic products. Tosh Tanaka heads a staff of 10.

Oroweat Foods Co.
1604 N. 34th
Seattle WA 98103
634-2700
Job openings at this bakery are often posted on the window by the retail outlet. Resumes can be sent to "Personnel." A subsidiary of Philip Morris, Oroweat employs about 250 locally.

Outdoor Empire Publishing Co., Inc.
511 Eastlake Ave. E.
Seattle WA 98109
624-3845
The weekly *Fishing and Hunting News*, with a circulation of nearly 140,000, is the flagship publication of this printing and publishing firm. Margaret Durante is the human resources director.

Overlake Hospital Medical Center
1035 116th Ave. N.E.
Bellevue WA 98004
454-4011
Jobline: 462-5150
This 225-bed facility posts its job openings outside the personnel office and on a board near the cafeteria. Many openings are also advertised.

Pabst Brewing Co.
P. O. Box 947
Olympia WA 948507
754-5000
This brewer of Olympia beer, located in Tumwater at the intersection of Schmidt Place and Custer Way, employs more than 400. The receptionist has applications.

PACCAR, Inc.
This Fortune 500 firm is the corporate parent for Kenworth and Peterbilt trucks as well as the Al's Auto Supply retail chain. PACCAR operates worldwide, so it's a company to consider if you have (or

would like) international experience. There also are a variety of opportunities in the company's finance and leasing subsidiaries. Besides the Bellevue corporate headquarters, locations in the Puget Sound area include Kirkland, Seattle, Renton and the PACCAR Technical Center in Mt. Vernon. Personnel contacts in the Seattle area include:

Corporate
P.O. Box 1518
Bellevue WA 98009

Regarding mid-management and professional positions:
Patty Cumming, Employee Relations Manager, 455-7547

Regarding support positions:
Melody Butenko, Human Resources Coordinator, 455-7375

Kenworth Division Headquarters
P.O. Box 1000
Kirkland WA 98083
Dan Snell, Human Resources Director, 828-5750

Kenworth Seattle Plant
8801 E. Marginal Way S.
Seattle WA 98108
Jim Britton, Personnel Manager, 767-8577

PACCAR Parts
750 Houser Way N.
Renton WA 98055
Bill Meyers, Employee Relations Manager, 251-7028

PACCAR Management Information Systems
P.O. Box 1518
Bellevue WA 98009

Regarding managerial positions:
Ree Laughlin, Human Resources Director, 251-7297

Regarding support positions:
Joan Stevens, Human Resources Coordinator, 462-4190

PACCAR Financial
P.O. Box 1518
Bellevue WA 98009

Regarding managerial positions:
Ree Laughlin, Human Resources Director, 251-7297

Regarding professional and technical positions:
Cheryl Nishimoto, Human Resources Manager, 462-6231

PACCAR Leasing
P.O. Box 1518
Bellevue WA 98009

Regarding managerial positions:
Ree Laughlin, Human Resources Director, 251-7297

Regarding professional and technical positions:
Jerry Huffman, Human Resources Manager, 462-6239

PACCAR Automotive, Inc.
(Al's Auto Supply)
1400 N. 4th
Renton WA 98055
Ingrid Rasch, Human Resources Director, 251-7692

Pacific Electro Dynamics Inc.
P.O. Box 97045
Redmond WA 98073-9745
881-1700
PED, a division of Olin Corp., makes aviation electronics. You
can consult the openings book in the lobby, 11465 Willows Road
N.E. Or submit your resume to Tica Gordon, the recruiter.

Pacific First Financial Corp.
P.O. Box 91029
Seattle WA 98111-9129
224-3000
Jobline: 224-3330 (Touchtone telephones only)
PFF owns the state's second largest thrift, Pacific First Bank. To
review openings, visit the human resources department, 1420 Fifth
Ave., 13th floor, between 9 a.m. and 4 p.m. weekdays. Or visit any
branch. Examples of recent openings: loan funder, cash management
services managers, accounting analyst and collections specialist.

Pacific Lumber & Shipping Co.

P.O. Box 21785
Seattle WA 98111
682-7262
This family-owned forest products manufacturing and distributing firm operates mills in Rochester, Morton, Packwood and Randle. Scott Stover is the personnel contact for the small staff at the corporate office.

Pacific Media Group

2314 Third Ave.
Seattle WA 98121
461-1300
This printing and publishing firm was created by a Houston investor group's purchase of Murray Publishing and Flaherty Newspapers. The company also runs a web and sheet-fed print shop. There are four publishers, each with responsibility for several publications; each is aware of openings throughout the firm. For information, contact Denis Law, one of the publishers. For opportunities in the printing operation, ask for the name of the person who should receive your resume.

Pacific Medical Center

1200 12th Ave. S.
Seattle WA 98144
326-2111
Jobline: 326-4120 (Touchtone telephones only)
This outpatient facility has six clinics. Its jobline lists job titles, locations and hours on the jobline. Recent openings were for registered nurses, pharmacy assistants, secretaries and lab assistants.

Pacific Northwest Bank

1111 Third Ave.
Seattle WA 98101
624-0600
Pat Fahey is president of this small bank, which opened branches in Seattle and Bellevue in 1987. According to *Washington CEO*, by 1992 the bank had assets of $75 million. Total employment: about 40.

Pacific Northwest Media, Inc.

701 Dexter Ave. N., #101
Seattle WA 98109
284-1750
This firm, a division of Micromedia Affiliates, publishes two glossy regional magazines: *Pacific Northwest* and *Greater Seattle*. Both

publications have small staffs supplemented by free-lancers. At press time, *Pacific Northwest* was edited by Ann Naumann and *Greater Seattle* by Giselle Smith.

Pacific Nuclear Systems
1010 S. 336th, #220
Federal Way WA 98003
874-2235
This firm processes, handles and disposes of low- and high-level nuclear waste. Many positions require engineering backgrounds, but some nontechnical positions exist. Alesa McCrory is the personnel contact.

Pacific Sound Resources
2801 S.W. Florida St.
Seattle WA 98126
932-0445
Ted DePriest is the president of this manufacturer of forest products. The corporate staff is very small. Formerly The Wyckoff Co.

Pacific Trail
1310 Mercer St.
Seattle WA 98109
622-8730
Kelly Case is the personnel manager at this family-owned manufacturer of outerwear (primarily skiwear and casual jackets).

Panlabs Inc.
11804 North Creek Parkway S.
Bothell WA 98011
487-8200
This contract research lab provides research for pharmacology and fermentation industries. You can ask the receptionist regarding current openings. Jane Ramsey is human resources manager.

Paradigm Press
2701 First Ave., #250
Seattle WA 98121
441-5871
Mimi Kirsch and Paul Temple head this firm, which publishes the Alaska and Horizon airlines in-flight magazines. Occasional free-lance writing opportunities exist; contact Paul Frichtl, who edits both publications.

Parametrix Inc.
13020 Northup Way
Bellevue WA 98005
455-2550
If you'd applying to this environmental and engineering consulting
firm, your resume should be directed to "Personnel."

Parenting Press
11065 5th N. E., #7
Seattle WA 98125
364-2900
Shari Steelsmith is the managing editor of this publishing firm, which
employs 11; some free-lance art opportunities exist.

Path
4 Nickerson St.
Seattle WA 98109-1699
285-3500
One of Seattle's largest nonprofits, with 160 employees total and 125
locally, Path (Program for Appropriate Technology in Health) makes
medical technology available to developing countries. The organization develops diagnostic and health-care devices and trains native
health care educators. Personnel director Jackie Sperry says staff falls
into three categories. The program staff usually has public health
training, often at the postgraduate level, and experience in developing
countries. Most are at least bilingual. The technical staff members
have bioscience or engineering training and work on diagnostic and
preventative product development. The third category is the administrative staff (personnel, purchasing, accounting, etc.). Check the job
listing book at the receptionist's desk. Unsolicited resumes are
welcome. All clerical applicants should have excellent communications and computer skills.

Paul Thomas Winery
1717 136th Pl. N.E.
Bellevue WA 98005
747-1008
This winery's staff is small (only four full-time) and openings are
infrequent. However, it's a great place to get started in the wine
industry, says Colleen Cave, sales and marketing manager.

Pay 'N Pak
Began liquidation of all stores in summer, 1992.

Pay 'n Save Drug Stores Inc.
Sold to Pay-Less Drug Stores in July, 1992.

Pemco Financial Center
325 Eastlake Ave. E.
Seattle WA 98109
628-4090
Jobline: 628-8740
Pemco Mutual Insurance, Evergreen Bank and Washington School
Employees Credit Union share a personnel office.

Peninsula Gateway
P.O. Box 407
Gig Harbor WA 98335
851-9921
A weekly paper published by Thomas Taylor, the *Gateway* has a paid
circulation of 10,000 and an editorial staff of five.

Perkins Coie
1201 Third Ave., #4000
Seattle WA 98101
583-8888
For this law firm, one of Seattle's largest, Janet Cunningham handles
recruiting of attorneys. Administrative staff is recruited by two
employment administrators, Joyce Herman and Ann Mary Oylear.

Perstort-Xytec Inc.
9350 47th Ave. S.W.
Tacoma WA 98499
582-0644
From Seattle: 623-4007
A manufacturer of industrial containers, this firm employs about 100.
Inquiries regarding openings on the office staff can be sent to Deborah
Feste-Kirk, accounting manager.

PGL Building Products
P.O. Box 1049
Auburn WA 98071
941-2600
When this building products distributor has openings, you'll find
them advertised in the daily papers and posted at local college
placement offices. Contact: Teresa Kaelin, personnel manager.

Phoenix Partners

1000 Second Ave., #3600
Seattle WA 98104
624-8968
Stuart Johnston is the managing partner for this venture capital firm.

Physio-Control Corp.

P.O. Box 97006
Redmond WA 98073-9706
867-4000
A division of Eli Lilly & Co., Physio produces cardiac care systems. Openings are advertised in the Seattle papers; resumes can be directed to "Personnel."

Pioneer Bank

P.O. Box M
Lynnwood WA 98046
771-2525
Jobline: through operator (Touchtone telephones only)
This thrift serves Snohomish and King counties.

Piper, Jaffray & Hopwood Inc.

Each office of this brokerage and investment banking firm handles its own recruiting.

Piper, Jaffray & Hopwood Inc.
P.O. Box 34930
Seattle WA 98124-1930
287-8700
Personnel manager: Sherry Allen

Piper, Jaffray & Hopwood Inc.
P.O. Box 97308
Bellevue WA 98009
646-7700
Personnel manager: Adrienne Coccia.

Piper, Jaffray & Hopwood Inc.
2828 Colby Ave., #405
Everett WA 92011
259-2930
Personnel manager: Eileen Dunster.

Plum Creek Timber Co.
999 Third Ave., #2300
Seattle WA 98104
467-3600
One of the largest private owners of Northwest timberland, Plum Creek was formed in 1989 to operate the forest products business formerly owned by Burlington Resources Inc. David Leland is president.

Portac Inc.
4215 East-West Road
Tacoma WA 98421
922-9900
From Seattle: 622-6387
Owned by Mitsui & Co. U.S.A., this is a lumber milling and exporting firm with operations on the Olympic Peninsula as well as in Tacoma. Mitsui & Co. also maintains a sales office in Seattle. Terry Mathern handles administrative recruiting.

POSdata
P.O. Box 1305
Gig Harbor WA 98335
851-6500
A subsidiary of Sensormatic Electronics Corp., POSdata supplies point-of-sale code scanning equipment. Employs 60. Sherryl Peterson handles human resources.

Precor Inc.
P.O. Box 3004
Bothell WA 98041
486-9292
Jobline: 486-9292, Ext. 444
Founded in 1980, Precor makes fitness equipment, including rowing machines, stationary bicycles and treadmills. Bill Potts is president.

Preston Thorgrimson Shidler Gates & Ellis
701 Fifth Ave., #5400
Seattle WA 98104
623-7580
This law firm also has offices in Bellevue, Tacoma, Spokane, Anchorage and Washington, D.C. Susan Jones is the hiring partner, handling the recruiting of attorneys; David Buckner, personnel director, hires for all other positions.

Price Waterhouse
1001 Fourth Ave. Plaza, #4200
Seattle WA 98154
622-1505
Rachelle Winkler is the human resources director for this "Big 6" accounting and consulting firm.

Princess Tours
2815 Second Ave.
Seattle WA 98121
728-4202
Owned by P & O, Ltd., this firm runs cruises and land tours to Alaska. There are both permanent and seasonal opportunities. Julie Huffar is the personnel director.

Proctor and Associates
15050 N.E. 36th
Redmond WA 98052
881-7000
Inquiries regarding openings at this telecommunications manufacturer can be directed to Debra Shute, human resources.

ProCyte Corp.
12040 115th Ave. N.E., #210
Kirkland WA 98034-6900
820-4548
Joseph Ashley is president of this publicly-traded biotech firm, which is developing peptide-copper compounds to promote healing, tissue repair and hair growth.

Professional Review Organization for Washington
10700 Meridian Ave. N., #100
Seattle WA 98133
364-9700
Nancy Dorsey handles personnel for this health care organization.

Providence Hospital
916 Pacific
P.O. Box 1067
Everett WA 98206
258-7267
Jobline: 258-7562
This 200-bed facility posts its job openings in the personnel office, located on the main floor.

Providence Medical Center
500 17th Ave.
Seattle WA 98122
320-2464
Nurse recruiter: 320-2476
Jobline: 320-2020
Use the jobline or review the postings in Providence's main hallway, near the cafeteria, or in the personnel office, located on the main floor near the gift shop. Positions in purchasing, accounting and child care are examples of the non-nursing opportunities at this 376-bed hospital. Providence also operates Hospice of Seattle and several clinics.

Prudential Securities
This brokerage firm's offices hire separately. Branch managers handle inquiries regarding broker positions and the office managers the applications for support jobs.

Prudential Securities
1201 Third Ave., #3500
Seattle WA 98101
464-8200
Branch manager: Paul Wonnacott.

Prudential Securities
P.O. Box 97314
Bellevue WA 98009
451-7170
Branch manager: Michael McQuaid.

PTI Communications
Western Division
8102 Skansie Ave.
Gig Harbor WA 98332-8415
851-8118
Jobline: 851-1376
A subsidiary of Pacific Telecom, Vancouver, this is the state's third largest telephone company (in annual sales). Openings are posted at state Job Service Centers; you can also inquire at the front desk.

Puget Sound Bancorp.
1119 Pacific Ave.
Tacoma WA 98411
593-3600
Joblines:
From Tacoma: 593-5307
From Seattle:, 447-2017, Ext. 5307
At press time, a sale to KeyCorp. was pending. See Key Bank of Washington.

Puget Sound Blood Center
921 Terry Ave.
Seattle WA 98104-1256
292-6500
Jobline: 292-2302
Shirley Durgan is the personnel director for this nonprofit clinical and research medical facility serving 10 Northwest Washington counties. Recent openings were for a systems analyst, lab courier and lab assistant.

Puget Sound Business Journal
101 Yesler Way, #200
Seattle WA 98104
583-0701
One of several weeklies owned by American City Business Journals, this publication has a circulation of approximately 20,000. Mike Flynn is publisher and Donald Nelson executive editor.

Puget Sound Hospital
215 36th St.
Tacoma WA 98408
474-0561
From Seattle: 623-1417
Jobline: Through operator, Ext. 103
Recent openings at this medical facility included nurse manager, mental health counselor, data entry clerk and radiology technician.

Puget Sound Power & Light Co. (Puget Power)
Employee Services
P.O. Box 0868
Bellevue WA 98009-0868
454-6363
Jobline: Ext. 2692
An investor-owned utility, Puget Power provides electric service within Washington state. Most operations are in the Puget Sound

area. Entry level openings are posted at the state Job Service Centers.

Puyallup Valley Bank
P.O. Box 578
Puyallup WA 98371
848-2316
David Brown is president of this multi-branch local commercial bank.

Quadrant Corp.
P.O. Box 130
Bellevue WA 98009
455-2900
A subsidiary of the Weyerhaeuser Co., Quadrant handles both commercial and residential development. Personnel director is Virginia Woods.

Quality Food Centers (QFC) Inc.
10116 N.E. 8th
Bellevue WA 98004
455-3761
Concentrated in King County, this upscale supermarket chain had about 30 stores at press time. The corporate office employs about 100. Resumes may be directed to specific departments. Adena Sanders, office manager, hires for accounting support positions.

Quicksoft Inc.
219 First Ave. N.. #224
Seattle WA 98109
282-0452
Leo Nikora is president of this 20-person firm, which provides word processing software.

Quinton Instrument Co.
2121 Terry Ave.
Seattle WA 98121
223-7373
A. H. Robins owns this manufacturer of high-tech medical instruments. Ed Schnebele is the personnel director.

Ragan MacKenzie, Inc.
999 Third Ave., #4300
Seattle WA 98104
343-5000
Brooks Ragan heads this investment banking firm. Judy Sterling is the personnel director.

Raima Corp.
3245 146th Pl. S.E., #230
Bellevue WA 98007
747-5570
Stephen Smith heads this 80-person firm, which produces database management software.

Rainier Brewing Co.
P.O. Box 24828
Seattle WA 98124
622-2600
A subsidiary of G. Heileman Brewing Co., this firm posts openings only internally. However, you're welcome to call the receptionist and inquire about current openings. Administrative staff: 100.

Rane Corp.
10802 47th Ave. W.
Everett WA 98204
355-6000
Linda Arink, chief executive officer, handles personnel for this manufacturer of professional audio products.

Raytheon Marine Corp.
1521 S. 92nd Pl., #D
Seattle WA 98108
763-7500
Frances Masters is the personnel manager for this marine electronics distribution operation.

Recreational Equipment Inc.
6750 S. 228th
Kent WA 98032
395-3780
Joblines:
Corporate headquarters: 395-4694
Distribution center: 891-2562
The country's largest consumer cooperative, REI operates 25 retail outlets across the U.S., a huge mail order sales department and a distribution center in Sumner. Corporate openings can be reviewed in the foyer of the headquarters office. Openings were recently posted in human resources, direct mail, purchasing, accounts payable, merchandising and catalog sales. For part-time or full-time retail positions, apply at the store of your choice.

Redhook Ale Brewery
3400 Phinney Ave. N.
Seattle WA 98103
548-8000
Established in 1981, this microbrewery employs 20 full-time. There's little turnover--and lots of competition for the few openings, warns the staff.

Redmond National Bank
P.O. Box 3430
Redmond WA 98073
881-8111
Keith Galpin is president of this community bank, which opened in late 1988. Current employment: 10.

Regis McKenna
601 Union St., #3100
Seattle WA 98101
292-4299
An affiliate of KPMG Peat Marwick, this firm provides public relations consulting to high-tech companies. The local branch, headed by Barbara Curtis, employs fewer than 10.

Reliance Insurance Co.
2505 S. 320th St., #C-2999
Federal Way WA 98003
952-5000
A regional headquarters for a nationwide property and casualty insurance company, this office employs about 200. Direct resumes to Robyn Layne, human resources. The commercial lines office, which employs 45 in downtown Seattle, hires its own staff. Contact:

Reliance Insurance Co.
701 Fifth Ave., #3850
Seattle WA 98104
386-5700

Renaware Distributors, Inc.
P.O. Box 97050
Redmond WA 98073
881-6171
Mary Porter is the personnel director for this direct sales company, known to many of us for the cookware it offers.

Restaurants Unlimited, Inc.
1818 N. Northlake Way
Seattle WA 98103
634-0550
Jobline: through operator
Cutter's Bayhouse, Pantana, Palisade and Triples are just four of the
more than 20 full-service restaurants owned by this regional chain. A
subsidiary, Cinnabon, operates cinnamon roll bakeries in shopping
malls. Tom Griffith is the corporate recruiter.

Revelation Technologies, Inc.
3633 136th Pl. S.E., #200
Bellevue WA 98006
643-9898
A division of the New York City-based Revelation, this software firm
employs 75.

Robbins Co.
P.O. Box 97927
Kent WA 98064-9727
872-0500
Dick Robbins is president of this firm, which employs more than 250
nationwide. Products include machines for cutting round tunnels
through mountains as well as rectangular holes on mining sites. Many
openings are advertised; you can also visit the reception desk at the
office, located at 22445 76th Ave. S.

Rocket Research Company/Olin
P.O. Box 97009
Redmond WA 98073
885-5000
A division of Olin Corp., this firm manufactures rocket engines.
About 50 per cent of its business is defense, the *Puget Sound Business
Journal* recently reported. Openings are posted in the lobby of the
main entrance, 11441 Willows Road N.E. Personnel recruiter: Ernest
Batiste.

The Rocket
2028 Fifth Ave.
Seattle WA 98121
728-7625
This free monthly music and entertainment magazine has a press run
of 70,000, but the full-time staff is small. If you're interested in free-
lance writing, check a sample issue and contact Grant Alden, managing editor.

The Rockey Co. Inc.
2121 Fifth Ave.
Seattle WA 98121
728-1100
Jay Rockey is chairman and Nancy Williamson personnel director of this firm, one of Seattle's oldest and largest in public relations.

Roffe Inc.
808 Howell St.
Seattle WA 98101
622-0456
Judy Chapman is the personnel director for this sportswear firm, which manufactures skiwear and sweaters under the Roffe and Demetre names. The corporate staff is small.

R.W. Beck & Associates
2101 Fourth Ave., #600
Seattle WA 98121
441-7500
This firm provides engineering consulting and services in planning, technical and financial feasibility, design and construction management. Van Finger is director, human resources.

The Sabey Companies
201 Elliott Ave. W., #100
Seattle WA 98119
281-8700
This privately held conglomerate includes Sabey Corp. and Berkley Construction.

Safeco Insurance Corp.
Safeco Plaza
Seattle WA 98185
545-5000
Jobline: 545-3233
One of Seattle's major service industry employers, Safeco is headquartered in the University District. Several operations are located in Redmond. Safeco's services include insurance, securities, annuities, credit and escrow. In the headquarters employment center and on the jobline, you'll learn of positions in Seattle. A few Redmond operations, including the print shop and supply center, also post their openings on the jobline.

Safeco Life Insurance Co.
15411 N.E. 51st St.
Redmond WA 98052
Personnel: 867-8101
Safeco's Redmond campus is the headquarters for its life insurance company, which employs approximately 725 in such areas as pension administration, information systems, accounting, underwriting and claims. There's no jobline, but you can call the personnel office.

Safeco Property and Casualty Co.
4909 156th Ave. N.E.
Redmond WA 98052
881-4500
About 500 work in the regional and branch offices of the property and casualty subsidiary, which also has offices in Portland and Spokane. Most positions are in claims, underwriting and customer service.

Safeway Stores Inc.
1121 124th N.E.
Bellevue WA 98005
455-6444
Jobline: 455-6501
Many Safeway positions, including those at the Bellevue division office and distribution center, are filled through referrals from the state Job Service Centers; for some entry level positions, you can apply directly at stores. Some positions in the administrative office are advertised in the Seattle papers. Susan Hitchcock is the human resources manager.

St. Claire Hospital
11311 Bridgeport Way S.W.
Tacoma WA 98499
588-1711
Jobline: 581-6419
Formerly Lakewood Hospital, this facility is now operated by Franciscan Health Services of Washington.

St. Francis Community Hospital
34515 9th Ave. S.
Federal Way WA 98003
838-9700
Jobline:
Seattle: 838-9700, Ext. 7930
Tacoma: 952-7930
This 110-bed hospital is owned by Franciscan Health Services.

St. Joseph Hospital and Health Care Center
P.O. Box 2197
Tacoma WA 98401
627-4101
Jobline: 591-6623
This 340-bed facility is owned by Franciscan Health Services of Washington. Special programs include a burn center and kidney renal dialysis.

St. Peter Hospital
413 Lilly Rd. N.E.
Olympia WA 98506
Personnel: 493-7439
Owned by the Sisters of Providence, this hospital has approximately 350 beds and more than 1,300 employee.

Salmon Bay Communications
1515 N.W. 51st
Seattle WA 98107
789-5333
This firm publishes *Pacific Fishing*, a periodical for commercial fishermen. The staff is small, but articles and photos are purchased from free-lancers. For information, contact Steve Shapiro, editor.

Sasquatch Publishing Inc.
1931 Second Ave.
Seattle WA 98101
441-5555
This firm publishes weekly news and arts tabloids, the *Seattle Weekly* and *Eastside Week* as well as several books about Northwest living and entertainment. David Brewster is editor-in-chief and publisher of the *Seattle Weekly*; Katherine Koberg is managing editor. There are opportunities for free-lance writing; inquire before submitting material. If you're interested in selling advertising, contact Ellen Cole, the display advertising manager. The book publishing staff is small; Chad Haight is publisher.

Satisfaction Guaranteed Eateries
419 Occidental S.
Seattle WA 98104
625-9818
Headed by Tim Firnstahl, this five-outlet upscale restaurant chain includes Von's and Jake's.

Schuck's Auto Supply Inc./Northern Automotive Corp.
2401 W. Valley Highway N.
Auburn WA 98002
833-1115
Schuck's is based in Phoenix, but Harry Lang, the human resources director in this office, handles much of the recruiting for regional offices and stores in the Northwest.

Schwartz Bros. Restaurants
300 120th Ave. N.E.
Bellevue WA 98005
455-3948
Jobline: 637-4864, #6 (Touchtone telephones only)
This restaurant and catering operation includes The Butcher, Gretchen's Of Course and Benjamin's. The corporate staff is small; most openings are at entry level. Camille Keefe is the personnel director.

Science Applications International Corp.
18706 North Creek Parkway, #110
Bothell WA 98011
485-5800
In the Puget Sound area, the San Diego-based SAIC has several offices, most focusing on environmental consulting. Total local employment is about 150. Most openings are for engineers and geologists. The Bothell operations are the largest; resumes can be sent to "Personnel" at the address above. If you're interested in the marine consulting handled by the Bellevue office, contact:

Science Applications International Corp.
13400-B Northup Way, #36
Bellevue WA 98005
747-7152

Seafair
2001 Sixth Ave., #2800
Seattle WA 98121-2574
728-0123
Bob Gobrecht is managing director of Seafair, a Seattle summer festival that includes neighborhood parades, downtown parades, special events and hydroplane races. The permanent staff is less than 10; internships are sometimes available for the summer.

Seafirst Corp.
Personnel
P.O. Box 3977
Seattle WA 98124
358-3000
Jobline: 358-7523
Owned by BankAmerica, this was Washington's largest commercial bank even before the 1992 merger with Security Pacific. Besides traditional banking jobs, Seafirst offers some unusual opportunities. For example, it has people who work in disaster recovery, the sale of repossessed property, printing and relocation. Like many other firms, it also has positions in telecommunications, charitable contributions, building security and purchasing. You can inquire about openings in the personnel office, 805 Fifth Ave., 33rd floor.

Sea-Land Service Inc.
3600 Port of Tacoma Rd., 44th Floor
Tacoma WA 98424
922-3100
From Seattle: 386-8786
Jobline: 593-8042
This containership giant pioneered year around container service to Alaska. It's also a trans-Pacific carrier. Sea-Land employs nearly 500 in the Puget Sound area.

Sears, Roebuck & Co.
The Western Region Administration office in Redmond was closed in early 1992, so most hiring is now done at the stores. Because Sears promotes from within, most openings are entry level. Many are part-time. For information about the management training program, call (312) 875-2500 and ask for the human resources department.

Seattle Daily Journal of Commerce
P.O. Box 11050
Seattle WA 98111
622-8292
Phil Brown is the managing editor of this 9,000-circulation business publication. The staff is small. However, besides general business news and legal notices, the *Journal of Commerce* has special industry pages of value to job-seekers.

Seattle-King County Economic Development Council
701 Fifth Ave., #2510
Seattle WA 98104
386-5040
A private nonprofit consortium of 150 private firms and several

government agencies, this group focuses on stimulating and maintaining growth in King County. Its current emphasis is on growth management, transportation planning and education planning. Limited turnover in the staff of 14. Kathie Kohorn, office manager, receives resumes.

Seattle Mariners Baseball Club
411 First S.
Seattle WA 98104
628-3555
Love sports? If you're interested in a job in baseball, consider the Mariners. The club has an office staff of about 50, including people who work in sales, stadium operations, marketing, community relations and ticketing services.

Seattle Pacific Industries
P.O. Box 58710
Seattle WA 98138
282-8889
Unionbay is one of the labels at this large sportswear manufacturer. Inquiries should be directed to Tina Diaz.

Seattle Post-Intelligencer
P.O. Box 1909
Seattle WA 98111
Human Resources: 448-8076
Owned by Hearst, this morning daily functions under a joint operating agreement with the Seattle *Times*, which handles all advertising sales, production and distribution. That means that virtually all of the 160 employees work in the newsroom. You can call the human resources department to check on openings; usually there's one or two. Daily circulation is about 204,000. The Sunday issue is a combined *Times/P-I* edition. Managing editor is Kerry Slagle.

Seattle Seahawks
11220 N.E. 53rd St.
Kirkland WA 98033
827-9777
Half-time entertainment, the Seagals, player statistics, equipment and scouting are examples of the responsibilities of the administrative staff for Seattle's pro football team. About 55 work for the Seahawks. All positions are full-time permanent except for the intern who works in the public relations department. If you're interested in a permanent position, contact Gayle Larse in human resources. If you're a college student in public relations or marketing who'd like to apply for the

internship, you should submit your resume to the public relations director anytime after March 1. The intern is selected in late spring.

Seattle Telco Federal Credit Union
800 Stewart St.
Seattle WA 98101
382-7000
One of Seattle's larger credit unions, this thrift employs about 80. Resumes can be directed to Sharon Sanford, vice president.

Seattle Times
P.O. Box 70
Seattle WA 98111
464-2111
Jobline: 464-2118
Seattle's evening newspaper has a circulation of about 233,000 (daily) and 503,000 (Sunday). Managing editor is Alex MacLeod and advertising director, Margi Ruiz. Subsidiaries include the Walla Walla *Union-Bulletin,* Rotary Offset Press, which offers printing and mailing services, and Times Community Newspapers, which publishes weekly papers in the south end. The subsidiaries do their own hiring; contact:

Rotary Offset Press
Dan Langdon, General Manager
18221 Andover Park W.
Tukwila WA 98188
575-0144

Federal Way News
Brad Broberg, Editor
P.O. Box 3007
Federal Way WA 98063
839-0700

Highline Times/Des Moines News
Jeff Dirks, Editor
P.O. Box 66518
Seattle WA 98166
242-0100

Security Pacific Bank Washington
Merged into Seafirst Bank in spring, 1992 through the combination of BankAmerica and Security Pacific. Some branches were sold to Key Bank and others to WestOne.

Shannon & Wilson Inc.
P.O. Box 300303
Seattle WA 98103
632-8020
This geotechnical and foundation engineering firm employs about 100 in the Seattle area. Contact: Joan Marie Gorans-Eggert.

Sharp Hartwig Inc.
100 W. Harrison Plaza
South Tower, #500
Seattle WA 98119
282-6242
Dave Sharp and Cynthia Hartwig head this advertising and public relations firm, which specializes in business-to-business work.

Shearson Lehman Bros.
Each office of this stock brokerage firm hires separately. If you're interested in a financial consultant position, write the branch manager. Resumes for other positions can be sent to the contacts noted.

Shearson Lehman Bros.
999 Third Ave., #3800
Seattle WA 98104
344-3500
Contact: Michelle Savage.

Shearson Lehman Bros.
411 108th Ave. N.E., #2100
Bellevue WA 98004
453-3450
Contact: Stacy Meister.

Sheraton Hotel and Towers
1400 Sixth Ave.
Seattle WA 98101
691-9000
Jobline: 287-5505
If you're interested in the hospitality industry, consider hotels. Applications are always welcome at the Sheraton; check the jobline for the personnel office hours. Recent openings were in accounts receivable, reservations, cashiering, the kitchen and the cocktail lounges.

Siemens Quantum Inc.
1040 12th Ave. N.W.
Issaquah WA 98027
392-9180
Jobline: 391-1231 (Touchtone telephones only)
Formed in 1991 through the merger of Siemens Ultrasound and Quantum Medical, this firm now employs nearly 400 in the Northwest. Founded in 1982, Quantum has been a leader in making ultrasound systems to access blood flow through the body and to specific organs.

Sierra Geophysics
11255 Kirkland Way, #300
Kirkland WA 98033
822-5200
Marlyse Cato handles personnel for this software developer, which employs about 200 in the Northwest.

Simpson & Fisher Companies, Inc.
1326 Fifth Ave., #646
Seattle WA 98101
621-1924
At press time this company and subsidiaries Westminister Lace and Yankee Peddler had filed for Chapter 11 bankruptcy protection. For information about management positions, contact Peter Revers, who succeeded founder Bob Camp as president in spring, 1992. Westminister Lace has 27 outlets in 14 states, including one store in downtown Seattle; Yankee Peddler has three stores, all in Seattle.

Simpson Timber Co.
1201 Third Ave., #4900
Seattle WA 98101-3009
224-5000
You can learn about all openings at this forest products firm—whether in the corporate office or at any of the mills—by reviewing the postings at the reception desk. No unsolicited resumes are accepted.

Ski Lifts, Inc.
7900 S.E. 28th St., #200
Mercer Island WA 98040
232-8182
Interested in working at Snoqualmie Summit, Ski Acres or Alpental? This firm operates these three Snoqualmie Pass ski areas. The corporate staff is very small, but a variety of seasonal opportunities exist. You can call the corporate office and ask that you be notified when interviews are scheduled.

Skinner Corp.
1326 Fifth Ave., #711
Seattle WA 98101
623-6480
The corporate headquarters for a family-owned firm, this office has fewer than 10 positions. For a support position, write Debbie Sokvitne, office manager. Resumes regarding other positions should be directed to the appropriate subsidiary: NC Machinery, Alpac Corp. or Skinner Development (see elsewhere in this chapter). Each hires its own staff.

Skinner Development Corp.
2350 Carillon Point
Kirkland WA 98033
822-1700
Headed by Dewey Taylor, this land development firm built Carillon Point, a Kirkland mixed-use project that includes office and retail space, housing, a hotel, restaurants, parks and a marina. Carolyn Ernst, the office manager, handles applications for support positions.

SpaceLabs, Inc.
15220 N.E. 40th
P.O. Box 97013
Redmond WA 98073-9713
882-3700
Until recently a subsidiary of Westmark International, SpaceLabs has been spun off as an independent public company. It manufactures hospital monitoring systems used with the critically ill. Local employment: about 500. Job openings are posted at the main reception desk.

Spectra-Lux Corp.
11825 120th Ave. N.E.
Kirkland WA 98034
823-6857
Eileen Hively handles personnel for this manufacturer of light panels and switches for aircraft. Local employment: about 110.

Spectrum Glass Co.
P.O. Box 646
Woodinville WA 98072
483-6699
About 150 are employed locally by this manufacturer of flat colored glass. Bruce Stapleton is the personnel manager.

Squire Shops Inc.
830 Fourth Ave. S.
Seattle WA 98134
624-5560
This retailer of young men's apparel employs about 35 in the corporate office. Resumes can be directed to Jamie Todd in personnel. If you're interested in a sales position, you can apply in any store.

Starbucks Coffee Co.
2203 Airport Way S.
Seattle WA 98134
447-1575
Jobline: 447-4123, Ext. 2
This fast-growing coffee roaster and retailer has more than 125 stores here and elsewhere in the country. Howard Schultz is president. Applications are accepted in stores or by human resources.

Stevens Memorial Hospital
21600 76th Ave. W.
Edmonds WA 98020
771-0188
Jobline: 672-0584
Nurse recruiter: 771-0189
This 217-bed facility has a variety of nursing, professional and support positions. Recent openings were in fundraising, pharmacy and physical therapy.

STI Optronics
2755 Northup Way
Bellevue WA 98004
827-0460
Joyce Anderson is the personnel director for this laser technology research and development firm. Local employment: about 115.

Stouffer Madison Hotel
515 Madison St.
Seattle WA 98104
583-0300
Jobline: Through operator
This hotel offers a variety of opportunities. Recent openings: PBX operator, security officer, garage cashier and room service server.

Sun Dog Inc.
712 N. 34th St.
Seattle WA 98103
547-2270

In Seattle for more than 10 years, this firm makes such soft-sided carriers as fanny packs and backpacks.

Sun Sportswear
6520 S. 190th St.
Kent WA 98032
251-3565
This is one of the country's largest producers of screen-printed casual sportswear for discount chains. Job openings are posted in the reception area. Robin Jaquish is the personnel manager.

Sunset Magazine
500 Union St., #600
Seattle WA 98101
682-3993
Part of Lane Publishing, a unit of Time Warner, Sunset maintains a small editorial and advertising sales office in Seattle. All hiring for these positions is done through Lane's headquarters. Write:

Lane Publishing Co.
80 Willow Rd.
Menlo Park CA 94025

Sundstrand Data Control, Inc.
15001 N.E. 36th St.
P.O. Box 97001
Redmond WA 98073-9701
885-3711
Joe Luce is employee relations manager for this manufacturer of electronic equipment. Job openings can be reviewed at the reception desk.

Swedish Hospital Medical Center
Personnel Office
601 Broadway, First Floor
Seattle WA 98104
Personnel: 386-2141
Jobline: 386-2888 (Touchtone telephones only)
One of Seattle's most specialized medical centers, this is a 650-bed hospital. Openings are posted in the personnel office.

Tacoma Boatbuilding Co.
1840 Marine View Dr.
Tacoma WA 98422
572-3600

This shipbuilding and repair operation advertises its openings in the *Morning News Tribune*. Resumes can be directed to Chuck Holmes in personnel.

Targeted Genetics Corp.
1201 Western Ave.
Seattle WA 98101
623-7612
(Ms.) H. Stewart Parker heads this biotech firm, which focuses on gene therapy. Spun off from Immunex in early 1992.

TCI West, Inc.
2233 112th N.E.
Bellevue WA 98004
462-2620
About 60 work in this regional headquarters for the Denver-based TCI, a cable television operation. Personnel director is Sally Howe.

Teltone Corp.
22121 20th Ave. S.E.
Bothell WA 98021-4408
827-9626
This manufacturer of electronic telecommunications and data communications equipment employs about 80 locally. You can ask the receptionist about current openings.

That Patchwork Place
P.O. Box 118
Bothell WA 98041
483-3313
This publisher of craft patterns employs about 25 in its Woodinville offices. Sue Ross handles personnel.

Thaw Corp.
P.O. Box 3978
Seattle WA 98134
624-4277
Thaw manufactures and imports recreational apparel and equipment. The receptionist at the main entrance (1212 First Ave. S.) has a folder with job announcements. Resumes can be directed to Metta Kramer.

Thousand Trails/NACO
12301 N.E. 10th Pl.
Bellevue WA 98005
455-3155

This campground company has a variety of positions in its corporate headquarters. There are also positions in the 75 recreation sites across the U.S. Most local openings are advertised in the Seattle papers. You can direct your resume to "Human Resources." If you're a writer seeking free-lance assignments, contact John Powers, the editor of *Trailblazer*, about the membership magazine.

Timeline Inc.
3055 112th Ave. N.E., #106
Bellevue WA 98004
822-3140
Paula McGee, the office manager, screens resumes for this producer of financial accounting software. Current employment: about 50.

Todd Shipyards Corp.
P.O. Box 3806
Seattle WA 98124
623-1635
Todd emerged from bankruptcy in December, 1991, according to the *Puget Sound Business Journal*, which quoted company officials as saying they are seeking more commercial ship repair business to compensate for the reduced military business. If you're interested in a professional, technical or administrative position, direct your resume to Michael Marsh, personnel director.

Tone Commander Systems, Inc.
4320 150th N.E.
Redmond WA 98052
883-3600
Job openings are posted in the entrance to the human resources office at this manufacturer of telephone intercom systems. The firm employs about 30.

Totem Ocean Trailer Express
P.O. Box 24908
Seattle WA 98124
628-4343
There's limited turnover at this privately-owned firm, which provides deep sea transportation between Washington and Alaska. It's one subsidiary of Totem Resources Corp. Hiring for both Totem's Seattle office of 60 and the Tacoma staff of 35 is done in Seattle. Openings are posted at the state Job Service Centers and advertised. Resumes can be directed to John Martin, vice president, human resources.

TRA
215 Columbia
Seattle WA 98104
682-1133
Amy Collis is the human resources director for this large design firm, which provides architectural, engineering, planning and graphic and interior design services.

TRAMCO, Inc.
11323 30th Ave. W.
Everett WA 98204
347-6969
Jobline: 347-6969, Ext. 2600
About 1,000 are employed by this firm, which provides commercial jet airplane maintenance and repair. It's located at Paine Field. Recent openings: engineering director, computer programmer, structural engineer, accounts payable clerk and carpenter.

Transamerica Insurance Group
2001 Sixth Ave., #1811
Seattle WA 98121
448-8442
Due to consolidation of offices, this branch office of an insurance company has reduced its staff to less than five. If you're interested in working in underwriting, marketing or excess coverage, you can contact the hiring office and ask that your resume be kept on file.

Transamerica Insurance Group
Carroll Roarty, Human Resources
P.O. Box 52101
Phoenix AZ 85072-2101
(800) 238-1970

Transamerica Title Insurance Co.
320 108th Ave. N.E.
Bellevue WA 98004
451-7301
Jody Schimke handles hiring for escrow staff in the Seattle-area offices of this firm and Louise Condon recruits for title insurance staff.

Travelers Insurance Co.
1601 Fifth Ave., #600
P.O. Box 91033
Seattle WA 98111-9133
464-3400

If you'd like information about openings at this financial services and insurance firm, check with the receptionist. Opportunities are limited, however; through consolidation, the local staff has been reduced to 30.

Traveling Software Inc.
18702 North Creek Parkway
Bothell WA 98011
483-8088
Barbara Thompson handles personnel for this software developer.

Trident Seafoods Corp.
5303 Shilshole Ave. N.W.
Seattle WA 98107
783-3818
Jobline (Hourly positions): Through the personnel office.
One of Washington's largest seafood processors, Trident operates in both the Northwest and Alaska.

Unico Properties
1215 Fourth Ave., #1010
Seattle WA 98161
628-5050
Dave Cortelyou heads this firm, which manages several downtown Seattle buildings, including the Cobb, Puget Sound Plaza, Skinner, and One and Two Union Square.

Unigard Security Insurance Co.
15805 N.E. 24th St.
Bellevue WA 98008
641-4321
Jobline: 644-5236 (Touchtone telephones only)
This property and casualty insurance firm employs 450 at its corporate headquarters alone.

UniSea Inc.
15110 N.E. 90th St.
Redmond WA 98073
881-8181
Jobline (Hourly positions): 883-0884
This large seafood processor does not accept unsolicited resumes. Openings—for both Alaska and Redmond operations—are listed on the jobline or advertised in the Seattle *Times*. Recent openings were for a buyer and an accounting supervisor.

United Airlines
Employment Office
P.O. Box 66100
Chicago IL 60666
Jobline: (708) 952-7077
To apply for a position at UA's local offices, request an application from the office above. In your cover note, indicate the kind of job in which you're interested. Enclose a stamped, self-addressed envelope.

United Graphics
21409 72nd S.
Kent WA 98032
325-4400
Jo Powers is the personnel manager for this large printing firm. Most of the work force is unionized.

United Marine International Inc.
1441 N. Northlake Way
Seattle WA 98103
632-1441
Personnel for this shipbuilder is handled by Sally Bergmann.

United Press International
101 Elliott W., #110
Seattle WA 98119
283-3262
This wire service employs fewer than five in Seattle. Summer internships are sometimes available for students. For information regarding free-lance work, contact Luke Hill, the Northwest regional manager.

United Olympic Life Insurance
P.O. Box 90055
Bellevue WA 98009
451-7441
This life insurance company employs about 70 in its corporate office. Openings are advertised. Contact: Sue Struck, human resources.

Univar Corp.
P.O. Box 34325
Seattle WA 98124-1325
889-3400
This distributor of industrial chemicals employs 2,700 nationwide and 300 in the Northwest, including its corporate headquarters in Kirkland. Contact: David Gentry, vice president, human resources.

University Savings Bank
6400 Roosevelt Way N.E.
Seattle WA 98115
526-1000
This thrift employs about 250. Job openings are advertised and posted at state Job Service Centers. Or call Jana Chard in human resources.

University of Washington Medical Center
1959 N.E. Pacific
Seattle WA 98195
Joblines:
Nursing: 548-4470
General: 543-6969 (Touchtone telephones only)
A unit of the University of Washington, this medical center employs about 1,800. Job openings, which include positions at Harborview Medical Center, are posted at:

University Hospital Personnel
BB130 University Hospital
1959 N.E. Pacific St.

UW Staff Employment Office
1320 N.E. Campus Parkway

Harborview Medical Center
319 Terry Ave.

URS Corp.
1100 Olive Way, #200
Seattle WA 98101
284-3131
This engineering firm, a branch of a San Mateo company, employs about 60 in Seattle. Resumes can be directed to Kathy Barrows in human resources.

U.S. Bank
P.O. Box 720
Seattle WA 98111
344-3619
Jobline: 344-5656
This Oregon-based bank is the successor to Peoples Bank and Old National Bank. It has more than 50 branches in the Seattle area alone. You can use the jobline or apply in person at any branch or at the corporate headquarters staffing office, 1415 Fifth Ave.

U S West Communications
Employment Office
520 Pike St., #1000
Seattle WA 98101
345-1234
Jobline: 345-6126
To learn about part-time and full-time telephone company jobs in the
Puget Sound area and elsewhere in the state, you can use the jobline
or review the postings in the U S West employment office.

U S West NewVector Inc.
3350 161st Ave. S.E., B-12
Bellevue WA 98008
747-4900
If you'd like to review opportunities at this cellular telephone and
mobile communications company, you can check the job postings
book in the human resources office, Suite 150. Unsolicited resumes
are routed to the appropriate manager.

U.S. Venture Partners
777 108th Ave. N.E., #2460
Bellevue WA 98004
646-7620
Dale Vogel is the local general partner for this venture capital firm.

UTILX Corp.
22404 66th Ave. S.
Kent WA 98032-4801
395-4537
Formerly named FlowMole for its major service, this utility renova-
tion firm provides a trenchless service through its own technology.
Sales are in excess of $13 million. Limited opportunities at press time.

Uwajimaya Inc.
A family-owned retailer and wholesaler of Asian groceries and gifts,
this firm was recently described as the U.S.'s leading Japanese-
American food merchant. Annual sales are estimated at $30 million.
Apply at either the Seattle or Bellevue store if you're interested in a
retail position; corporate recruiting is handled by the human resources
manager, who maintains her office at Seasia, a subsidiary. Resumes
are always accepted.

Seasia
Diane Rasmussen, Human Resources Manager
4601 6th Ave. S.
Seattle WA 98108
624-6380

Valley Daily News
P.O. Box 130
Kent WA 98032
872-6600
The 29,000-circulation newspaper serving Kent, Renton and Auburn, the *Daily News* employs about 160.   If you're a journalist, your inquiry should go to Bob Jones, the executive editor. Circulation is handled by Shirley Jacobs and advertising sales by Rick Riegle. Owned by Persis Corp.

Valley Medical Center
400 S. 43rd
Renton WA 98055
251-5160
Jobline: 251-5190 (Touchtone telephones only)
The jobline for this 300-bed hospital lists job titles, hours and shifts. No unsolicited resumes are accepted.

Vernon Publications Inc.
P.O. Box 96043
Bellevue WA 98009
827-9900
Vernon publishes several business periodicals. The editorial staff is small; inquiries regarding full-time positions and free-lance assignments can be addressed to Michelle Dill, editorial director.

Virginia Mason Clinic
P.O. Box 900
Seattle WA 98111
223-6600
Jobline: 223-6496
To learn about job openings at VM, one of Seattle's largest medical facilities, you can use the jobline or visit the human resources office on the third floor of the clinic's Health Resource Building. Unsolicited resumes are routed and filed for three months.

Virginia Mason Hospital
P.O. Box 900 G-3-HR
Seattle WA 98111
583-6503
Nurse recruiter: 583-6072
Jobline: 223-6798
At this 300-bed hospital, you'll find full-time, part-time, seasonal and permanent positions ranging from carpenter and storeroom coordinator to accountant, systems analyst, nurse midwife, pharmacist, child care teacher and credit union assistant. Unsolicited resumes are not accepted.

Walden Investors
5302 143rd Ave. S.E.
Bellevue WA 98006
643-7572
Ted Wight is the managing partner for this venture capital firm.

Walker Richer & Quinn Inc.
2815 Eastlake Ave. E.
Seattle WA 98102
324-0407
Doug Walker and Mike Richer are two of the partners in this firm, which develops communications software. Often cited as one of the country's fastest growing software firms.

Wall Data Inc.
17769 N.E. 78th Pl.
Redmond WA 98052
883-4777
Wall markets Rumba, a software program that connects personal computers with mainframes and allows applications from mainframes to be accessed with Microsoft Windows. The firm has offices in several U.S. cities as well as overseas. Job openings are advertised in papers and on the Washington Software Association jobline.

Washington CEO/Fivash Publishing
2505 Second Ave., #602
Seattle WA 98121-1426
441-8415
This slick monthly magazine is distributed free to company presidents and top managers. It's available by subscription for others (see "*Job Bulletins and Valuable Publications*"). Circulation is about 20,000. The small staff is headed by publisher Scott Fivash; free-lance writers can query editor Kevin Dwyer regarding writing assignments.

Washington Credit Union League

P.O. Box 6279
Bellevue WA 98008
885-1121
Tami Craig handles personnel for this nonprofit association of credit unions. It provides such services as educational programs and group buying.

Washington Dental Service

P.O. Box 75688
Seattle WA 98125
522-1300
If you've worked in a dental office or in dental insurance claims processing, you'll have the experience you need for a position in this dental insurance firm's claims processing/customer service department. That's where the most opportunities occur at WDS, which employs 175.

Washington Education Association

33434 8th Ave. S.
Federal Way WA 98003
941-6700
The nonprofit professional association for education employees and the union for state school employees, WEA employs nearly 100 in its Federal Way office. An additional 50 work in regional offices across the state. Many employees have education experience, although several job functions do not require that. Personnel director: Kristi Bruhahn Mills.

Washington Energy Co.

P.O. Box 1869
Seattle WA 98111
622-6767
Jobline: 622-6767, Ext. 2800
This firm distributes natural gas, explores for oil and gas, develops coal and also sells home security systems. Its major subsidiary is Washington Natural Gas. You'll find the job openings posted in the lobby at 815 Mercer; applications are available from the cashier.

Washington Federal Savings and Loan Association

425 Pike St.
Seattle WA 98101
624-7930
This thrift employs 70 in its corporate headquarters in addition to branch staff. You can send a resume to Laurie Ware, vice president,

personnel, or call the personnel office to check on current openings. You can also inquire in branches regarding openings.

Washington Mutual Savings Bank
Employment Department
P.O. Box 834
Seattle WA 98111
Human Resources: 461-6400
Jobline: 461-8787 (Touchtone telephones only)
One of Washington's largest banks, this firm also offers insurance, travel planning, securities and brokerage services. Subsidiaries include Murphey Favre, Inc., Composite Research and Management and Mutual Travel. You can check listings in the personnel office (located at 1191 Second Ave., first floor), which is open Monday through Thursday. The jobline, which includes job titles, requirements, location and salary ranges, recently listed opportunities for underwriters, appraisers and paralegals. There are both part-time and full-time openings.

Washington State Bar Association
2001 Sixth Ave, #500
Seattle WA 98121-2599
448-0441
The bar association employs about 60—and many are not lawyers or paralegals. This nonprofit organization administers the bar exam and handles the discipline process, including consumer complaints about attorneys. The association also provides continuing legal education and publishes a monthly newsletter and many different pamphlets (on such topics as selecting an attorney and the landlord-tenant act). There's also a speakers' bureau and a series of law-related programs offered in schools. It also helps county bar associations establish pro bono programs. Personnel: Pat Dieken, director, administration.

Washington State Labor Council
314 First W.
Seattle WA 98119
281-8901
The umbrella organization for the AFL-CIO in Washington, the labor council employs 15. All officers are elected by unions. The staff is comprised of two groups. The first includes the directors of such programs as education, which conducts workshops and provides materials on workplace issues; political action; research, which studies issues and pricing for members; public relations; and job training, which works with apprenticeship programs and encourages

the development of both apprenticeship and alternative training programs. The second staff includes support departments, which provide clerical support, database management and accounting. Interns are welcome. Written inquiries should be directed to Lawrence Kenney, president.

Washington Wine Institute
1932 First Ave., #510
Seattle WA 98101
441-1892
This private industry group is the lobbyist for several state wineries. It has a staff of two. It shares space with the Washington Wine Commission, the promotional agency for state wineries, which employs three.

Waterfront Press
1115 N.W. 46th
Seattle WA 98107
789-6506
Seafood Leader, which covers the commercial seafood industry, *Simply Seafood,* a new consumer-oriented magazine, and *Alaska Fisherman's Journal* are the three publications of this firm. Peter Redmayne is editor and publisher; contact him regarding free-lance opportunities.

West Coast Grocery Co.
P.O. Box 2237
Tacoma WA 98401
593-3200
Jobline: 593-5876
Nearly 2,000 are employed by this wholesale grocery supplier. Examples of positions are accountants (CPAs preferred), retail counselors (retail store management preferred) and international traders (fluency in Asian languages is important). Contact: Les Soltis, human resources manager. Applications are available at 1525 E. D St., second floor.

Western Washington Fair
P.O. Box 430
Puyallup WA 98371
845-1771
This nonprofit fair association employs more than 1,500 on a temporary basis during the fall fair season. The seasonal employment office opens in August. There's limited turnover in the permanent staff of 55, but resumes are always welcome. Contact Bob Carlson, fair manager.

Westin Hotel
1900 Fifth Ave.
Seattle WA 98101
728-1000
Jobline: 728-1000, Ext. 5766
One of Seattle's largest hotels, the Westin offers a variety of job opportunities, both managerial and entry-level.

West One Bank Washington
P. O. Box 1987
Seattle WA 948111
585-3840
This bank, part of the Boise-based Moore Financial Group, purchased several small Puget Sound banks and then significantly increased its presence with 38 Security Pacific branches. After this purchase is complete in late 1992, a personnel department may be established. In the interim, visit a branch or contact Janet Carter, assistant to the president.

West Seattle Herald, Inc.
P.O. Box 16069
Seattle WA 98116
932-0300
Spun off from Robinson Publishing when that firm was sold to the Seattle *Times*, the West Seattle *Herald* and the White Center *News* are two community papers published by Jerry Robinson. Shauna Brown is editor.

Westwood Shipping Lines
P.O. Box 1645
Tacoma WA 98401
924-4399
Effenus Henderson handles personnel for this subsidiary of the Weyerhaeuser Co. Employment: about 50.

Weyerhaeuser Co.
Recruitment and Staffing QP 4
Tacoma WA 98477
924-2345
Jobline: 924-5347
Established as a timber company, Weyerhaeuser planted the country's first tree farm and has been recognized for its programs in fire prevention, perpetual-harvest forestry and intensive forest management. Today this Fortune 500 firm remains one of the largest forest products companies. Its Quadrant real estate subsidiary handles both

commercial and residential development. (See listing earlier.) The address above is for Weyerhaueser's central screening office; you can send it your resume with a cover letter explaining the kind of position you seek.

Weyerhaeuser Information Systems
Personnel CH2, E25
Tacoma WA 98477
924-4200
Terri Dion is the personnel manager for this software development subsidiary. Total employment is estimated at more than 400.

Weyerhaeuser Video Communications
PC2-23
Tacoma WA 98477
661-9728
This division produces corporate videos, primarily for Weyerhaeuser. Kathy Budinick, one of the producers, receives resumes.

The Wright Group
19201 120th Ave. N.E.
Bothell WA 98011
486-8011
This publisher, which recently moved to the Puget Sound area, employs about 65. It produces materials for the "whole language" classroom.

Wright Runstad & Co.
1201 Third Ave., #2000
Seattle WA 98101
447-9000
One of the largest U.S. real estate developers, Wright Runstad has offices in Bellevue, Portland, Anchorage and Los Angeles. Contact: Carol Briant, personnel director.

Wright Schuchart Inc.
P.O. Box 3764
Seattle WA 98124
447-7545
Each unit of this construction firm handles its own personnel. Greg Woodward, vice president, operations, receives resumes. You may also contact Howard S. Wright Construction (see earlier in this chapter) or Wright Schuchart Harbor Co., the heavy construction firm.

Wright Schuchart Harbor Co.
P.O. Box 3764
Seattle WA 98124
447-7593
This unit has no personnel manager; hiring is handled by department managers. Call for the name of the person to whom your inquiry should be directed.

Xerox Corp.
6400 Southcenter Blvd.
Tukwila WA 98188
241-1200
Office machine sales and service are handled in this Xerox location. Personnel coordinator: Sandra Dolan.

Zenith Administrators, Inc.
201 Queen Anne Ave. N., #100
Seattle WA 98109
282-4100
A third party administrator of employee health and pension plans, this office employs nearly 200 people in five areas: management, health claims, client services (including customer service and sales), finance (including trust accounting) and computer programming. Dean Kalahar is president. Resumes can be directed to Kathy Klavin in human resources.

Zimmer Gunsul Frasca Partnership
1191 Second Ave., #800
Seattle WA 98101
623-9414
This branch of a Portland architectural firm employs about 40 in Seattle. One local project: the Fred Hutchinson Cancer Research Center. Daniel Huberty heads this office.

ZymoGenetics, Inc.
4225 Roosevelt Way N.E.
Seattle WA 98105
547-8080
Jobline: through operator (Touchtone telephones only)
This biotechnology firm employs about 165. Most openings are in research and development and require training in the sciences. Recent opportunities: summer internships, inventory control clerk, regulatory affairs clerk and research associate. Resumes can be directed to Jamie Rector, the assistant human resources manager.

8. Employers:
Government Agencies

In King County alone, government agencies—federal, state, county and city—employ more than 100,000. Thousands more work in civilian jobs in Snohomish, Pierce, Kitsap and Thurston counties. Many of the jobs are in downtown office buildings; others are on research vessels or disaster sites, in parks, classrooms or test labs. Some government employees work alone; others are part of very large agencies. Government employees plant trees, sell marriage licenses, kill weeds, appraise buildings, teach swimming, write and design publications, administer preschool programs and collect taxes. They are pilots, police officers, counselors, attorneys, accountants, firefighters, mechanics, nurses and umpires.

ACTION
915 Second Ave., #3190
Seattle WA 98174
553-1558
This federal agency, which many of us know as Vista, has only 13 on its staff in Seattle; all openings are posted through the U.S. Office of Personnel Management (see later). If you're interested in public service, consider a year (the minimum) in Vista. You'll receive a stipend, usually $600-700 monthly, plus a relocation allowance at the end of your service. In screening prospects, recruiter Simon Conner looks for people with volunteer experience who demonstrate a commitment to alleviating the problems of poverty. Examples of Vista jobs in Seattle: setting up recreational programs for the elderly; establishing family centers for the homeless; and handling such projects as infant mortality prevention and AIDS education.

City of Algona
402 Warde
Algona WA 98001
833-2897
Near Auburn, this city of 1,700 employs about 30.

City of Auburn
25 W. Main St.
Auburn WA 98001
Personnel: 931-3040
Jobline: 931-3077
A city of more than 33,000, Auburn offers part-time, full-time and seasonal opportunities. On the jobline, you'll learn of administrative positions and receive instructions for applying for the police and fire jobs that require civil service tests. Detailed job descriptions are available in the personnel office.

City of Bainbridge Island
625 Winslow Way E.
Bainbridge Island WA 98110
842-7633
Formerly Winslow, a city which encompassed only part of Bainbridge Island, this community in 1991 annexed the rest of the island and changed the city name. It now has a population of 17,000 and employs 75. Job openings are posted at the city hall.

City of Bellevue
11511 Main St.
Bellevue WA 98004
Human Resources: 455-6838
Jobline: 455-7822
About 1,000 work for this fast-growing Eastside city, which currently has about 90,000 residents. Job opportunities are posted in the human resources office on the third floor of City Hall.

City of Black Diamond
P.O. Box 599
Black Diamond WA 98010
886-2560
When openings occur in this small city's staff of nine, they are advertised in the Enumclaw *Courier-Herald* and the *Valley Daily News*.

Bonneville Power Administration
Puget Sound Area Office
201 Queen Anne Ave. N., #400
Seattle WA 98109
553-1910
Jobline: 553-7564
In western Washington, this federal agency employs about 200. Responsible for transmitting electrical power from dams to utilities,

BPA builds and maintains lines and substations. Many BPA employees work primarily with utilities, even in consumer affairs. For example, the conservation specialists help utilities develop conservation programs . Most hiring is done through the Office of Personnel Management (see later). Engineers and some economists can submit applications directly to the BPA.

City of Bonney Lake
19306 Bonney Lake Blvd.
P.O. Box 7380
Bonney Lake WA 98390
862-8602
When this city of 8,200 has job openings, they're advertised in the local papers and posted in the city hall.

City of Bothell
18227 101st Ave. N.E.
Bothell WA 98011
489-3437
Jobline: 486-9473
This city of 25,000 employs 130. Openings are posted in the personnel and city clerk's offices.

City of Bremerton
Personnel
239 4th St.
Bremerton WA 98310
478-5283
Jobline: 478-5241
Because most nonmanagerial city positions are civil service, you'll find the openings posted in the civil service department. There's also a bulletin board outside the personnel office.

Port of Bremerton
8850 S.W. State Highway 3
Port Orchard WA 98366
674-2381
When the port has openings, you'll find the jobs posted at the Job Service Center in Bremerton and advertised in the Bremerton *Sun* and the Port Orchard *Independent*. The port employs about 30, with 10 in the office and others at the airport and marina.

City of Brier
2901 228th S.W.
Brier WA 98036
775-5440

This city of 5,500 near Lynnwood employs about 20. Openings are posted on the readerboard outside the city hall.

City of Buckley
P.O. Box D
933 Main
Buckley WA 98321
829-1921
This city of 3,560 employs about 60, including the summer help. Openings are posted at the post office and clerk's office.

City of Burien
Incorporation of this nine-square-mile community (estimated population 27,000) was approved by voters in March, 1992, with the city council to be elected in September, 1992.

Town of Carbonado
P.O. Drawer 91
818 8th Ave.
Carbonado WA 98323
829-0125
This community of 500 employs only one full-time, with three additional part-time staff members. Openings are posted at the town hall.

Town of Clyde Hill
9605 N.E. 24th
Clyde Hill WA 98004
453-7800
Because this community of 3,000 employs only 14 full-time, openings are infrequent. When they occur, they're posted on the kiosk outside the town hall.

Community Transit
1133 164th St. S.W., #200
Lynnwood WA 98037
348-7100
From Seattle: 745-1600
Jobline: 348-2333
A unit of Snohomish County, Community Transit employs about 300. About 140 are bus drivers (some full-time, some part-time). There's also a large bus maintenance staff. The small administrative staff includes human resources, marketing, planning and accounting personnel. If you're interested in a position for which there are currently

no openings, complete a "job interest" card so you'll be notified when there is a vacancy.

Congress

All members of the U.S. Congress maintain local offices in their districts. If you'd like to work or intern for a member of the Senate or House of Representatives, contact the local district manager for the appropriate Congressperson. You'll find the offices listed in the telephone book under "U.S. Government-Congress." If you're considering a career in government, it's important to remember that these positions in the offices of members of Congress are not civil service jobs and carry no seniority within the federal system. You may also be interested in a position on a member of Congress' campaign staff. These jobs are temporary, usually starting in April or June (depending on the position) and continuing through November. Senate races, like such other statewide races as governor, require larger staffs. Members of the House of Representatives, who have smaller districts, will have fewer people on their campaign staffs. Typical positions include campaign manager, finance manager, district organizer, press secretary, bookkeeper and data entry clerk. Some of these positions are often part-time or combined with other jobs. To inquire about campaign positions, call the member of Congress' local office. The campaign office will not be located there, but the staff will be able to refer you.

Cooperative Extension

Run in cooperation with Washington State University's College of Agriculture and Home Economics, the extension offices provide information on agriculture and family life (through the Master Gardener program, for example) and run educational programs (4-H is the best known). Most support personnel are hired through county personnel offices; for example, in King, Pierce and Snohomish counties, openings are listed on the county joblines. The largest counties sometimes have additional support or technical positions funded by WSU. All extension agents are funded by and hired by WSU. You can inquire at your local extension office regarding openings or contact WSU. Send resumes for all WSU positions (support, technical and extension agent) to:

Barbara Scott, Employment Coordinator
Washington State University
305 Hulbert Hall
Pullman WA 99164-6230
(509) 335-2888

If you're interested in an agent position, which carries faculty status, you'll need a master's degree. For more information about such positions, you can contact Ms. Scott, your local extension office or the district director for your area:

For King, Pierce and Kitsap counties:
Mary Kohli, Director, Northwest District

For Thurston County:
Robert Butler, Interim Director, Southwest District

Both supervisors can be contacted at:

Washington State University-Puyallup
7612 Pioneer Way E.
Puyallup WA 98371
840-4552

The Puget Sound co-op extension offices are:

King County Cooperative Extension
Smith Tower
506 Second Ave., #612
Seattle WA 98104
296-3900
Employment: about 50.

Snohomish County Cooperative Extension
600 128th S.E.
Everett WA 98208
338-2400
Employment: about 25.

Pierce County Cooperative Extension
3049 S. 36th, #300
Tacoma WA 98409
591-7180
Employment: about 20.

Thurston County Cooperative Extension
921 Lakeridge Drive S.W., #216
Olympia WA 98502
786-5445
Employment: about 10.

Kitsap County Cooperative Extension
P.O. Box 146
Courthouse Annex
614 Division St.
Port Orchard WA 98366
876-7157
Employment: about seven.

City of Des Moines
21630 11th S.
Des Moines WA 98198
878-4595
This city of 18,000 employs about 100. Openings are posted at the library and in the courtyard outside City Hall.

City of DuPont
P.O. Box 455
DuPont WA 98327
964-8121
Openings are infrequent in this south Pierce County community, because there are fewer than 10 full-time positions. The city itself has about 600 residents. When openings do occur, they're posted at City Hall.

City of Duvall
31 Main St.
P.O. Box 1300
Duvall WA 98019
788-1185
A community of 3,000, Duvall employs about 35. The occasional openings are advertised.

City of Edmonds
Personnel Office
505 Bell St.
Edmonds WA 98020
775-2525
Jobline: 771-0243, #1
About 185 work full-time for the City of Edmonds, which today has a population of 31,000. Openings are posted in the police and fire building at 250 Fifth and at the personnel office.

Port of Edmonds
336 Admiral Way
Edmonds WA 98020
774-0549

About 15 work full-time for this port, with summer employment adding as many as another 20 temporary positions.

City of Enumclaw
1339 Griffin Ave.
Enumclaw WA 98022
825-3591
This growing community (7,300 population at press time) accepts applications at all times.

Enumclaw Library
1700 First St.
Enumclaw WA 98022
825-2938
This municipal library has a small staff and openings are limited; you can complete an application at any time.

City of Everett
Mailing Address
3002 Wetmore
Everett WA 98201
259-8767
Jobline: 259-8768
More than 72,500 live in Everett, where the city employs about 1,000. Job openings are posted at the personnel office, located at 2927 Colby.

Everett Public Library
Mailing Address
2702 Hoyt
Everett WA 98201
259-8790
Of the library's 80 employes, most are hired through the City of Everett personnel office. You can complete a "job interest card" and when an opening in that function occurs, you'll be notified. Library openings are also posted on the Everett city jobline. If you're interested in part-time work, you can apply directly to the library for a "page" position. These are support jobs involving shelving and checking out books. Applications are available at the downtown and Evergreen branches.

Port of Everett
P.O. Box 538
Everett WA 98206
259-3164
Most port openings are posted at the Job Service Centers. There are

about 50 full-time positions and some part-time jobs, usually for summer.

City of Federal Way
33530 1st Way S.
Federal Way WA 98103
Personnel: 661-4083
Jobline: 661-4089
This community of 71,000 just north of Tacoma was incorporated in 1990. Openings are posted on a counter in the back lobby in City Hall.

City of Fife
5213 Pacific Highway E.
Fife WA 98424
922-2489
When this city of 4,000 has an opening, it'll be advertised in the *Morning News Tribune*. Even when no openings exist, you can complete an application at City Hall. Total city employment is nearly 90.

Town of Fircrest
115 Ramsdell St.
Fircrest WA 98466
564-8901
Adjacent to Tacoma, this town of 5,000 employs 35 full-time. Job openings are advertised in the *Morning News Tribune*.

City of Gig Harbor
P.O. Box 145
3105 Judson
Gig Harbor WA 98335
851-8136
This city of 3,000 employs 35. Openings are posted at City Hall.

Town of Hunts Point
3000 Hunts Point Rd.
Bellevue WA 98004
455-1834
This small community neighboring Bellevue has only one full-time employee: the clerk. Other positions are part-time or contract.

Intercity Transit
526 S. Pattison St.
Olympia WA 98506
786-8585

Thurston County's bus service employs 200. Openings are posted at several agencies, including the Olympia Job Service Center. Applications, available from the Intercity receptionist, are accepted only for open positions.

City of Issaquah
P.O. Box 1307
Issaquah WA 98027-1307
391-1000
This city of 8,150 employs about 100. Openings are posted in the lobby at City Hall South, 135 E. Sunset Way.

City of Kent
220 4th Ave. S.
Kent WA 98032
859-3300
Jobline: 859-3375
This city of 35,000 employs more than 600. Openings are posted at the city hall.

King County
Human Resource Management
500 Fourth Ave., Room 450
Seattle WA 98104
296-7340
Jobline: 296-5209.
Some 6,000 people work for King County full-time—in jobs ranging from AIDS prevention and Kingdome management to stream stewardship and traffic engineering. As many as another 4,000 may be hired during the summer. Openings are posted in the hallway outside the personnel office, at entrances to the King County Courthouse and at the Fourth Avenue entrance to the King County Administration Building.

King County Library System
Personnel Office
300 Eighth N.
Seattle WA 98109
684-6601
Serving communities from Algona, Bellevue and Maple Valley to Carnation, North Bend and Skykomish, the King County system operates 37 branch libraries, with several facilities scheduled to be added or expanded in the next five years. Total library system employment is currently about 600. Besides the librarians, library assistants and clerks who work in the branches, the system employs accountants, video specialists, graphic designers, printers and archi-

tects. All librarian positions require a master's degree in library science. Professional openings are posted in all branch libraries and on the Pacific Northwest Library Association jobline, 543-2890. If you'd like to work part-time as a page (a support position), apply at the branch in your area.

King County Parks and Recreation
The parks department employs about 250 full-time and offers many seasonal positions. All hiring is handled by King County Human Resource Management (see above).

King County Department of Public Safety (Police)
Headed by the sheriff, this agency employs more than 800 full-time. Most positions are civil service; all are listed on the King County jobline and posted in the King County Human Resource Management office and the police personnel office in the courthouse. For more information, call the recruiter at 296-4069.

City of Kirkland
123 Fifth St.
Kirkland WA 98033
828-1100
Jobline: 828-1161
This city of 41,000 employs 250. Openings are posted at the front desk at City Hall.

Kitsap County
614 Division St.
Port Orchard WA 98360
876-7169
Jobline: Through switchboard (Touchtone telephones only)
You can use the jobline or look outside the personnel office in the courthouse to learn of job openings.

Kitsap Regional Library
1301 Sylvan Way
Bremerton WA 98310
377-7601
This library has 10 branches that serve such communities as Bremerton, Bainbridge Island, Little Boston, Silverdale and Poulsbo. Openings are posted at each branch.

Kitsap Transit
234 S. Wycoff
Bremerton WA 98312
479-6962

The Kitsap County bus service employs nearly 160. Job openings are posted at the front desk.

City of Lacey
P.O. Box B
420 College St. S.E.
Lacey WA 98503
491-3214
Jobline: 491-3213
This city of 21,000 near Olympia posts its openings on the jobline and at the personnel office counter in City Hall.

City of Lake Forest Park
17711 Ballinger Way N.E.
Seattle WA 98155
364-7711
This city of 4,000 employs about 20. Openings are posted on a bulletin board in City Hall.

City of Lynnwood
19100 44th Ave. W.
Lynnwood WA 98036
775-1971
Jerry Witzel is personnel director for this city of 29,000, which employs about 300 in full-time and part-time positions. Job openings are posted in the City Hall reception area.

City of Medina
501 Evergreen Pt. Rd.
P.O. Box 144
Medina WA 98039
454-9222
A community of 3,000, Medina employs about 15. Openings are posted at City Hall.

City of Mercer Island
9611 S.E. 36th
Mercer Island WA 98040
236-3561
About 165 work full-time for this city of 21,000. Openings are posted at the personnel counter (simply ask one of the staff for help).

METRO
Self-Service Application Office
821 Second Ave., Fourth Floor
Seattle WA 98104
684-1175
Jobline: 684-1313
The Municipality of Metropolitan Seattle employs more than 4,600 in two programs: transit and water pollution control (including sewage treatment). Nearly 85 per cent of the employees work in the transit division, half of them as bus or trolley drivers. Other job opportunities include positions in vehicle maintenance, water quality engineering and public information.

City of Mill Creek
15728 Mill Creek Blvd.
Mill Creek WA 98012
745-1891
Mill Creek has a population of about 8,300 and employs about 45. Openings are posted in the city hall lobby.

City of Milton
1000 Laurel
Milton WA 98354
922-8733
When this city of 5,000 has openings, they're posted in the city hall.

City of Mountlake Terrace
23204 58th Ave. W.
Mountlake Terrace WA 98043
776-1161
When this city of 19,000 has vacancies in its full-time and part-time staff of 220, they're posted on a clipboard in the city hall.

City of Mukilteo
P.O. Box 178
304 Lincoln Ave.
Mukilteo WA 98275
355-4151
This city of 12,500 employs about 50 full-time. Applications are accepted at any time.

City of Normandy Park
801 S.W. 174th St.
Normandy Park WA 98166
248-7603

This community of 6,300 employs 22, half of whom are police officers hired from civil service registers. When openings do occur, notices are posted in the city hall lobby.

City of North Bend
P.O. Box 896
North Bend WA 98045
451-2259
A city of 2,500 with a staff of 30, North Bend advertises openings in local papers and posts them on a clipboard in City Hall, 211 Main Ave. N.

City of Olympia
Personnel
P.O. Box 1967
Olympia WA 98507
753-8442
When this city of 34,000, the state capitol, has openings in its staff of 400, announcements are posted at city hall, 900 Plum S.E.

Port of Olympia
P.O. Box 827
Olympia WA 98507
586-6150
The port employs about 40 total, but only about 15 in its offices. Turnover is limited.

Olympic Air Pollution Control Agency
909 Sleater-Kinney Rd., #1
Lacey WA 98503
438-8768
A regional agency funded by federal, state, county and city governments, the OAPCA enforces, implements and provides public education on the state Clean Air Act in Thurston, Clallam, Jefferson, Mason, Pacific and Grays Harbor counties. There are fewer than 10 staff positions; employees range from engineers to support staff. Internships (usually unpaid) are often available for college and technical college students; an engineering background is not required. Contact: Charles Peace, control officer.

City of Orting
P.O. Box 489
110 E. Train
Orting WA 98360
893-2219

About 2,300 live in this community. Openings are posted at City Hall.

City of Pacific
100 3rd Ave. S.E.
Pacific WA 98047
833-2660
A community of 5,000 near Auburn, Pacific employs 35. Openings are posted at City Hall, post office and supermarket.

Pierce County
Personnel Office
615 S. 9th St., #200
Tacoma WA 98405
591-7480
Jobline: 591-7466
The county posts its openings in the personnel office and just outside the office doors; on the jobline, recent openings included nurse practitioner, pharmacist, attorney and planner.

Pierce County Library
Processing and Administrative Center
3005 112th St. E.
Tacoma WA 98446-2215
536-6500
This library system has 17 branches in the suburbs of Tacoma as well as such communities as Bonney Lake, Buckley, Orting, Steilacoom and Sumner. Job openings are on a clipboard available from the receptionist at the administrative center and on bulletin boards in each branch. The few professional openings are also listed on the Pacific Northwest Library Association jobline, 543-2890. Total employment, full-time and part-time: 285.

Pierce Transit
3701 96th S.W.
P.O. Box 99070
Tacoma WA 98499
581-8080
Jobline: 581-8097
This transit authority posts its job openings on the jobline and just inside the main entrance to its office.

Pike Place Development Authority
85 Pike St., #500
Seattle WA 98101
682-7453

Funded by rents from Public Market tenants and by the City of Seattle, this agency has a small administrative staff, which includes property managers. Most positions are in security, maintenance and secretarial support. Total employment is about 80. Openings are posted in the office.

Puget Sound Air Pollution Control Agency
110 Union St., #500
Seattle WA 98101
434-8800
Toll-free within Washington: (800) 552-3565
A regional agency, the PSAPCA enforces, implements and provides public education on the state Clean Air Act in four counties: King, Kitsap, Pierce and Snohomish. It regulates more than 3,000 industrial sources of pollution, indoor and outdoor burning and asbestos removal. Established in 1967, it employs 56, ranging from engineers to inspectors to public information and education staff. Dee Endelman is the human resources manager.

Puget Sound Regional Council
216 First S.
Seattle WA 98104
464-7524
Formerly the Puget Sound Council of Governments, this is a voluntary organization of local government agencies (counties, cities and Indian tribes) in King, Pierce, Snohomish and Kitsap counties which focuses on regional transportation planning. Organized in 1957, it also maintains a regional database for economic, demographic and travel data. When vacancies occur in the 45-member staff, they are posted internally and advertised. Contact: Mark Gulbranson, administrative services officer.

Puget Sound Water Quality Authority
P.O. Box 40900
Olympia WA 98504-0900
493-9300
A state agency established in 1985 to preserve and protect Puget Sound and the waters that flow into it, this office employs about 30. Many are environmental planners who work on education, industrial pollution and wetlands. There's also a public information and outreach staff. Hiring is handled by the state personnel office. Contact: Betty Stewart, the PSWQA's administration director.

City of Puyallup
218 W. Pioneer
Puyallup WA 98371
Human Resources: 841-5551
Jobline: 841-5596
About 250 work for this city of 25,000. Job openings are described
in a notebook at the City Hall reception desk.

City of Redmond
15670 N.E. 85th St.
Redmond WA 98052
Human Resources: 556-2120
Jobline: 556-2121
More than 350 work full-time for this fast-growing suburban community, which now has 39,000 residents. Openings (full-time, part-time
and full-time seasonal) are posted in the City Hall lobby and in the
third floor personnel office.

City of Renton
200 Mill Ave. S., Sixth Floor
Renton WA
235-2500
Jobline: 235-2514
This city of 43,000 employs 510 full-time and part-time, with additional seasonal positions available.

Town of Ruston
5117 N. Winnifred
Tacoma WA 98407
759-3544
A neighbor of Tacoma, this community has 700 people and employs
fewer than 10.

City of SeaTac
19215 28th Ave. S.
SeaTac WA 98188
878-9100
Incorporated in February, 1990, SeaTac is another of the state's
newest cities. Located south of Seattle, near the airport, it has a
population of 23,000. When personnel openings occur, they are
advertised in local papers and posted at City Hall. City offices will
relocate in late 1993 or early 1994.

City of Seattle
Personnel Department
710 Second Ave., Fourth Floor
Seattle WA 98104
684-7664
Jobline: 684-7999
Except for civil service positions, most of the City of Seattle's 11,200 jobs are filled through this office. (Some exceptions are noted below.) Positions range from a sound equipment technician for Seattle Center and a zookeeper at Woodland Park to building inspectors, carpenters and electrical engineers. You can review openings and pick up an application form weekdays. Applications are also mailed if you provide a large stamped, self-addressed envelope.

Seattle Center
Personnel
Center House
305 Harrison, #112
Seattle WA 98109
684-7221
Jobline: 684-7218
A City of Seattle facility, Seattle Center hires most of its staff through the city personnel office. Temporary and on-call positions are filled by the center personnel staff; apply at the Job Information Center on the first floor of the Center House weekdays during business hours. Permanent, temporary and on-call positions are listed on the Seattle Center jobline.

Seattle City Light
Personnel
1015 Third Ave., #103
Seattle WA 98104
684-3273
Jobline: 233-2181
Most City Light jobs are filled through the city personnel office (see above). For a few positions—for example, managers and line workers—City Light recruits directly. Openings are posted in its office.

Seattle Fire Department
Personnel
301 Second Ave. S., Fourth Floor
Seattle WA 98104
386-1470
For information about firefighting and the civil service test necessary for firefighter applicants, this office has an information sheet.

Seattle Housing Authority
120 6th Ave. N.
Seattle WA 98109
443-4400
Jobline: 443-4376

A public corporation created by the City of Seattle and funded primarily by the federal government, SHA manages housing developments for the low-income, elderly and disabled; administers the federal voucher program for privately-owned housing; and manages the Seattle Senior Housing Program. Total employment is approximately 500. Besides administrative and maintenance personnel, positions include managers and resident assistant managers, interviewers (who determine eligibility), inspectors, accounting and public information staff. Openings are posted in the reception area of the SHA office.

Seattle Police Department
610 Third Ave., 15th Floor
Seattle WA 98104
684-5470

The police department employs some 500 in civilian positions and approximately 1,200 as police officers. All civilian positions are filled through the city personnel office. For police officer positions, the civil service exam must be taken; applications are available at the police department or by calling the Seattle civil service commission at 386-1303.

Seattle-King County Department of Public Health
110 Prefontaine Pl. S., Sixth Floor
Seattle WA 98104
296-4618

Most health department positions are filled through the King County Human Resource Management office. Applications for two positions—dentists and nurses—are accepted by this office.

Seattle Parks and Recreation
Employment Services
100 Dexter Ave. N.
Seattle WA 98109
684-0991

Most park department jobs are filled through the city personnel office. About 600 temporary seasonal positions are filled through this office; although a third require experience and skill (for example, in teaching or program development), about two-thirds of the jobs are appropriate for students. A few examples: supervisors and assistants for the 24 city playgrounds, cashiers, zookeepers and lifeguards. If you seek summer employment in a community center, apply directly with a center. You'll find them listed in the blue pages of the Seattle telephone book, under "Seattle Parks and Recreation." Parks and Recreation uses many seasonal volunteers—1,100 in 1991. Some positions were short-term; other volunteers worked all summer. Volunteer work for the city is an excellent way to obtain experience that will help you in obtaining a paid position.

Port of Seattle
Pier 66, 2201 Alaskan Way
P.O. Box 1209
Seattle WA 98111
728-3000
Jobline: 728-3290
About 1,200 work for the Port, at Seattle-Tacoma International Airport, at the piers, at Shilshole Marina or in the port offices. To learn of current openings, you can visit the Port's personnel office or use the jobline.

Seattle Public Library
Personnel Office
1000 Fourth Ave., Fifth Floor
Seattle WA 98104
386-4121
Jobline: 386-4120
All of the library's 525 positions are filled through this office. Openings are posted at the office and in each branch. Besides the 140 librarians (managers and "public service"), there are 40 administrative and managerial positions and a variety of "library associate" (support) positions; some are technical and involve no public interaction. The administrative staff includes finance, facilities and resource development.

City of Snohomish
116 Union Ave.
Snohomish WA 98290
568-3115
When this city of 6,500 has job openings, they're posted on the City Hall bulletin board.

Snohomish County
Personnel Office
3000 Rockefeller, First Floor
Everett WA 98201
388-3642
Jobline: 388-3686
Detailed job descriptions and official application forms are available
in the personnel office.

Snohomish County P.U.D.
Employee Resources
P.O. Box 1107
Everett WA 98206
258-8655
Toll-free within Washington: (800) 562-9142, Ext. 8655
Jobline: 347-5599, Ext. 9151
This public utility district, which employs 900, provides electric and
water service. Job openings are posted in the personnel office, located
at 2401 Hewitt.

Sno-Isle Regional Library
Service Center
7312 35th Ave. N.E.
Marysville WA 98271-9164
659-8447
Brier, Edmonds, Lynnwood, Mill Creek, Mountlake Terrace, Mukilteo
and Snohomish are examples of the communities served by this
library system. You'll find job openings posted at the service center
and in each of the branches. Professional positions are also listed on
the Pacific Northwest Library Association jobline, 543-2890.

Town of Steilacoom
1715 Lafayette St.
Steilacoom WA 98388
581-1900
One of Washington's oldest communities, Steilacoom has a population of about 5,600 and employs 50. Job openings are posted in the
administrative building and on the bulletin board by the local bank
branch.

City of Sumner
1104 Maple
Sumner WA 98390
863-8300
When this city of 7,500 has openings in its staff of 70, you'll find the
jobs posted on the City Hall bulletin board.

City of Tacoma
Human Resources
747 Market St., #1336
Tacoma WA 98402
591-5400
Jobline: 591-5795
You'll find city openings posted in the personnel office.

Tacoma Public Library
1102 Tacoma Ave. S.
Tacoma WA 98402
591-5602
The library handles its own recruiting; it does not use the city personnel office. Openings are posted in each branch. The library system, which includes nine branches, employs 180 total; however, professional vacancies are infrequent. When they occur, they are advertised and listed on the Pacific Northwest Library Association jobline, 543-2890.

Port of Tacoma
P.O. Box 1837
Tacoma WA 98401
383-5841
From Seattle: 838-0142
Jobline: Ext. 244
The Port openings are advertised in the Seattle and Tacoma Sunday papers and posted in the personnel office of Port headquarters, 1 Sitcum Plaza (on East 11th Street, directly north of Brown & Haley).

Thurston County
Personnel
County Courthouse
921 Lakeridge Dr. S.W.
Olympia WA 98502
786-5498
Jobline: 786-5499
Temporary, permanent and civil service jobs are available with Thurston County; recent openings included public health educator, camp counselors, summer recreational workers, off-road vehicle park manager and attorney. Postings can be reviewed at the courthouse information desk.

Timberland Regional Library
Service Center
415 Airdustrial Way S.W.
Olympia WA 98501
943-5001
Twenty-eight libraries in five counties (Thurston, Pacific, Grays
Harbor, Mason and Lewis) are operated by this agency, which
employs about 325. When vacancies occur, they are advertised.
Professional openings are also listed on the Pacific Northwest Library
Association jobline, 543-2890.

City of Tukwila
6200 Southcenter Blvd.
Tukwila WA 98188
433-1831
Jobline: 433-1828
This city of 14,600, which is located at the intersection of Interstates
5 and 405 and State Route 518, near Southcenter, employs 250.

U.S. Department of Agriculture
Forest Service
Mount Baker-Snoqualmie National Forest
21905 64th Ave. W.
Mountlake Terrace WA 98043
775-9702
One of three national forests in western Washington, this agency
employs about 300 full-time. Positions include foresters, biologists,
civil engineers, personnel specialists, contract specialists, computer
programmers and clerks. Some positions are filled internally or
through the Office of Personnel Management. An increasing number
of positions is filled directly. All openings are posted at state Job
Service Centers.

Interns are also hired through the national forest's personnel office.
The internships, called "co-op programs," are for natural resources
and engineering students who wish to make careers of the forest
service. The co-op program, which allows students to work in the
national forest while attending college or between terms, is administered in Mount Baker-Snoqualmie by Judy Mooney. Contact her at
the address above.

If you're interested in a summer job in a national forest, Mount Baker-
Snoqualmie hires more than 100 natural resource technicians each
year. Recruiting is handled by the following Job Service Centers:
Mount Vernon Job Service Center for the Mount Baker Ranger

District; Everett Job Service Center for the Darrington and Skykomish Ranger Districts; Bellevue Job Service Center for the North Bend Ranger District; Auburn Job Service Center for the White River Ranger District; Lynnwood Job Service Center for the Mountlake Terrace forest headquarters; and Seattle Rainier Avenue Job Service Center for the Pacific Northwest Research Station.

U.S. Air Force
McChord Air Force Base
There are two kinds of civilian jobs—and two personnel offices—at McChord. Those jobs funded by the Department of Defense are subject to periodic freezes; other positions are supported by user fees and, although not subject to the freezes, may not offer civil service benefits.

Department of Defense-funded Positions
Although at press time a freeze had been imposed, some civil service opportunities existed for current and previous federal employees. Applicants must be U.S. citizens. Openings can be reviewed and official application forms picked up at the personnel office, located inside the front gate of the base, which adjoins Tacoma.

Civilian Personnel Office
Building 773
McChord AFB WA 98438
984-3803
Jobline: 984-2277

Nonappropriated Fund Personnel
These are the people who handle fee-supported activities at McChord— for example, the golf course, officers' club and child care center. Some jobs are permanent full-time or part-time with full benefits. Others are "flexible;" they may offer regular work schedules but no benefits. Many positions are appropriate for students; the minimum age is 16. You need not be a U.S. citizen. About 150 openings occur each year. Examples: lifeguard, recreational aide, food service, maintenance mechanic, clerk and golf pro. A jobline is to be installed soon. You can also walk in the office and check the bulletin boards.

Human Resources Office
Nonappropriated Fund Personnel
Building 100, Room 1009
McChord AFB WA 98438
984-3838

U.S. Department of the Army

Corps of Engineers
4735 E. Marginal Way S.
Seattle WA 98124
Human Resources: 764-3416
Jobline: 764-3739
If you're an engineer, you can apply directly to Anita Wilcox, corps human resources. Other positions are filled through the U.S. Office of Personnel Management, Seattle Area Office (see below). All positions are listed on the corps jobline and in its human resources office.

Fort Lewis
Logistics Center
Building 9503, Room 100-A
Fort Lewis WA 98433
967-5091
Jobline: 967-5377 (Touchtone telephones only)
Despite the   civilian hiring freeze imposed at press time, some openings existed at Fort Lewis, which adjoins Tacoma. Some jobs are part-time, temporary, seasonal or intermittent; others are full-time permanent. You can review postings in the personnel office, which is open Monday through Friday 9 to 4. To reach it, take the Tillicum exit (#123) from Interstate 5.

U.S. Department of Commerce

Western Regional Administrative Support Center
7600 Sand Point Way N.E., Building 1
Seattle WA 98115-0070
526-6053
Jobline: 526-6294
Interested in the weather service? Or the National Marine Fisheries Services? Or the Economic Development Administration? This is where you'll learn about opportunities in these agencies and many others in several western states. All positions require U.S. citizenship. Many openings are limited to current federal employees with "career" or "career conditional" status. Job openings are posted in the building lobby and at the Office of Personnel Management.

National Oceanic and Atmospheric Administration (NOAA)
Personnel Office, Building 1
7600 Sand Point Way N.E.
Seattle WA 98115
Joblines:
General personnel information (taped message): 526-6053
Shipboard jobs: 526-6051
If you're interested in an entry-level shipboard position, you must apply in person. Applications for more advanced positions can be submitted by mail or in person. For information on NOAA jobs in Seattle, check the Western Regional Administrative Support Center jobline.

U.S. Environmental Protection Agency (EPA)
Human Resources Management Branch
1200 Sixth Ave., Seventh Floor, Mailstop MD-077
Seattle WA 98101
553-2959
Jobline: 553-1240
Many EPA jobs are open to the public, but most require specialized experience. To learn of openings, visit the EPA or Office of Personnel Management offices. Applications must be submitted using the Application for Federal Employment—SF 171 available in either office.

U.S. Federal Aviation Administration (FAA)
Northwest Mountain Region
1601 Lind Ave. S.W., Mailstop NM-14E
Renton WA 98055
Joblines:
General: 227-2014
Air traffic controllers: 227-1012
Test pilots, engineers, airport planners and, of course, air traffic controllers are examples of FAA jobs. Many positions are filled from registers maintained by the Office of Personnel Management (OPM). Others, including engineer, electronic technician, maintenance mechanic and air traffic controller, are filled by FAA human resources. Openings are posted in the FAA office and at OPM. Applications are accepted only for open positions and only with the SF 171.

U. S. Federal Bureau of Investigation (FBI)
915 Second Ave., #710
Seattle WA 98174
622-0460
Interested in the FBI? You'll find informational material in the

reception area of the local office. For special agents, the investigative positions, the FBI seeks people with college degrees who are at least 23. You'll need three years of work experience unless you have an accounting degree (for work in white-collar crime) or fluency in a language such as Chinese, Russian, Spanish or the Arabic dialects. Note: special agents can be assigned anywhere in the U.S.; you can't specify location. This office also employs entry-level clerk-typists.

U.S. Federal Emergency Management Agency (FEMA)
130 228th St. S.W.
Bothell WA 98020
487-4600
Jobline: #4
This facility houses two units: the staff for Region X and the Mobile Emergency Response Support Detachment. FEMA Region X activities include the natural and technical hazards program, which covers problems such as flood plains, chemical spills and radioactive wastes; civil defense preparedness; and disaster assistance, which has both full-time permanent and full-time intermittent employees. The permanent staff establishes disaster assistance programs which are implemented by experienced personnel who work on-call, often on two- to four-month assignments. FEMA has about 65 permanent employees and approximately 200 intermittent. Most are hired through the registers established by the Office of Personnel Management. Openings are posted at OPM and in the FEMA office lobby.

U.S. Government Services Administration
400 15th St. S.W.
Auburn WA 98001
931-7542
Jobline: (415) 744-5182
Former and current federal employees may apply directly for GSA openings; others must first take an exam administered by the Office of Personnel Management. Openings are posted in the Henry M. Jackson Federal Building in downtown Seattle and in the cafeteria of the GSA's Auburn office.

U.S. Department of Health and Human Services
Regional Personnel
2201 Sixth Ave., Mailstop RX-05
Seattle WA 98121
553-0566
This federal agency has both full-time and part-time positions. Some hiring is done directly and other positions are filled from registers maintained by the Office of Personnel Management. Some recent

openings: Social Security insurance representatives, chemists and consumer safety inspectors. Programs include the Public Health Service, Child Support Enforcement, Food and Drug Administration, Social Security, Human Development Services, and the Family Support Administration. You'll find openings posted at the HHS office, Office of Personnel Management, Job Service Centers and sometimes on the federal jobline. You must use the SF 171.

U.S. Department of Housing and Urban Development
1321 Second Ave., Eighth Floor, Mailstop 10-AP
Seattle WA 98101-2058
553-7581
Jobline: 442-8184
Applications are accepted at any time by this federal agency. You must use the SF 171; resumes are not accepted. Some positions require that you take a test. For information on current openings, use the jobline or speak to a personnel staffing specialist at the HUD office. Openings are posted at HUD, Job Service Centers and college placement offices. HUD positions include jobs in loan management, where you would work with VA and FHA loans, and property management, where you might oversee the management or rehabilitation of government-owned property. At press time there was a hiring freeze.

U.S. Department of the Interior
National Park Service
Pacific Northwest Regional Office
83 S. King St., #212
Seattle WA 98104
553-4409
Like to be a park ranger? It's a great job—and there are very few openings. Turnover is limited and most openings are for career status employees, those who have served a minimum of three years with the park service. You'll have a better chance at a park ranger job if you start with a summer seasonal position. To apply, request and complete a "seasonal packet" from the office above between Sept. 1 and Jan. 15 any year. There are two packets available: park ranger and laborer. Besides park rangers, the park service has other positions; for example, in science, landscape design, engineering, finance and public affairs. Some jobs are in the regional headquarters, others are in the parks. Openings are posted at the National Park Service and the Office of Personnel Management; most require a test (see below).

You may also be interested in the seasonal park jobs available from the concessions that provide food, lodging and tourist services. These jobs do not lead to park service positions. See below for concession-aires' winter addresses.

Mount Rainier National Park Concessions
Guest Services, Inc.
Elizabeth Marzano
General Manager
Star Route
Ashford WA 98304

North Cascades National Park (Ross Lake National Recreational Area)
Ross Lake Resort
Hal Tye
Yakima WA 98908

North Cascades National Park (Lake Chelan National Recreational Area)
North Cascades Lodge
Steve Gibson
P.O. Box 1779
Chelan WA 98816

Olympic National Park Concessions
Kalaloch Lodge
Star Route 1, P.O. Box 1100
Forks WA 98331

Log Cabin Resort
Bette Linenkugel
6540 E. Beach Road
Port Angeles WA 98362

National Park Concessions, Inc.
HC 62, Box 11
Port Angeles WA 98362-9798

Sol Duc Hot Springs Resort
Steve Olsen
P.O. Box 2169
Port Angeles WA 98362-0283

U.S. Internal Revenue Service (IRS)
915 Second Ave.
Seattle WA 98174
553-4774
Jobline: 553-2639
You'll find permanent and seasonal positions at the IRS.

U.S. Office of Personnel Management
Seattle Area Office
915 Second Ave.
Seattle WA 98174
Jobline: 442-4365
Many Seattle area federal government positions are filled through this office, which accepts applications in two different ways. For those positions in which openings occur frequently, the government maintains registers, lists of people with the necessary qualifications. For those positions in which openings seldom occur, the government occasionally issues a vacancy announcement and then creates a short-term list. Getting on a register may require taking a test. There is no one exam for all federal positions.

For information, call the jobline or visit the Job Information Center in Room 110 (First Avenue lobby) of the Henry M. Jackson Federal Building. (There is no telephone service.) Job openings are posted and detailed announcements are compiled in notebooks. For many of the jobs in this area, you'll be instructed to contact the hiring agency directly.

The Job Information Center can also provide information about Administrative Careers with America, a new program that recruits for entry-level positions in six general occupational areas: Health, Safety and Environmental; Writing and Public Information; Business, Finance and Management; Personnel, Administrative and Computers; Benefits Review, Tax and Legal; and Law Enforcement and Investigation. If you cannot visit a federal Job Information Center, you can obtain information from the Career America College Hotline, (900) 990-9200. Charge: 40 cents per minute. If you are a recent college graduate with a minimum grade point average of 3.5 or if you graduated in the top 10 per cent of your college class, you may be eligible for direct placement in an Administrative Careers position without taking the usual test.

For information about federal jobs anywhere in the country, you have three other options. First, you can simply call federal agencies in the city where you'd like to work and ask about openings. Second, you can formally request (in writing or in person) that OPM staff check the Federal Employment Data Service (FEDS) for openings in your occupation. Finally, you can use a personal computer and modem to access an electronic bulletin board listing job openings. Call (912) 471-3771 any day of the week.

U.S. Department of the Navy

Puget Sound Naval Shipyard
Reception Center
223 First St.
Bremerton WA 98314-5000
476-2958
Jobline: (800) 562-5972

Engineer, electrician and child development technician are examples of recent openings at the shipyard, which has both permanent and temporary positions. Applicants must be U.S. citizens. The reception center is open limited hours; check the jobline for the schedule.

U.S. Naval Station Puget Sound
There are different kinds of civilian jobs—and different personnel offices—at the Sand Point Naval Station. Those jobs funded by the Department of Defense are subject to freezes; other positions are supported by user fees and, although not subject to the freezes, may not offer civil service benefits. The naval station will be closed by September, 1994.

Department of Defense-funded Positions
Although at press time a freeze had been imposed, some permanent opportunities existed for current federal employees and some temporary positions for the general public. The only permanent positions open to the general public were police and fire. Applicants must be U.S. citizens. Check the jobline or the notebook on the front desk in the office below:

Human Resources Office, Building 30
7500 Sand Point Way N.E.
Seattle WA 98115-5007
526-3895
Jobline: 526-3598

Morale, Welfare and Recreation (MWR)
This department employs about 160 who handle many fee-supported activities. When the naval station moves to Everett, employment may reach 200. About a third of the jobs are permanent full-time with

Bureau of Naval Personnel benefits. The balance are "flexible;" they may offer regular work schedules but no benefits. Many positions are appropriate for students. Examples of MWR positions: lifeguard, recreational aide, chef, waiter, purchasing agent, public affairs specialist and personnel specialist. To learn of openings, visit the MWR personnel office at:

Naval Station Puget Sound
7500 Sand Point Way, Building 224
Seattle WA 98115
524-0828

Navy Exchange
The exchange operates retail stores, so most of the 200 jobs are for clerks and cashiers. Many are part-time and appropriate for students. You must be at least 16 years old; U.S. citizenship is not required. Applications are accepted at all times. For information about openings, visit the office:

Navy Exchange Personnel Office
Naval Station Puget Sound
7500 Sand Point Way, Building 193
Seattle WA 98115-5006
527-7836

U.S. Postal Service
Employment and Placement Office
415 First Ave. N., #240
P.O. Box 9000
Seattle WA 98109
442-6242
Joblines:
Seattle and Everett positions: 442-6240
Tacoma, Bremerton and Olympia positions: 756-6148
Not everyone who works for the U.S. Postal Service sells stamps or carries mail. Recently applications were being accepted for nurses, stenographers and elevator mechanics as well as rural carriers. There are also full- and part-time opportunities for clerks, mail handlers and carriers. Part-time temporary positions do not require a test.

U.S. Small Business Administration
Region X Office
2615 Fourth Ave.
Seattle WA 98121
553-7646

District Office
915 Second Ave.
Seattle WA 98174
553-5534

The SBA employs about 40 in the regional office, its management operation, and another 40 in the district office, where most programs are implemented and most client interaction takes place. Most clerical positions require that you be tested at the Office of Personnel Management and receive a "notice of rating." You can apply for more specialized positions (for example, business opportunities specialist or loan servicing specialist) without taking an exam. Openings are posted in the SBA offices and in Job Service Centers.

U.S. Department of Transportation
Coast Guard
915 Second Ave.
Seattle WA 98174
Civilian Personnel: 553-5155

The Coast Guard has very few civilian positions in the Northwest, which means there's limited turnover. When openings do occur, they are posted on bulletin boards on the 33rd, 34th and 35th floors in the Henry M. Jackson Federal Building (see U.S. Office of Personnel Management). They are not listed on the OPM jobline. Coast Guard civilian employment includes a variety of positions (for example, architects, engineers, vessel traffic controllers, field secretaries), but only a few positions of each type.

U.S. Department of Veterans Affairs

VA Regional Office
915 Second Ave.
Seattle WA 98174
553-4073

The VA has extremely limited openings; most are for clerical positions. For information, check the Office of Personnel Management postings.

VA Medical Center
1660 S. Columbian Way
Building 18, Room 103
Seattle WA 98108
764-2135

VA hospital openings are posted in its office and listed on the federal employment jobline. Some positions require testing.

Washington State Convention and Trade Center
800 Convention Place
Seattle WA 98101
447-5000
Jobline: 447-5039
The convention center is a state facility, but employees are not part of the state merit system, which means they do not have seniority when applying for positions in other state agencies. It also means that the convention center handles its own hiring. The full-time convention center staff is 75. In addition, there are 70 on-call positions in such areas as maintenance, admissions, parking and security. Openings are posted at the service entrance at the southeast corner of Pike and Ninth, where job applications are available.

State of Washington
Personnel Office
600 S. Franklin
Olympia WA 98504
753-5368
Joblines:
From Seattle: 464-7378
From Spokane: (509) 456-2889
From Olympia: 586-0545
Olympia is the state capital, but that isn't where all the state jobs are. In the three counties north of the capital—King, Pierce and Snohomish—there are 57,000 state employees. Positions range from accountant and affirmative action officer to fish biologist, college professor, social worker, truck driver and volunteer resource coordinator. Review the personnel announcements at Job Service Centers, libraries, community colleges and in the Olympia personnel office. Applications can be picked up at Job Service Centers and mailed directly to the state personnel office in Olympia. A separate application is required for each position. All hiring is handled through the Olympia office.

Governor's Internship Program
Created to recruit and train managers for state agencies, internships provides valuable experience for undergraduate and graduate students in any discipline. Permanent state employees are also eligible for this management training program. If you are not a state employee, you must be in school to apply. The number of positions available varies each year, but there are usually 60 to 100 positions ranging in length from three to 12 months for undergraduates. Most are in Olympia. There are 15 to 20 executive fellowships for graduate students, ranging in length from one to two years. Internships are

advertised in the same places you'll find information on other state jobs. They're usually listed on the green sheet at the end of the job announcements. These are paid positions, with full benefits. However, interns are exempt from the state merit system and so have no seniority for other state positions. For more information, contact the program manager, 753-3208.

Commodity Commissions
You may also be interested in the commodity groups funded by farmers. The larger Puget Sound-area commodity commissions established by the state but funded by farmers on a mandatory basis are listed below. The mission of these commissions may be promotion, research or grades and standards. These commissions range in size from the Seed Potato Commission, which has no paid staff, to the Apple Commission, which employs 16 in the state and has trade representatives across the U.S. and overseas. If you work for a commodity commission, you are a state employee—but not part of the state merit system. This means you do not have seniority when applying for other state positions. Commission openings are not included in the general state listings; you'll need to contact each commission separately.

Washington Beef Commission
2200 Sixth Ave., #105
Seattle WA 98121
464-7403
Executive director: Patti Brumbach

Washington Dairy Products Commission
(Dairy Farmers of Washington)
1107 N.E. 45th St., #205
Seattle WA 98105
545-6763
General manager: Stephen Matzen

Washington Fryer Commission
2003 Maple Valley Highway
Renton WA 98055
226-6125
Manager: Pam Williams. Employs three; internships possible.

Washington State Historical Society
315 N. Stadium Way
Tacoma WA 98403
593-2830

This museum has limited turnover, but when openings occur, they are filled through the state personnel office. Announcements are available at all Job Service Centers. The staff of 30, of which only nine are full-time, includes photographic and exhibition curators, volunteer and education coordinators, a publicist, librarians and museum assistants.

Washington State Patrol
(800) 888-8384
The state patrol has both commissioned (troopers) and civilian employees. Employment as a trooper is very competitive; at press time, 300 to 500 applicants were tested each month for an average of 10 positions. To apply, call the number above and ask for the application packet; you can also pick up the packet at any state patrol office. If you're determined to be qualified based on your application, you'll be sent information regarding the application tests conducted at the patrol's Shelton academy. All commissioned employees start as highway patrol officers; later you'll have the opportunity to specialize in narcotics, organized crime, auto theft or other functions. Civilian positions include clerks, the people who staff commercial vehicle scales and communications officers. Most jobs are listed on the state jobline and in the state's weekly employment bulletins. Hiring is handled by the state personnel office.

Western State Hospital
9601 Steilacoom Blvd.
Tacoma WA 98494
582-8900
Jobline: 756-3933
Typical openings at this state hospital for the mentally ill are for recreation leaders, speech pathologists, occupational therapists, physical therapists, LPNs, RNs, pharmacists, psychiatric social workers and internists. Openings are posted in the personnel office, Room 116, Central Administration Building.

City of Woodinville
Incorporation of this northeast King County community was approved by voters in spring, 1992. City council members will be elected in November and begin hiring staff, including a city manager, in early 1993. Population is expected to be about 9,000. At press time, there was no city hall. Watch local papers for information about the election of the city council (from which the mayor will be elected) and recruiting.

Woodinville Water District
17238 Woodinville-Duvall Rd.
Woodinville WA 98072
483-9104
About 25 work for this utility, in jobs ranging from engineer, operations director and finance director to customer service and engineering technician. Most openings are advertised in local papers. Personnel director: Diane Clark.

Town of Yarrow Point
4030 95th Ave. N.E.
Bellevue WA 98004
454-6994
This community of 1,000 has only two full-time employees: the clerk and treasurer-deputy clerk. Other positions are part-time or contract. When openings occur, notices are posted in Town Hall.

9. Employers:
Schools, Colleges and Universities

Work in a school? Yes, thousands of people in the Puget Sound area do—and they don't all have teaching certificates or graduate degrees. Some teach in hands-on vocational programs where expertise and the ability to teach are more important than degrees. Others work far from classrooms—in accounting, admissions, food service, facilities, transportation, public relations or fund-raising. A final choice: some train teachers—not only in college and university programs, but in educational service districts and in special programs that provide training resources to private schools and home-schooling parents.

How well do school jobs pay? You can earn $5 an hour—or $75,000 a year. Although some positions, especially in smaller schools, offer low salaries and limited benefits, you'll find that pay in schools and colleges has improved significantly. This is most obvious in administrative positions that require the same credentials as similar positions in business.

If you're considering a job in the academic world because you'd like every summer off, check job descriptions carefully. Today many positions, especially in administration, operate on a business schedule; there are no extended summer or Christmas vacations.

This chapter begins with colleges, universities and other post-secondary programs. Listings for elementary and secondary schools, educational service districts and in-service programs start on page 256.

Colleges, Universities and Other Post-Secondary Schools

Here are the public and private institutions that provide education for those who have completed high school or the equivalent. Some of these schools are very small and offer few employment opportunities. Others are huge and employ more staff than faculty.

If you'd like to teach, you'll need an advanced degree for most academic programs and specialized skills for most vocational programs (for example, the vo-tech courses in upholstery and auto mechanics). Many schools offer part-time, temporary teaching jobs (often in evening courses) as well as full-time, permanent positions.

What kind of positions can you expect to find in Seattle colleges? First, there are student- and classroom-related jobs: teachers, classroom aides, admissions counselors, registrars, curriculum designers and continuing education program designers. There are also the same positions that exist in any organization: purchasing managers, personnel directors, accountants, telephone operators and general administrative and support staff. Many Puget Sound colleges and universities also have full-time catalog editors, career counselors, printers, graphic designers, photographers, publicists, caterers, doctors, nurses, gardeners, parking and police departments, attorneys and architects.

Antioch University-Seattle
2607 Second Ave.
Seattle WA 98121-1211
441-5352
Jobline: Dial switchboard and then select 2, 3, 4 and 1.
This branch of a midwestern university offers a baccalaureate completion and four master's degree programs. Most classes meet evenings or on Fridays. Some staff positions are part-time.

Art Institute of Seattle
2323 Elliott Ave.
Seattle WA 98121
448-0900
This vocational school offers several programs: visual communications, photography, music-video business, interior design, industrial design technology and fashion merchandising. Classes meet during the day.

Bastyr College
144 N.E. 54th
Seattle WA 98105
523-9585
This naturopathic college and its affiliated clinic employ as many as 300 in a year's time, in part because many of its specialized medical courses are taught on a part-time basis by doctors. Some support and technical positions (for example, receptionist, lab technician, ac-

counting clerk) are part-time. Jennifer Brown, human resources manager, handles recruiting for both the college and the Natural Health Clinic of Bastyr College, which employs about 35.

L. H. Bates Technical College
1101 S. Yakima
Tacoma WA 98405
596-1598
Jobline: 596-1652
Training, apprenticeships and home and family life education are offered by Bates, a vocational school that is now part of the community college system. Examples of courses: automobile mechanics, boat building, bookkeeping and medical transcription. For information, contact Sally Cofchin, personnel director, or her assistant, Rose Kibbe.

Bellevue Community College
P.O. Box 92700
Bellevue WA 98009
641-2271
Jobline: 643-2082
This public two-year college offers university-transfer and Associate of Arts programs and continuing education. To apply for a BCC position, you must complete the official application available in the personnel office, B-103. (Enter the campus at Landerholm Circle from 148th Avenue Southeast.) All openings are posted in the personnel office.

Business Computer Training Institute
Administrative Office
15928 Mill Creek Blvd., #1
Mill Creek WA 98012
337-4426
(800) 752-2284
BCTI operates five schools in the Puget Sound area—at Bellevue, Northgate, Southcenter, Everett and Tacoma. The 10 or 12-week courses, offered both days and evenings, are in secretarial skills and medical claims. You can inquire about a teaching position by contacting the Curriculum Department at the administrative office or by calling a school location.

Central Washington University
Extended Degree Centers
Although based in Ellensburg, this regional state university offers selected programs in the Seattle area on the South Seattle Community

College and Edmonds Community College campuses. Both locations have full-time staff and part-time and full-time faculty. Staff openings are usually advertised. Faculty members are hired by Ellensburg administrators in two different ways: full-time instructors are hired by the appropriate department (for example, education or psychology) while part-time instructors are recruited by the Office of Extended University Programs. For more information, contact the coordinator at:

Central Washington University, South Seattle
764-6422

Central Washington University, Lynnwood
771-1574

Chapman University
This Orange, Calif. institution provides classes on four Puget Sound area military bases. Each location averages two or three teaching openings each term. For information, contact:

Chapman University-Bangor
P.O. Box 2120
Silverdale WA 98383-2120
779-2040

Chapman University-McChord/Fort Lewis
P.O. Box 4039
McChord AFB WA 98434
584-5448

Chapman University-Whidbey
Building 126, Room 137
Oak Harbor WA 98278
257-1277

City University
335 116th Ave. S.E.
Bellevue WA 98004
643-2000
This private school, with branches in the western U.S. and British Columbia, employs more than 225 staff. Management opportunities are limited. All teaching positions are part-time, usually evenings. At least a master's degree is required. Subject areas include business, nursing and paralegal. For staff positions, contact Nancy Johnson; for teaching positions, Priscilla Lewis.

Clover Park Technical College
4500 Steilacoom Blvd. S.W.
Tacoma WA 98499-4098
Human Resources: 589-5834
Now a part of the community college system, this vocational school accepts applications only for open positions. You'll find openings posted in the Human Resources office. If you'd like to teach through the college's continuing education program, contact Roger Mullen, continuing education director, 589-5833.

Cornish College of the Arts
710 E. Roy
Seattle WA 98102
323-1400
This four-year college offers degrees in art, dance, design, music, performance production and theater. Many openings are posted in the personnel office. Faculty openings are most likely to occur in late summer and in December. Applications are accepted only when openings exist.

Council of Presidents' Office
P.O. Box 40932
Olympia WA 98504-0932
753-5107
This state agency represents the state's six public four-year colleges and universities. The COP's staff of five carries out projects of benefit (for example, legislative liaison) to the university presidents as a group. Employees are hired directly by the COP, not by the state personnel office. Terry Teale is executive director.

Dominion College
P.O. Box 98947
Seattle WA 98198
878-1010
This new (1992-93 is its third year) liberal arts college offers general studies, theology and ministry degrees. Its enrolls about 60 and employs fewer than 10 full-time. There are occasional openings for adjunct faculty. Contact Don Wile, senior vice president, with a letter of interest and a resume.

Edmonds Community College
Human Resources Office
Mailing Address
20000 68th Ave. W.
Lynnwood WA 98036
771-1500
Jobline: 771-1510
Most ECC job openings are posted in the college's registration area and career placement office. A formal ECC application must be used for each opening; applications are accepted only for open positions.

Eton Technical Institute
This vocational school has two Seattle-area programs; for information regarding teaching you can contact:

Vivian Wilcox, Director
Eton Technical Institute
31919 6th Ave. S.
Federal Way WA 98003
941-5800

Allen Vernon, Director
Eton Technical Institute
209 E. Casino Rd.
Everett WA 98208
353-4888

Everett Community College
801 Wetmore
Everett WA 98201
259-7151
Jobline: 388-9229 (Live voice)
You'll find most openings (staff and faculty) posted outside the college personnel office.

The Evergreen State College
Employee Relations Office
Library 3238
Olympia WA 98505
866-6000
Jobline: Ext. 6361 (Touchtone telephones only)
Evergreen posts its openings on the jobline, in the employee relations office and in many agencies. Applications are accepted only when an opening is posted.

Golden Gate University
1326 Fifth Ave., #310
Seattle WA 98101
622-9996
This satellite of the San Francisco school has offered a master's degree in taxation in Seattle since 1974. The program offers as many as 18 evening courses a semester. All faculty positions are part-time and require an advanced degree in taxation.

Green River Community College
12401 S.E. 320th
Auburn WA 98002
833-9111
From Seattle: 464-6133
From Tacoma: 924-0180
Jobline: Ext. 86
Part-time instructors are hired directly by departments at this public two-year school. If you'd like advice on which dean to contact, ask the switchboard operator for the office of the Vice President of Instruction. GRCC's personnel office hires full-time faculty and administrative and support staff; positions are posted in the administration building.

Griffin College
Both vocational and academic programs are offered by this school. Tom Miller, the president, handles hiring for administrative and managerial positions; you can write him at the Seattle address. Each campus recruits its own teachers and support staff.

Dave Yocum, Academic Dean
Griffin College
2505 Second Ave.
Seattle WA 98121
728-6800

Steve Johnson, Academic Dean
Griffin College
10833 N.E. 8th
Bellevue WA 98004
455-3636

Glen Wyman, Academic Dean
Griffin College
2111 S. 90th
Tacoma WA 98444
537-0833

Highline Community College

P.O. Box 98000, MS 9-7
Des Moines WA 98198
Personnel: 878-3710, Ext. 751
If you'd like to work at this public two-year college, you can call or
visit the personnel office. The staff there handles applications for full-
time faculty and administrative and support staff and it can refer you
to the appropriate division chairperson if you're interested in a part-
time teaching job. Highline openings are posted at the HCC personnel
office reception desk, 2400 S. 240th.

ITT Technical Institute

12720 Gateway Dr., #100
Seattle WA 98168
244-3300
Electronics engineering and CAD drafting are the courses offered by
this school, which holds daytime and evening classes. If you're
interested in working in admissions, contact Toby Stanley, the sales
manager. For other administrative positions, contact Tom Hauser, the
center director. For faculty positions, contact Jim Shambo, the
education director.

Lake Washington Technical College

11605 132nd Ave. N.E.
Kirkland WA 98034
Human Resources: 828-2307
Now part of the community college system, this vo-tech school offers
vocational programs, continuing education and several classes for
job-seekers. Many openings are advertised in the Seattle and Bellevue papers. All are posted in the personnel office. If you'd like to
teach, call the personnel office; you'll be referred to the appropriate
academic department. Applications are accepted only when positions
are open.

Lutheran Bible Institute

4221 228th Ave. S.E.
Issaquah WA 98027
392-0400
This school offers several programs, most with a religious orientation.
Examples are Biblical studies, gerontology and missionology. The 40
employees include a few part-time staff and some adjunct faculty. If
you're interested in an administrative position, contact Ray Harbolt,
executive director, finance and administration. If you'd like to teach,
contact the Rev. Bob Moylan, academic dean.

Northwest College of the Assemblies of God
5520 108th Ave. N.E.
Kirkland WA 98033
822-8266
This small church-affiliated college offers both associate of arts and bachelor's degrees. If you're interested in a support position, you can pick up an application at the front desk. Inquiries regarding teaching positions should be directed to Academic Affairs.

Olympic College
Personnel Office
16th and Chester
Bremerton WA 98310-1699
478-4980
This public two-year college posts its nonacademic job openings in the Administration Building near the first floor mailroom. If you'd like to teach, you should complete a faculty application and submit it to the personnel office with a cover letter indicating whether you're interested in full-time or part-time positions.

Pacific Lutheran University
Administration Building
121st and Park Ave.
Tacoma WA 98447
535-7185
Jobline: 535-8598
This private liberal arts college affiliated with the Lutheran church enrolls approximately 3,000 full-time and more than 800 part-time students. There are both full-time and part-time faculty positions. You'll find both faculty and staff positions listed on the jobline; applications can be picked up in the administration building.

Pierce College
Personnel Services, Room 324
9401 Farwest Dr. S.W.
Tacoma WA 98498
964-6585
This public two-year college operates two campuses, Fort Steilacoom and Puyallup, and several extension sites. Classified openings are posted outside the personnel office. If there are no current openings for the position you'd like, you can complete an "interest card" that will be mailed to you when an appropriate position opens. To be considered for a part-time teaching position, submit your resume to Personnel Services. It'll be filed for review by division chairpeople when openings occur.

Renton Technical College

3000 N.E. 4th St.
Renton WA 98056
235-2352
Jobline: 227-5312

This vo-tech school enrolls approximately 23,000 annually in day, evening and continuing education classes. Job announcements are posted near the cafeteria on the first floor of the administration building. If you submit a letter and resume regarding teaching to the personnel office, your materials will be circulated to the appropriate associate dean.

St. Martin's College

5300 Pacific Ave. S.E.
Lacey WA 98503-1297
491-4700

This small Catholic college posts its occasional openings at the campus information center.

Seattle Community Colleges

Administrative Office
1500 Harvard Ave.
Seattle WA 98122
587-4155
Jobline: 587-5454

All full-time faculty positions and all administrative (managerial) and classified (support) positions at North Seattle, Seattle Central and South Seattle community colleges are filled through this office. The openings are posted on each campus, in the personnel office, in state Job Service Centers and in many other agencies. The part-time faculty positions (an estimated 800) are hired by division chairpeople or deans on the respective campuses. For information about teaching opportunities, obtain a copy of the catalog for the campus in which you're interested. Then call the office of the Dean of Instruction for the name of the department to which your resume should be sent. Each campus has academic (college-transfer), vocational and continuing education programs.

Seattle Pacific University

502 W. Emerson
Seattle WA 98119
281-2000
Jobline: 281-2065

When this private undergraduate and graduate school has staff openings, they're posted inside the personnel office and listed on the jobline. For information about teaching, contact Academic Affairs, 281-2125.

Seattle University
Broadway and Madison
Seattle WA 98122
296-5870
This Jesuit school posts openings outside the personnel office, located in the University Services Building. For faculty positions, you should contact the department in which you'd like to teach. For more information, consult the college catalog or call the office of the Assistant Provost for Academic Administration, 296-6140.

Seattle Vocational Institute
315 22nd Ave. S.
Seattle WA 98144
587-4800
Now part of the community college system, SVI provides vocational training for youth and adults. Classes include business computers, dental and medical assisting, medical transcription, job search skills and GED preparation. Total employment: about 40. Many job openings are posted in the school job center. Inquiries regarding teaching can be directed to LeRoy Drake, executive director.

Shoreline Community College
16101 Greenwood Ave. N.
Seattle WA 98133
546-4769
Both staff and faculty openings at this public two-year college are posted on campus, in the entry of the 1000 Building and in the student placement center.

South Puget Sound Community College
2011 Mottman Rd. S.W.
Olympia WA 98502
754-7711
Jobline: Dial switchboard and then select 1, 3, 3, 2 and 1.
This public two-year school lists its job openings on a board on the second level of the administrative building, just outside the personnel office. If you're interested in a part-time teaching job, you can submit a resume and cover letter to the personnel office; it will be retained for review by division chairs when appropriate openings occur.

Tacoma Community College
5900 S. 12th St.
Tacoma WA 98465
566-5000
At this public two-year college, you'll find classified openings posted in the lobby of Building 4. For faculty positions, full-time or part-time, pick up an application in the personnel office or ask that you be mailed one. Division chairpeople review the applications and select candidates for interviews.

University of Puget Sound
P.O. Box 7297
Tacoma WA 98407
756-3369
Jobline: 756-3368
This private liberal arts college and law school posts its faculty and staff openings in the personnel office, located at 1218 N. Lawrence.

University of Washington
Jobline: 543-6969 (Touchtone telephones only)
The UW employs an estimated 12,500 in the greater Seattle area—on the main campus, in Tacoma and Bothell branch campuses, at KUOW, in the medical centers and at the Washington Technology Center, Henry Art Gallery and Burke Memorial Washington State Museum. You can learn of many job openings by checking the listings posted in each employment office and at many libraries and public agencies. Some positions are advertised in the Seattle papers and in such professional publications as the *Chronicle of Higher Education.*

The university has about 8,000 classified (nonacademic, support) positions. Examples are admissions counselor, psychiatric outreach worker, University Press editor, cook, gardener, plumber, word processor and secretary. In addition, the UW employs about 2,000 in professional staff positions. These include directors (for example, of development or continuing education) and curriculum-related positions such as curriculum developers and research scientists. There are also approximately 2,500 faculty positions. Finally, the UW has many temporary employees, both in staff and teaching positions.

To be considered for a classified position, you must submit a standard UW employment application, available at:

Staff Employment Office
1320 N.E. Campus Parkway

Harborview Medical Center
319 Terry

University Hospital Personnel
BB130 University Hospital
1959 N.E. Pacific St.

There is no centralized hiring for faculty. You must contact the academic department in which you're interested. All departments and their chairpeople are listed in the UW Bulletin, available for purchase at the University Book Store. (The bookstore accepts telephone orders with bankcards; call 634-3400.) Most departments require doctorates.

Many departments hire temporary and contract staff. Such employees are paid on an hourly basis and have none of the benefits provided to permanent employees. Some contract-basis teaching opportunities exist, often through continuing education or staff training programs.

The University also runs an in-house "temp" agency. You can work in a support position (possibly while applying for classified positions) through University Temporary Services. This office has jobs as short as a half day and as long as six months. You'll find it easier to be placed through UTS if you have good word processing, spreadsheet and dictating machine skills and can type at least 55 words per minute. UTS also has frequent calls for medical transcriptionists and for those experienced with UW billing systems. The UTS staff points out that it has difficulty placing people who are not available during the entire UW workday (typically 8 to 5) and all five days of the work week. To obtain a UTS application, stop by the UW Visitors Information Center, 4014 University Way N.E., or call 543-5813 weekdays.

Washington State University
Besides the cooperative extension programs in each county (see *"Employers: Government Agencies"*), WSU has two offices in Seattle. One is academic, the other administrative.

Washington State University
Hotel and Restaurant Administration Program
Mailing Address
1108 E. Columbia
Seattle WA 98122
464-6349
Located at 914 E. Jefferson, #2300, on the Seattle University campus, the hotel administration program offers several undergraduate classes.

The staff is small, but there are support as well as full-time and part-time faculty positions. Openings are usually advertised. For information about faculty positions, contact Dr. Carl Riegel, the director.

WSU West
2001 Sixth Ave., #100
Seattle WA 98121-2521
448-1330
Fundraising, alumni special events and the sale of Cougar memorabilia are the primary functions of this office, which has a staff of five. Most openings are advertised. You can also call the office; if an opening exists, you'll be sent a position description and application instructions.

Western Washington University
The Bellingham-based regional state university offers two programs in Seattle.

Western Washington University
Seattle Urban Center
1801 Broadway, NP 101
Seattle WA 98122
464-6103
About 300 attend WWU classes on the campus of Seattle Central Community College, where WWU offers programs in human services, school administration and teacher certification. Prospective instructors must submit applications to the Faculty Vacancy Pool, which is opened each summer. Division directors screen the applications and then select candidates for interviews.

Western Washington University
Center for Apparel Design and Fashion Marketing
217 Pine St., #600
Seattle WA 98101
467-9968
The full-time staff at this program is small, but occasional openings occur for part-time instructors. All inquiries should be directed to:

Dr. Rosalie King
Department of Home Economics
Western Washington University
Old Main 560, MS 9001
Bellingham WA 98225-9001
676-3370

Educational Service Districts

Washington has nine regional agencies that serve as liaison between the schools in their geographic areas and the state Superintendent of Public Instruction. In the Puget Sound area, the ESDs are:

Puget Sound Educational Service District
400 S.W. 152nd
Seattle WA 98166
439-3636

This ESD's service area includes the 35 school districts and all state-approved private schools in King and Pierce counties and on Bainbridge Island. It serves about 40 per cent of the K-12 students in the state. Programs: in-service training, direct services to children (including Head Start and Indian education), teacher certification, technical assistance to school districts on both administrative and curriculum questions, and insurance co-ops. The ESD responds to particular district needs; for example, with programs about gangs, campus violence and substance abuse. The extensive health education programs cover such topics as sexually transmitted diseases. Many positions require an education background; examples of others are nurses, nutritionists, insurance claims representatives and safety officers, and computer programmers. Total employment: 145. Dr. Sonja Hampton handles personnel. You'll find openings described in a book at the reception desk; you can also call and ask the receptionist about job opportunities.

Olympic Educational Service District 114
105 National Ave. N.
Bremerton WA 98312
479-0993

About 100 work for this ESD, which serves Kitsap County (except Bainbridge Island), the North Mason School District, Jefferson and Clallam counties. Because several member districts are small, there is an emphasis on providing direct services—in working directly in the schools. For example, the ESD manages drug and alcohol intervention for several districts and operates two drug and alcohol abuse treatment centers. It also offers the ECAP (Head Start) program in Kitsap County. Science, particularly marine biology, is a special emphasis; the ESD hires science specialists to create science kits that are then leased to districts, it runs teacher-training programs in science and it maintains lab sites on the Olympic Peninsula. For 14 districts, the ESD also operates a personnel co-op. For information about job opportunities, contact Anna Alexander, executive secretary and personnel manager.

Educational Service District 113
601 McPhee Rd. S.W.
Olympia WA 98502
586-2933

Depending on the season, as many as 110 work for this ESD, which serves 45 school districts in Grays Harbor, Mason, Lewis, Thurston and Pacific counties. Through a youth employment program, the district also provides work for as many as 600 students. Assistance for member districts with fiscal services, curriculum development, staff development, transportation services and traffic safety education are examples of the ESD's programs. ESD 113 also operates insurance and data processing cooperatives. It manages the Cispus Environmental Center and the Public Schools Personnel Cooperative, which serves as a personnel clearinghouse for 10 districts (see below, under Public Schools). For more information, contact Fred Tidwell, superintendent.

Home-Schooling Resources

Hundreds of children in the Puget Sound area are home schooled—taught at home by their parents. Parents who need advice on developing curricula can call on the teachers who serve as parent consultants through programs such as Family Academy. A private school extension program, it offers education services rather than correspondence courses. Most of the 35 parent consultants work on a part-time basis. For information about working as a parent consultant, contact Candace Oneschak or Diane McAlister at

Family Academy
146 S.W. 153rd, #290
Seattle WA 98166
246-9227

Elementary and Secondary Schools

Here you'll find many of the public school districts and the state-approved private schools in Seattle, Tacoma, Bremerton, Olympia, Everett and Bellevue. Private elementary schools are listed if they provide at least kindergarten through fifth grade and enroll at least 50 students. For more information about public and private schools, especially those more distant from Seattle, consult the Washington Education Association (WEA) directory, available from Barbara Krohn and Associates, 835 Securities Building, Seattle WA 98101-1162, 622-3538. Approximate cost: $15. This book also lists all state colleges and universities, public institutions for the handicapped and many associations for educators.

Many current job openings for administrators, teachers and support staff are listed in bulletins available from the WEA Position Listing Service. A three-month subscription is $10 for WEA members and $35 for nonmembers. To subscribe, contact the Washington Education Association at 33434 8th S., Federal Way WA 98003. Telephone 941-6700 or, within Washington, (800) 622-3393.

A similar listing is available from the University of Washington placement center. The cost is $40 per academic quarter per list (with lower rates for UW alumni subscribing for at least two quarters). The lists, which are ordered by number, include: 1. Nonadministrative positions in K-12 educational programs (most positions require a valid Washington teaching certificate); and 2. Administrative positions in K-12 educational programs and higher education. To subscribe, contact the Placement Center, 301 Loew Hall FH-30, University of Washington, Seattle WA 98195, 543-9104.

Another list of openings for certified staff is published by Seattle Pacific University on a weekly basis. At press time the cost was $25 per three-month subscription (with lower rates for SPU alumni and students). Subscriptions are sold by quarter: the first is February, March and April; the second is May, June and July; the third August, September and October. No bulletin is published November through January. To subscribe, contact the Educational Vacancy Bulletin, Career Development Center, Seattle Pacific University, Seattle WA 98109, 281-2018.

A listing of openings in Catholic schools is also available to teachers registered with the Archdiocese of Seattle. See Catholic Schools in the Private Schools section of this chapter.

Public Schools

What opportunities do public schools offer? You can be a lifeguard, a librarian or a secretary, a principal, business manager or playground monitor. You can work the academic calendar or year 'round, a few hours each day or full-time. Or you may work on-call, substituting in the classroom, office or kitchen or on the bus route. You may spend all of your time in one office or classroom—or you may switch assignments and desks in midday.

As you review the employers listed below, remember that "administrative" positions in schools are usually management jobs; "certified" (or "certificated") positions are faculty jobs usually requiring a Washington state teaching certificate; and "classified" positions are technical, professional and clerical jobs.

Auburn School District
915 4th St. N.E.
Auburn WA 98002
931-4900
Jobline (Live voice): 931-4916
You'll find both certified and classified positions posted in the personnel office. You can also call the jobline number to discuss specific openings with the personnel staff.

Bainbridge Island School District
8489 Madison Ave. N.E.
Bainbridge Island WA 98110-2990
842-4715
Jobline: 842-2920
Certified and classified openings are posted in the administrative office.

Bellevue School District
P.O. Box 90010
Bellevue WA 98009-9010
455-6096
Jobline: 455-6009
Administrative, certified and classified openings are listed on this jobline. For the necessary district application forms, visit the personnel services office at 12111 N.E. 1st.

Bethel School District
Educational Service Center
516 E. 176th
Tacoma WA 98387
536-7272
Jobline: 536-7270
You'll find certified and classified openings as well as summer opportunities on the jobline. Applications are available in the service center.

Bremerton School District
300 N. Montgomery
Bremerton WA 98312
478-5107
This Kitsap County district enrolls about 6,000. Openings are seldom advertised, but they're posted on a bulletin board near the personnel office.

Carbonado Historical School District
P.O. Box 131
Carbonado WA 98323
829-0121
This district has one K-8 school that enrolls 140. Turnover is limited.

Central Kitsap Schools
9210 Silverdale Way N.W.
Silverdale WA 98383
692-3118
Jobline: 698-3470
Certified and classified openings are listed on the jobline and posted in the personnel office and in district schools.

Clover Park School District
10903 Gravelly Lake Dr. S.W.
Tacoma WA 98499
589-7433
Jobline: 589-7436
Certified and classified openings are listed on this jobline.

Dieringer School District
1320 178th Ave. E.
Sumner WA 98390
862-2537
This small K-8 district enrolls about 900 in two schools. You'll find openings posted in the district office.

Edmonds School District
Human Resources Office
20420 68th Ave. W.
Lynnwood WA 98036
670-7000
Jobline: 670-7021
You'll need official district application forms for both certified and classified positions at Edmonds. If you cannot visit the human resources office to pick up a form, you can request one by sending a large self-addressed, stamped envelope to the address above.

Enumclaw School District
2929 McDougall Ave.
Enumclaw WA 98022
825-2588
About 3,600 attend class in Enumclaw, where the job openings are posted in the administrative office.

Everett School District
4730 Colby Ave.
Everett WA 98203
339-4200
Jobline: 259-2935
Both certified and classified positions are listed on this jobline.
Recent openings included high school automotive trade teacher, high
school math teacher and school psychologist.

Federal Way School District
Personnel Office
31405 18th S.
Federal Way WA 98003
941-0100
From Tacoma: 927-7420
Jobline (Certified): 941-2058
Jobline (Classified): 941-2273
To apply for a teaching position, you'll need a resume and copy of
your Washington state teaching certificate. For a classified position,
you'll need an official school district application.

Fife Public Schools
5602 20th E.
Tacoma WA 98424
922-6697
You'll find openings posted in the school administration building.

Fircrest School
15230 15th Ave. N.E.
Seattle WA 98155
364-0300, Ext. 371
Jobline: 364-0300, Ext. 244
This residential state program for the developmentally disabled
enrolls about 500. Job openings are posted in the personnel office.

Franklin Pierce School District
Administrative Office
315 S. 129th St.
Tacoma WA 98444
535-9896
Jobline: 535-8829
Both certified and classified openings are posted in the personnel
office.

Highline School District
P.O. Box 66100
Seattle WA 98166
433-2281
Jobline: 433-6339
Job openings (teaching, coaching, classified and substitute) are listed on the jobline and posted in the district office at 15675 Ambaum Blvd. S.W.

Issaquah School District
565 N.W. Holly St.
Issaquah WA 98027
392-0700
Jobline: 392-0707
This fast-growing Eastside district employs about 1,000. You'll find both certified and classified positions posted in the district office.

Kent School District
12033 S.E. 256th
Kent WA 98031-6643
Human Resources: 859-7209
Jobline (Classified): 859-7508
Although Kent lists only the nonacademic positions on the jobline, all positions are posted in the personnel office.

Lake Stevens School District
12708 20th St. N.E.
Lake Stevens WA 98258
335-1500
This north end district enrolls 3,500. Openings are posted in the administrative office.

Lake Washington School District
P.O. Box 2909
Kirkland WA 98083
828-3220
Jobline: 828-3243
This district serves Redmond and Kirkland. Classified openings are posted in the personnel office at 10903 N.E. 53rd.

Mercer Island School District
4160 86th Ave. S.E.
Mercer Island WA 98040
Personnel: 236-3331
Jobline: 236-3302

This district serves the 3,200 public school students on Mercer Island. Job openings are posted in the administrative offices.

Mukilteo School District
9401 Sharon Dr.
Everett WA 98204
356-1217
Jobline: 356-1237
Job openings are posted in the administrative office.

Northshore School District
18315 Bothell Way N.E.
Bothell WA 98011
489-6356
Jobline (Certified): 489-6381
This district, which serves communities on the north end of Lake Washington, lists its faculty positions on the jobline. You'll find classified positions on the bulletin board outside the personnel office.

Orting Schools
P.O. Box 460
120 N. Washington
Orting WA 98360
893-6500
All openings for this district of 1,400 students are posted in the administrative office. Teaching positions are also advertised through the Washington Education Association and in college placement offices.

Peninsula School District
Educational Service Center
14015 62nd Ave. N.W.
Gig Harbor WA 98332
857-6171
Jobline: 857-3565
Both certified and classified job openings are posted in the educational service center.

Public Schools Personnel Cooperative
601 McPhee Rd. S.W.
Olympia WA 98502
753-2855
Operated by Educational School District 113, this agency posts openings and accepts applications for certified and classified positions in 10 school districts, including Olympia, Griffin (located in

Olympia), Tumwater, North Thurston, Toledo and Yelm. Districts with openings screen the applications and conduct their own interviews.

Puyallup School District
P.O. Box 370
Puyallup WA 98371
841-1301
Jobline: 841-8666
To learn of openings in this growing district, you can stop at the main desk in the administration building, 109 E. Pioneer, and check the notebooks for certified and classified positions.

Rainier School
P.O. Box 600
Buckley WA 98321
829-1111
This state institution for the developmentally disabled posts its openings outside the personnel office on the schoolgrounds, located at 2120 Ryan Rd., and at the Buckley Job Service Center.

Renton School District
Administrative Office
435 Main Ave. S.
Renton WA 98055
235-2385
Jobline: 235-5826
If you live outside the Renton area and wish to apply for a teaching position, you can ask that an application be mailed to you.

Seattle Public Schools
Personnel Services
815 Fourth Ave. N., #138
Seattle WA 98109
298-7365
Jobline: 298-7382
The state's largest district, Seattle enrolls some 40,000 students in a wide variety of programs and settings. Recent listings included secretary, office machine repair technician, business manager, drug intervention specialist and interpreter for the deaf. All job openings are posted in the personnel office and in all Seattle schools.

Shoreline School District

18560 1st Ave. N.E.
Seattle WA 98155
361-4223
Jobline: 361-4367

This North Seattle district posts its openings on the jobline and in the personnel office. Official district application forms can be picked up at the office. Applications are also mailed to those who provide self-addressed, stamped business-size envelopes.

Snohomish School District

301 Union Ave.
Snohomish WA 98290
568-3151

Snohomish enrolls some 7,000 students. Job openings are posted on a bulletin board in the administration office and in each district school.

South Central School District

4640 S. 144th
Seattle WA 98168
244-2100
Jobline: 244-2100 (Live voice)

About 1,700 are enrolled in this district, which serves the Tukwila/Southcenter area. Openings are posted in the district office.

South Kitsap School District

1962 Hoover Ave. S.E.
Port Orchard WA 98366
876-7300
Jobline: 876-7389

You'll need an official district application form to be considered for South Kitsap positions. If you live outside the area, ask that an application be mailed to you. Specify certified (academic) or classified (nonacademic).

Steilacoom Historical School District 1

510 Chambers
Steilacoom WA 98388
588-1772

Steilacoom, which enrolls about 1,500, posts its openings in the district office.

Sumner School District
1202 Wood Ave.
Sumner WA 98390
863-2201
Jobline: 863-2232
About 5,500 attend Sumner schools, where the district posts certified and classified job openings in the personnel office. Recent openings were for junior high English teachers, junior high principal, child care teacher, a physical therapist and school psychologist.

Tacoma School District
Personnel Office
P.O. Box 1357
Tacoma WA 98401
596-1250
Joblines:
Certified: 596-1300
Classified: 596-1265
To apply for a classified position, you'll need an official school district application; check the jobline or call the personnel office to determine when applications will be distributed for the position in which you're interested. All openings are also posted in the personnel office, located at 601 S. 8th St.

Tahoma School District
23015 S.E. 216th Way
Maple Valley WA 98038-8412
432-4481
Notices of faculty openings are routed to the Washington Education Association and area colleges. There are limited classified openings. All openings in this district of 4,000 students are posted in the administration building.

University Place School District
8805 40th St. W.
Tacoma WA 98466
566-5600
About 4,200 students are enrolled in University Place, which posts its openings in the district office.

Vashon Island School District
20414 Vashon Highway S.W.
Vashon WA 98070
463-2121

No unsolicited resumes are accepted by this district, which serves Vashon Island. Many openings are advertised in the Vashon Island paper. You can also call the district personnel office for information.

White River School District
P.O. Box G
240 N. A
Buckley WA 98321
829-0600
This district enrolls about 3,000 students. Openings are posted in each school and in the administrative office, located in the high school annex.

Private Schools

Adventist Schools
For Seventh Day Adventist schools, resumes are accepted and teaching candidates recommended to individual schools by the conference office. You should contact:

Education Department
Washington Conference of Seventh Day Adventists
20015 Bothell-Everett Highway
Bothell WA 98012
481-7171

All Saints School
504 Second St. S.W.
Puyallup WA 98371
845-5025
Alice Milam is the principal at this Catholic elementary school.

Amazing Grace Lutheran
10056 Renton Ave. S.
Seattle WA 98178
723-5526
Gary Gable, principal, handles personnel for this preschool-grade 8 program.

Annie Wright School
827 N. Tacoma Ave.
Tacoma WA 98403
272-2216
Annie Wright has coeducational Lower and Middle schools and a girls' college prep program.

Assumption School
6220 32nd Ave. N.E.
Seattle WA 98115
524-7452
Mike Foy, principal, handles personnel for this Catholic elementary school.

Bellarmine Preparatory School
2300 S. Washington
Tacoma WA 98405
752-7701
Christopher Gavin, principal, hires staff for this Catholic high school.

Bellevue Christian School
1601 98th Ave. N.E.
Bellevue WA 98004
454-4028
Bobbi Mead serves as personnel director for this preschool-12 Christian school.

Bertschi School
2227 10th Ave. E.
Seattle WA 98102
324-5476
Nancy Osborne, the assistant administrator, handles personnel for this preschool-5 independent school.

Blanchet High School
8200 Wallingford Ave. N.
Seattle WA 98103
527-7711
Inquiries regarding openings at this Catholic high school should be directed to the principal.

Bright and Early School
21316 66th Ave. W.
Lynnwood WA 98036
672-4430
JoAnn Nelson handles personnel for this preschool-4 program.

Buena Vista Seventh Day Adventist School
3320 Academy Dr. S.E.
Auburn WA 98002
833-0718
Hans Krenz, principal, hires staff for this K-8 program.

The Bush School
405 36th Ave. E.
Seattle WA 98112
322-7978
Fred Dust is headmaster of this K-12 program, one of Seattle's oldest private schools.

Calvary Lutheran School
3420 S.W. Cloverdale
Seattle WA 98126
937-6590
This school enrolls about 110 in grades K-8.

Catholic Schools
If you'd like to apply for positions in Puget Sound Catholic schools, contact the Archdiocese of Seattle's school department for an application packet. This office serves as a clearinghouse, maintaining applicants' files and notifying applicants of specific openings with a weekly bulletin. When an opening occurs, you'll send a resume and letter of interest to the school principal, who can then request your file from the Archdiocese. For more information, contact

Office of Superintendent of Schools
Archdiocese of Seattle
910 Marion
Seattle WA 98104
382-4861

Cedar Park Christian
16300 112th Ave. N.E.
Bothell WA 98011
488-9778
Stan Friend, principal, handles personnel for this preschool-grade 9 program.

Central Lutheran Christian School
409 Tacoma Ave. N.
Tacoma WA 98403
383-5595
Janie Lineberger is the personnel contact for this school, which enrolls 75 to 100.

Charles Wright Academy
7723 Chambers Creek Rd. W.
Tacoma WA 98467
564-2171
Pam Dunlap handles personnel for this preschool-12 program.

Chief Leschi School
2002 E. 28th
Tacoma WA 98404
597-6200
Amy Ackley is the personnel director for this elementary and secondary program, formerly known as the Puyallup Tribal School System. Most of the 550 students are enrolled tribal members.

Christian Faith School
P.O. Box 98800
Seattle 98198
878-6036
Carole Wile handles personnel for the elementary and secondary program at this school.

Christ the King School
415 N. 117th
Seattle WA 98133
364-6890
Carol Lamberger is the principal of this Catholic elementary school.

Concordia Lutheran School
7040 36th N.E.
Seattle WA 98115
525-7407
Keith Brosz, administrator, handles personnel for this preschool-grade 8 program.

Concordia Lutheran School
202 E. 56th
Tacoma WA 98404
475-9513
Henry Hays, principal, hires staff and faculty for this preschool-grade 8 program.

Cornerstone Christian School
21705 58th Ave. W.
Mountlake Terrace WA 98043
776-0760

To learn of openings in this 165-student K-grade 8 program, you can write John Bennett, principal.

Cougar Mountain Academy
5410 194th Ave. S.E.
Issaquah WA 98027
641-2800
Christie Tandy is the director of this pre-kindergarten-grade 5 program, designed for children "with high expectations."

Cypress Adventist School
21500 Cypress Way
Lynnwood WA 98036
775-3578
Address inquiries regarding this elementary and secondary program to the principal, David Tripp.

Eastside Catholic High School
11650 S.E. 60th
Bellevue WA 98006
644-7737
Dee McKeehan handles personnel for this Catholic high school.

Epiphany School
3710 E. Howell
Seattle WA 98122
323-9011
Jean Augustine, headmistress, hires faculty, and Sally Amey, business manager, coordinates the hiring of staff for this pre-kindergarten-grade 6 program.

Eton School
2701 Bellevue-Redmond Rd.
Bellevue WA 98008
881-4230
Dr. Patricia Feltin, director, handles personnel at this school for children 3-14.

Everett Christian School
2221 Cedar St.
Everett WA 98201
259-3213
Ken Swets, principal, is in charge of personnel for this K-grade 8 program.

Forest Ridge School
4800 139th Ave. S.E.
Bellevue WA 98006
641-0700
If you're interested in teaching or working at this Catholic girls' school (grades 5-12), an inquiry can be directed to "Personnel."

Harbor Montessori School
5415 68th St. Ct. N.W.
Gig Harbor WA 98335
851-5722
Terry Taylor directs this preschool through elementary program.

Heritage Christian School
19527 104th Ave. N.E.
Bothell WA 98011
485-2585
C. Randy Nading, principal, does the hiring for this interdenominational program for preschool through grade 9.

Heritage Christian School
5412 67th Ave. W.
Tacoma WA 98467
564-6276
John Battle is principal of this elementary school.

Hillside Student Community
5027 159th Pl. S.E.
Bellevue WA 98006
747-6448
Edith Sherrard, director, handles personnel for this program for grades 4-12.

Holy Family School
505 17th S.E.
Auburn WA 98002
833-8688
Kathleen Cowin is the principal of this Catholic elementary school.

Holy Family School
7300 120th Ave. N.E.
Kirkland WA 98033
827-0444
Maureen Blum is principal of this Catholic elementary school.

Holy Family School
2606 Carpenter Rd. S.E.
Lacey WA 98503
491-7060
Judith Martin is the principal of this Catholic elementary school.
Most staffing is volunteer, so the only openings are for teachers.

Holy Family School
9615 20th S.W.
Seattle WA 98106
767-6640
William Hoppes is the principal of this Catholic elementary school.

Holy Names Academy
728 21st Ave. E.
Seattle WA 98112
323-4272
Sr. Mary Tracy, principal, handles personnel for this Catholic girls'
high school.

Holy Rosary School
P.O. Box 206
Edmonds WA 98020
778-3197
Mary Gerrish is the principal of this Catholic elementary school.

Holy Rosary School
4142 42nd Ave. S.W.
Seattle WA 98116
937-7255
Kris Brown is the principal of this Catholic elementary school.

Holy Rosary School
504 S. 30th
Tacoma WA 98402
272-7012
Sr. Margaret Ann Rohling is the principal of this Catholic elementary
school.

Hope Lutheran School
4446 42nd Ave. S.W.
Seattle WA 98116
935-8500
James Knittel is the principal of this preschool-grade 8 program.
Enrollment: about 260.

Immaculate Conception/Our Lady of Perpetual Help
2508 Hoyt Ave.
Everett WA 98201
252-5175
Inquiries regarding positions at this Catholic elementary school can be directed to the principal.

Jewish Day School of Metropolitan Seattle
15749 N.E. 4th St.
Bellevue WA 98008
641-3335
Allen Silver is the principal of this K-8 elementary school.

John F. Kennedy Memorial High School
140 S. 140th
Seattle WA 98168
246-0500
John C. Schuster, principal, handles personnel for this Catholic high school.

Kent View Christian Schools
930 E. James
Kent WA 98031
852-5145
Wes Denison, administrator, hires staff and faculty for the junior and senior high school. Cathy Guy, the elementary principal, hires for her program.

King's Schools
19303 Fremont Ave. N.
Seattle WA 98133
546-7241
Jobline (Live voice): 546-7533
Operated by Crista Ministries, this preschool-12 program enrolls more than 1,000. Linda Montgomery is the junior-senior high school principal, Evelyn Sherwood the elementary principal and Karen Weber head of the early childhood program.

King's West School
4012 Chico Way N.W.
Bremerton WA 98312
479-2969
Frank Washburn is the secondary principal and Joanna Schoenknecht the elementary principal at this K-12 program, formerly Bremerton Christian.

Kirkland Seventh Day Adventist School
5320 108th N.E.
Kirkland WA 98033
822-7554
Inquiries regarding openings at this K-10 school can be directed to the principal.

Lakeside School
14050 First Ave. N.E.
Seattle WA 98125
368-3600
Missy Poirier is the contact person regarding openings at Lakeside, which divides its fifth graders through seniors into Middle and Upper schools.

Life Christian School
1717 S. Puget Sound
Tacoma WA 98405
756-5317
This preschool-grade 8 program enrolls about 500. Inquiries regarding openings can be addressed to the principal.

The Little School
2812 116th Ave. N.E.
Bellevue WA 98004
827-8708
Pat Sommers, business manager, coordinates hiring for this ungraded school for children 3-12.

Maple Valley Christian School
16700 174th Ave. S.E.
Renton WA 98058-9599
226-4640
If you'd like to apply at this K-6 school, send your cover letter and resume to the administrator, Elmer Bisset.

Neighborhood Christian School
625 140th Ave. N.E.
Bellevue WA 98005
746-3258
Richard Jessup is the principal at this school for preschoolers through eighth graders.

New Hope Christian School
25713 70th Ave. E.
Graham WA 98338
847-2643
This preschool and elementary school enrolls 100.

A New School for Children
4649 Sunnyside Ave. N.
Seattle WA 98103
632-8445
Kathryn Cooper, director, hires staff and faculty for this K-5 program, which enrolls 90.

North Seattle Christian School
12345 8th N.E.
Seattle WA 98125
365-2720
Hal Drake, administrator, is the personnel contact for this K-12 program. Your cover letter should indicate the grade level and subjects in which you're interested.

The Northwest School
1415 Summit Ave.
Seattle WA 98122
682-7309
Inquiries regarding work at this program for grades 6-12 should be directed to the headmaster.

O'Dea High School
802 Terry Ave.
Seattle WA 98104
622-6596
Dr. Dennis Elwell, vice principal, handles personnel for this boys' Catholic high school.

Olympia Junior Academy
1416 26th Ave. N.E.
Olympia WA 98506
352-1831
The principal at this Seventh-Day Adventist elementary and secondary school can be contacted for information regarding job openings.

Our Lady of Fatima School
3301 W. Dravus
Seattle WA 98199
283-7031

Susan Burdette is the principal at this Catholic elementary school.

Our Lady of the Lake School
3520 N.E. 89th
Seattle WA 98115
525-9980
For information about this Catholic elementary school, contact the principal.

Our Lady Star of the Sea School
517 Veneta Ave.
Bremerton WA 98310
373-5162
Shawna Bliss is the principal of this Catholic elementary school.

The Overlake School
20301 N.E. 108th St.
Redmond WA 98053
868-1000
Genie Benson is the personnel contact at this school for grades 5-12.

Parkland Evangelical Lutheran School
P.O. Box 44006
Tacoma WA 98444
537-1901
Larry Rude is the principal of this preschool-grade 8 program.

Peace Lutheran School
1234 N.E. Riddell Rd.
Bremerton WA 98310
373-2116
Mark Smith is the administrator of this preschool-grade 8 program.

Peoples Christian School
1819 E. 72nd
Tacoma WA 98404
473-0590
Contact the principal of this preschool-grade 11 program.

Perkins Elementary School
4649 Sunnyside Ave. N.
Seattle WA 98103
632-7154
If you're interested in this private school's program for grades 1-5, send your resume to Ellen Toole, director. Perkins also operates a separate preschool and kindergarten.

Puyallup Valley Christian School
601 9th Ave. S.E.
Puyallup WA 98372
841-2091
Don Johnson heads this preschool-grade 6 program.

Redmond Christian School
P.O. Box 3337
Redmond WA 98052
641-1351
Direct inquiries regarding this elementary and secondary program to the administrator, Jo Farris.

Renton Christian School
221 Hardie Ave. N.W.
Renton WA 98055
226-0820
Karen Sanderson is the administrator for this elementary program.

Sacred Heart School
9450 N.E. 14th
Bellevue WA 98004
451-1773
Dr. Karen Matthews is the principal of this Catholic elementary school.

St. Alphonus School
5816 15th N.W.
Seattle WA 98107
782-4363
Kathryn Palmquist-Keck is the principal of this Catholic elementary school.

St. Anne School
101 W. Lee St.
Seattle WA 98119
282-3538
Anna Kemper is the principal of this Catholic elementary school.

St. Anthony School
336 Shattuck Ave. S.
Renton WA 98055
255-0059
Douglas C. Arthur is the principal of this Catholic elementary school.

St. Benedict School
4811 Wallingford N.
Seattle WA 98103
633-3375
Chuck Secrest is the principal of this Catholic elementary, which enrolls about 270.

St. Bernadette School
1028 S.W. 128th
Seattle WA 98146
244-4934
Sr. Marie Colarossi is the principal of this Catholic elementary school.

St. Catherine School
8524 8th Ave. N.E.
Seattle WA 98115
525-0581
Dr. Kristine Brynildsen-Smith is the principal of this Catholic elementary school.

St. Christopher Academy
318 3rd Ave. S.
Kent WA 98032
852-1515
Contact the director, Darlene Jevne, for information about job openings at this elementary and secondary program.

St. Edward School
4212 S. Mead St.
Seattle WA 98118
725-1774
Les Newvine is the principal at this Catholic elementary school.

St. Frances Cabrini School
5621 108th S.W.
Tacoma WA 98499
584-3850
Stephanie Van Leuven is the principal of this Catholic elementary school.

St. Francis of Assisi School
P.O. Box 870
Seahurst WA 98062
243-5690
Joseph W. Moore heads this Catholic elementary school in the Highline area.

St. George School
5117 13th Ave. S.
Seattle WA 98108
762-0656
You can contact Glen Lutz, the principal, regarding job openings at this Catholic elementary school.

St. John School
120 N. 79th
Seattle WA 98103
783-0337
Daniel Sherman is the principal of this Catholic elementary school.

St. Joseph School
700 18th Ave. E.
Seattle WA 98112
329-3260
George Hofbauer is principal of this Catholic elementary school.

St. Louise School
133 156th S.E.
Bellevue WA 98007
746-4220
Inquiries regarding job openings at this Catholic K-8 elementary school can be directed to the principal.

St. Luke School
17533 St. Luke Pl. N.
Seattle WA 98133
542-1133
You can contact the principal of this Catholic elementary school.

St. Mark School
18033 15th Pl. N.E.
Seattle WA 98155
364-1633
This Catholic elementary school enrolls about 235.

St. Mary Magdalen School
8615 7th Ave. S.E.
Everett WA 98208
353-7559
If you'd like to work at this Catholic elementary school, you can direct your resume to the principal.

St. Matthew School
1230 N.E. 127th
Seattle WA 98125
362-2785
You can contact the principal regarding openings at this Catholic elementary school.

St. Monica School
4320 87th Ave. S.E.
Mercer Island WA 98040
232-5432
Ken Dorsett is the principal of this Catholic elementary school.

St. Patrick School
1112 N. G St.
Tacoma WA 98403
272-2297
Inquiries regarding openings at this Catholic elementary school can be directed to the principal.

St. Paul School
10001 57th Ave. S.
Seattle WA 98178
725-0780
This Catholic elementary school enrolls about 270.

St. Philomena School
1815 S. 220th St.
Des Moines WA 98198
824-4051
Contact the principal for information about this Catholic elementary school.

St. Pius X School
22105 58th Ave. W.
Mountlake Terrace WA 98043
778-9861
Dorothy Hamilton is the principal of this Catholic elementary school.

St. Therese School
900 35th Ave.
Seattle WA 98122
324-0460
You can contact the principal of this Catholic elementary school regarding job openings.

St. Thomas School
P.O. Box 124
Medina WA 98039
454-5880
Ron Smallman, headmaster, handles personnel for this Episcopal preschool-grade 6 program.

Seattle Academy of Arts and Sciences
1432 15th Ave.
Seattle WA 98122
323-6600
Canfield Smith, head of the upper school, handles inquires regarding teaching positions at this school for grades 6-12. Gayle Pearl, the registrar, coordinates the hiring of staff.

Seattle Christian School
19639 28th Ave. S.
Seattle WA 98188
824-1310
Judy Jennings is superintendent of this program, which enrolls 550 in elementary and secondary classes.

Seattle Country Day School
2619 4th Ave. N.
Seattle WA 98109
284-6220
(Ms.) Wilder Dominick, the admissions director, handles faculty hiring for this K-8 school for gifted children; Nancy Hanneman, business manager, hires the staff.

Seattle Hebrew Academy
1617 Interlaken Dr. E.
Seattle WA 98112
323-5750
Rabbi Shmuel Lopin heads this preschool-eighth grade program.

Seattle Lutheran High School
4141 41st Ave. S.W.
Seattle WA 98116
937-7722
Robert Christian, headmaster, is the personnel contact at this high school.

Seattle Preparatory School
2400 11th Ave. E.
Seattle WA 98102
324-0400
Therese Billings, the registrar, coordinates the hiring of faculty for this Catholic high school. (Ms.) Riley Martin, the admissions secretary, handles staff openings.

Seattle Waldorf School
2728 N.E. 100th
Seattle WA 98125
524-5320
Bev Younge handles personnel for this preschool-grade 8 program.

Silver Lake Christian School
2027 132nd S.E.
Everett WA 98208
337-6992
Ingrid Hornung is the administrator of this K-8 program.

Snohomish County Christian School
Administrative Office
23607 54th Ave. W.
Mountlake Terrace WA 98043
774-7773
Ron Pearson is the secondary principal and Debbie Schindler heads the elementary program in this K-12 program, which enrolls 470.

Spanaway Christian School
P.O. Box 579
Spanaway WA 98387
537-9339
For information regarding this K-6 elementary school, contact the principal.

Tacoma Adventist School
P.O. Box 8190
Tacoma WA 98408
472-3204
Jim Weller is the administrator for this K-8 school.

Tacoma Baptist Schools
2052 S. 64th
Tacoma WA 98409
475-7226
Douglas Bond is the superintendent for this elementary and secondary program.

Tacoma Christian School
1801 N. Pearl
Tacoma WA 98406
752-2752
Sue Beard is the principal for this prekindergarten-grade 7 program.

Thomas Academy
8207 S. 280th St.
Kent WA 98032-8616
852-4438
David Selby is the headmaster at this Episcopal pre-kindergarten, elementary and middle school, formerly known as St. James of Thomas School.

University Child Development School
5062 9th N.E.
Seattle WA 98105
547-5059
John Adelsheim, director, handles personnel for this preschool and elementary program for gifted children. Enrollment: nearly 200.

University Preparatory Academy
8000 25th N.E.
Seattle WA 98115
525-2714
Pam Brown is the personnel contact at this school for grades 6-12.

Valley Christian School
1312 2nd St. S.E.
Auburn WA 98002
833-3541
Don Hodson is the administrator for this K-6 school.

Villa Academy
5001 N.E. 50th St.
Seattle WA 98105
524-8885
If you'd like to work at this independent K-8 Catholic school, contact the headmaster regarding faculty openings or the business manager regarding staff positions.

Visitation School
3306 S. 58th
Tacoma WA 98409
474-6424

Evergreen Academy/Montessori House School
16017 118th Pl. N.E.
Bothell WA 98011
488-8000
Kathy Bergstrom handles hiring for the preschool portion of this program and Sue Hedlund hires for the elementary staff. Total enrollment, preschool through grade 4, is 320.

Evergreen Christian School
1010 Black Lake Blvd.
Olympia WA 98502
357-5590
Elizabeth Funk and Rebecca Morse are the administrators for this elementary and junior high program.

The Evergreen School
15201 Meridian Ave. N.
Seattle WA 98133
364-2650
Inquiries regarding this preschool-grade 8 program should be directed to Barbara Jordan, director of education (faculty positions), or Ray Reinbolt, business manager (staff positions).

Fairview Christian School
844 N.E. 78th
Seattle WA 98115-4202
526-1880
(Ms.) Don Deena Johnson is the administrator for this elementary school.

Faith Lutheran School
7075 Pacific Ave.
Olympia WA 98503
491-1733
Paul Bergman, the principal, is the personnel contact at this school for preschoolers through seventh graders.

Faith Lutheran School of Redmond
9041 166th Ave. N.E.
Redmond WA 98052
882-2778
Bob Short heads this K-6 program of 80 children.

Patty Mitchell is the principal of this Catholic elementary school.

Watson Groen Christian School
2400 N.E. 147th St.
Seattle WA 98155
364-7777
Tim Visser, the administrator, handles personnel for this preschool-grade 12 school.

West Seattle Christian School
4401 42nd Ave. S.W.
Seattle WA 98116
938-1414
Beth Rice is principal of this elementary school.

West Seattle Montessori
4536 38th Ave. S.W.
Seattle WA 98126
935-0427
This preschool through grade 6 program is owned by five of the instructors, so teaching opportunities are limited. If you'd like to work as a classroom assistant, contact Dolores Atwood to inquire about openings.

Woodinville Montessori
13965 N.E. 166th
Woodinville WA 98072
481-2300
Mary Schneider and Sherri Nick, the administrators, handle hiring for this preschool-grade 6 program.

Zion Lutheran School
3923 103rd Ave. S.E.
Everett WA 98205
334-5064
This preschool-8 program enrolls more than 270. Direct inquiries regarding employment to the principal.

Zion Preparatory Academy
620 20th S.
Seattle WA 98144
322-2926
This private Christian school enrolls more than 450 in preschool through eighth grade. The school's staff is headed by administrator-founder Bishop Eugene Drayton.

10. Employers:
Nonprofits

What do nonprofits offer you? Experience, responsibility, autonomy...and the chance to support an important cause or program. The low budgets and lean staffs typical of nonprofits mean you'll probably get to tackle a variety of tasks--for example, public speaking, media relations, copywriting, grantwriting and budgeting. In between, you may set up exhibits and stuff envelopes or pinch hit as a cashier or stagehand.

Volunteers are important to most of the groups listed. If your academic program requires an internship or if you need work experience in a particular field or job function to increase your marketability, consider contacting one of these organizations regarding an assignment. In most cases, internships are unpaid or involve only modest stipends.

A Contemporary Theatre
100 W. Roy
Seattle WA 98119
285-3220
Accounting, marketing, development, box office and operations are examples of the administrative positions on this theater's 20-person staff. Openings are usually advertised; resumes can also be sent to Susan Trapnell Moritz, managing director.

Allied Arts of Seattle
107 S. Main, #201
Seattle WA 98104
624-0432
Focused on support of the arts, historic preservation and urban design, this nonprofit and its affiliate, the Allied Arts Foundation, have only a one-person staff supplemented by contract employees. But if you're interested in the arts, Allied Arts can provide a valuable resource: *Access,* a listing of Washington arts organizations, available for $10.

Allied Arts also offers unpaid internships. Usually the same length as an academic quarter, these provide exposure to the Seattle arts community. Contact Richard Mann, director.

Alzheimer's Association of Puget Sound
120 Northgate Plaza, #316
Seattle WA 98125
365-7488
One of 207 chapters of a national organization, this group covers 22 western and central Washington counties with seven paid positions. Nearly 300 volunteers are also involved—and occasionally, volunteer positions do become part-time or full-time paid jobs. Sandra Lewis, the association director, said volunteers are especially welcome on publications projects (newsletters and brochures) and for office support work; many of these positions are appropriate for teenagers.

American Association of Retired Persons
Area 10 Office
9750 3rd Ave. N.E., #400
Seattle WA 98115
526-7918
With 1.3 million members (all 50 or older) to serve in the states of Washington, Oregon, Idaho and Alaska, the 15 regional AARP employees have to know how to work through volunteers. There's limited turnover in the staff, but when openings do occur, the area representative (who heads the office) looks for people with experience in gerontology as well as specific functions (for example, public relations). Most AARP positions involve heavy travel. All applications for paid positions should be sent to: AARP Human Resources, 3200 E. Carson, Lakewood CA 90712.

American Cancer Society
2120 First N.
Seattle WA 98109
283-1152
The cancer society offers educational programs; services to cancer patients and their families; and fellowships and grants to research institutions. This location houses both the state office, which includes 27 staff members in such areas as program (education), Crusade (fund-raising) and communications, and the two-member Seattle Metro office. If you're interested in a particular department, call for the name of that manager.

American Cancer Society
Northwest Area Office
14450 N.E. 29th Pl., #220
Bellevue WA 98007
867-5588
Dan Burleigh is the area vice president for this office, which covers
nine counties. His staff includes the two Seattle Metro employees and
12 additional positions located in the Bellevue office.

American Cancer Society
Southwest Area Office
1551 Broadway, #200
Tacoma WA 98402
272-5767
David Sokolowski is the area vice president for this office, which
supervises activities in 12 counties. Total staff: 13.

American Civil Liberties Union (ACLU)
705 Second Ave., #300
Seattle WA 98104
624-2184
Kathleen Taylor is executive director of the ACLU, which employs
12.

American Diabetes Association, Washington Affiliate
557 Roy St.
Seattle WA 98109
282-4616
Toll-free within Washington: (800) 628-8808
Statewide programs are coordinated by this office, which has a staff
of about 10. Positions include public relations, education and accounting. Resumes can be directed to Carl Knirk. There are smaller
chapter offices in Everett and Olympia. The Tacoma group, not
affiliated with the ADA, is the Diabetes Association of Pierce County.

American Diabetes Association
6315-A Fleming
Everett WA 98203
347-8875
Toll-free within Washington: (800) 950-8875

American Diabetes Association
3434 Martin Way N.E.
Olympia WA 98506
456-6677
Toll-free within Washington: (800) 456-6017

American Heart Association, Washington Affiliate
4414 Woodland Park Ave. N.
Seattle WA 98103
632-6881
More than 30 work in this facility, which houses both the state and
Northwest area offices of the heart association. Mark Rieck is
executive director of the state association; Lori Gangemi is the
executive director of the Northwest area office. Most hiring is done
by department heads. Examples of positions: field representatives
(fundraisers), communications, education and financial services (accounting). About a third of the staff is support. Volunteers are
welcome, especially for office jobs.

American Heart Association
Southwest Area
16 Tacoma Ave. N.
Tacoma WA 98403
272-7854
Juanita Porso is the executive director of this office, which employs
five.

American Lung Association of Washington
2625 Third Ave.
Seattle WA 98121
441-5100
In Washington the Lung Association has both a state office and four
regional offices. Seattle is the site of the state headquarters and one
regional office. Headed by Sara Swanson, the regional office serves
eight northwestern Washington counties. Rochelle Hughes is the
state program director, responsible for the Lung Association's health
and public awareness programs. Astrid Berg, executive director,
manages the entire operation, including the administrative functions.
Positions include fundraisers, a public relations coordinator and a
business manager. Another important position is health educator.
Openings are often posted on the Society for Public Health Education
jobline (see *"Professional Associations: How to Network Even If You
Know No One"*). Internships may be available and there's a wide
range of volunteer opportunities, including data entry, photography,
writing and organization of the Bicycle Trek. Kathy Rexford, office
manager, routes job applications and volunteer inquiries to the appropriate departments.

American Lung Association
Southwest Area
2203 N. 30th St.
Tacoma WA 98403
272-8777
Chris Parent is the program manager for this office, which has a staff of three.

American Red Cross, Seattle-King County Chapter
1900 25th Ave. S.
Seattle WA 98144
323-2345
David Siebert manages this agency, which offers disaster preparedness and relief, health and safety education, aid to aging and military, camps for low-income children and senior volunteer recruitment and placement (RSVP). There are 85 full-time employees in positions ranging from accounting and public affairs to camp manager, volunteer coordinator and disaster caseworkers. Classes such as first aid, CPR, HIV-AIDS education, swimming and water safety are taught by volunteers and by contract employees, who work either full-time temporary or part-time. Human resources director: Patricia VandenBroek.

American Red Cross, Tacoma-Pierce County Chapter
1235 S. Tacoma Way
Tacoma WA 98409
572-4830
About 50 work for this chapter, which also has contract opportunities. Nancy Mendoza, development director, handles personnel. Besides disaster preparedness and health and safety education, this chapter has a RSVP program, which uses volunteers for an elder abuse information referral program, for health benefit advice and home repair activities. It also offers a senior citizen nutrition program, including Meals on Wheels and 14 meal sites. Internships are available throughout the agency.

American Red Cross, Snohomish-Island County Chapter
P.O. Box 5672
Everett WA 98206
252-4103
Besides disaster preparedness and health and safety education, this chapter's programs include Project Pride, which helps those in need with payment of utility bills; emergency housing; and Carrier Alert, which monitors the safety of shut-ins with the cooperation of the U.S. Postal Service. These programs employ about 15 full-time; there are

also part-time and contract opportunities. In addition, the chapter runs two senior day centers which together employ about a dozen. Contact: Gloria Ruthruff, human resources director.

American Red Cross, Kitsap-North Mason County Chapter
605 Washington Ave.
Bremerton WA 98310
377-3761
Fewer than 10 work full-time for this chapter, which also employs part-time and contract staff. Internships are possible. Like all Red Cross chapters, Bremerton offers health and safety education, disaster preparedness and service (especially of a human services nature) to the military. Inquiries regarding paid positions should be directed to Neil Molenaar, manager; for internships, contact Dianne Lipscomb, volunteer chairperson.

American Red Cross, Thurston-Mason County Chapter
P.O. Box 1547
Olympia WA 98507
352-8575
Kay Walters manages this chapter, which has a full-time staff of four. Internships are possible.

American Youth Hostels, Washington State Council
419 Queen Anne N., #101
Seattle WA 98109
281-7306
This office, part of Hosteling International, oversees the 10 hostels in Washington and serves as liaison to the national and international hostel programs. The staff is very small (three), but volunteers are welcome, especially for data entry and office support. Contact Amy McBroom. Job opportunities also sometimes occur at the Seattle International Hostel.

Seattle International Hostel
84 Union St.
Seattle WA 98101
622-5443
Louise Kipping, who manages the hostel, accepts resumes at all times. Most positions are for front desk or maintenance people. Customer service skills are important; fluency in foreign language is not required, but it's a significant asset.

Arthritis Foundation, Washington State Chapter
100 S. King St., #330
Seattle WA 98104
622-1378
Fundraising, public relations and program administration are examples of the positions at this nonprofit, which employs fewer than 10. Cindy Fitzpatrick is executive director.

Artists Unlimited
20000 68th Ave. W.
Lynnwood WA 98036
775-7290
Founded in 1981 to help disabled artists reach their full creative potential, this program now employs six and uses 50 volunteers. Interns are welcome. In addition, many artists volunteer their time to help teachers in classes. The program currently enrolls about 30 disabled artists. For information about internships and volunteering, contact Paula Griff, artistic director. To inquire about job openings, contact Celia Gartenberg, executive director.

Artist Trust
1402 Third Ave., #415
Seattle WA 98101
467-8734
Artist Trust administers fellowship and grant programs that fund individual artists and issues the quarterly Artist Trust newsletter (see *"Job Bulletins and Valuable Publications"*). The staff is small—usually three full-time permanent employees. Volunteers and interns are welcome. For information, contact the executive director.

Asian Counseling and Referral Service
1032 S. Jackson, #200
Seattle WA 98104
461-8414
With its staff of 74, this agency provides a number of services to the King County Asian and Pacific Island community. The primary programs are mental health counseling, including a semi-independent housing program; and help for the elderly. Job applicants should have social service or mental health care experience; a M.S.W. is desirable. Because most clients have limited or no English skills, job applicants should speak at least one Asian or Pacific Island language or dialect. Most interns are M.S.W. candidates. Personnel director: Jodi Haavig.

Bathhouse Theater
7312 W. Greenlake Dr. N.
Seattle WA 98103
524-3608
Most positions here require extensive experience in the theater; however, the Bathhouse does employ specialists in marketing, accounting and fundraising. Some jobs are full-time temporary or part-time permanent. Volunteers are always needed. Resumes—for paid or volunteer positions—should go to Steven Lerian, managing director.

Bellevue Art Museum
301 Bellevue Square
Bellevue WA 98004
454-3322
Like all other organizations, whether business or nonprofit, museums have accountants, public relations directors and secretaries. But they also offer some more unusual opportunities: for example, education coordinator and volunteer coordinator. In many museums, the gift shop manager/buyer provides an important—and growing—source of income. The registrar, the person who documents and protects borrowed exhibit pieces from the time they leave their owners until they're returned, is another example of a position specific to the museum world. Diane M. Douglas is director/chief curator and heads a staff of 13, including full-time, part-time and contract. Unpaid internships are available in nearly every department. Contact: Linda Krouse, chief financial officer, who handles personnel.

Bellevue Philharmonic Orchestra
400 108th Ave. N.E.
Bellevue WA 98004
455-4171
R. Joseph Scott, general manager, founded this arts group in 1967. Today it has a paid staff of six, supplemented by volunteers.

Big Brothers/Big Sisters
Merged on the national level, these organizations operate local programs that are sometimes combined—and, in other communities, separate. Based on the concept of one-to-one relationships between adult volunteers and a child or teenager (often from a single-parent family), Big Brothers matches men with boys and Big Sisters matches women with girls. The goal is to provide positive role models for youth.

Big Brothers of King County
8511 15th N.E.
Seattle WA 98115
461-3630

Recruiting and screening adult volunteers, recruiting young participants, matching volunteers with boys, monitoring the matches (which is done by Big Brothers caseworkers), fundraising (through special events and a Federal Way bingo operation), working with a board of 40 volunteers and general administration are examples of the responsibilities handled by this unit. It has five satellites: North Seattle, Central Seattle, Kirkland, Burien and Kent. Internships are possible. There are 22 permanent, full-time employees in addition to the bingo staff. Contact: Christopher Breen, executive director.

Big Sisters of King County
1100 Virginia, #210
Seattle WA 98101
461-3636

Patricia Frank, executive director, heads this program, which serves girls from both two-parent and single-parent homes. Besides matching girls with women, the program matches teen mothers and pregnant girls with older volunteers. Activities include recruitment of volunteers; outreach to girls, especially those younger than 12; public relations; and fundraising. There are 24 program staff members and an additional 14 in the bingo operation. Interns are welcome; there are opportunities for social work students and for those interested in public relations and development. The chapter also employs high school students in paid clerical positions.

Big Brothers/Big Sisters of Tacoma/Pierce County
8200 Tacoma Mall Blvd.
Tacoma WA 98409
581-9444

Besides matching boys with men and girls with women, this chapter has a Sisters Plus program to pair teenage girls, especially young mothers or pregnant teenagers, with adult women. There's an office staff of 14 in addition to the 30 who work on bingo. Interns are welcome. If you're interested in working in social services, contact Linda Mason; Sylvia Anderson handles inquiries regarding administrative positions.

Bing Crosby Historical Society
P.O. Box 216
Tacoma WA 98401
627-2947

Ken Twiss is president of this group, which hopes to eventually open a museum about the Washington state entertainment industry. There is no paid staff. Volunteers and interns are welcome.

Boyer Children's Clinic
1850 Boyer Ave. E.
Seattle WA 98112
325-8477
The Boyer Clinic runs outpatient programs in Seattle and Lynnwood for children (usually younger than 3) who have cerebral palsy and other neuromuscular delays. All administration is handled in Seattle; most program staff work at both sites. The 25 employees include the program staff (doctors, nurses, speech therapists, physical therapists, occupational therapists and certified special education teachers who provide services) as well as the accountant, development director, medical secretary, bus drivers, administrative assistants and maintenance staff who provide the administrative services. Internships are available. No unsolicited resumes are accepted, but you can call the clinic to inquire about openings or internships.

Boy Scouts of America, Chief Seattle Council
3120 Rainier Ave. S.
Seattle WA 98144
725-5200
Character development, physical fitness and citizenship are the programs for youth and young adults in King, Kitsap, Jefferson and Clallam counties provided by this council, which employs 48 in Seattle. The office is headed by Dean Lollar, scout executive. Nearly half of the staff work in direct service to the field. Others work in fundraising, accounting, camping and support. You can apply at any council office and arrange to be interviewed by a regional representative of the national office.

Boy Scouts of America, Mount Rainier Council
1722 S. Union St.
Tacoma WA 98405
752-7731
This council employs a total of 11 in the office, with an additional two working as camp caretakers/rangers. Norman Stone is scout executive.

Boy Scouts of America, Evergreen Council
1715 100th Pl. S.E.
Everett WA 98208
338-0380
Fred LaCase is scout executive.

Boy Scouts of America, Tumwater Area Council
P.O. Box 1308
Olympia WA 98507
357-3331
This council employs seven. Jim Phillips is the scout executive.

Boys & Girls Clubs of King County
107 Cherry, #200
Seattle WA 98104
461-3890
Part of a national organization for those between 6 and 18, the Boys
& Girls Clubs provides facilities, programs and staff to help youth
develop self-esteem, values and skills. Cary Bozeman is the executive director and Quincy Robertson the personnel and training director
for the Seattle-based affiliate, which has about 60 full-time permanent
positions in its administrative offices and nine branches (including
Kirkland/Redmond and Mercer Island). Each branch has an executive director, a program director, and an athletic director. The Boys
& Girls Club also operates seven sites for before- and after-school
care. The administrative staff includes fundraising, marketing, budget, accounting, data processing and grantwriting positions. There are
part-time and seasonal positions, especially in the summer camp
program. Interested in an internship? Contact Robertson.

Bellevue Boys & Girls Club
209 100th N.E.
Bellevue WA 98004
454-6162
Similar programs are offered by the Bellevue club, which employs 15
on a permanent basis. During the summer, day camp counselors are
also hired. Resumes should be directed to Marc Dosogne, executive
director.

Boys & Girls Clubs of Tacoma
2005 S. 64th, #316
Tacoma WA 98409
474-3590
Besides many of the programs offered in Seattle, this club provides
aquatics classes and a program for latchkey children. There are also
teen centers, each with a director. Jim Hatch, executive director,
heads a staff of 32, which expands with seasonal help and interns.

Boys & Girls Clubs of Snohomish County
P.O. Box 5224
Everett WA 98206
258-2436

Twenty work full-time and 16 part-time for the Snohomish organization, which adds another 20 during the summer. The programs includes seven club sites, each with its own director, program director and athletic director. Some larger sites also employ cultural arts directors, usually part-time staff who direct music, fine arts, arts and crafts and drama activities. There's also the before- and after-school care programs and the administrative center. For most positions, a background in recreation or education is helpful. For others, training in business (especially budgeting) is valuable. Internships are available. Contact: Bill Tsoukalas, executive director.

Broadway Center for the Performing Arts
901 Broadway
Tacoma WA 98402
591-5890

Formerly the Pantages Centre for the Performing Arts, this arts center is now one of two operated by the nonprofit Broadway Center Corp. in City of Tacoma facilities. A third theater, for the Tacoma Actors Guild, will open in 1993. Together the Pantages and Rialto theaters present 34 touring shows during the October-May season. Their facilities are also rented for other programs. The managing director is a city employee; the other 17 staff members, both permanent and seasonal, are employed by the Center. Department managers in finance, development, marketing and operations hire their own staff and select their own interns. Other positions include volunteer coordinator, programming assistant (to negotiate contracts with shows), systems manager, ticket office manager, maintenance staff and stage manager. The staff is supplemented by more than 100 volunteers.

Camp Fire, Central Puget Sound Council
8511 15th Ave. N.E.
Seattle WA 98115
461-8550

Lee Drechsel is the executive director of this group, which provides personal development programs for boys and girls ages 5-18. Camp Fire activities include camping and the clubs as well as before and after school care, teen parent programs and Saturday programs for children with disabilities. The Central Puget Sound council, which has a staff of about 45 in its Seattle, Redmond, Bremerton and Kent offices, has full-time, part-time and seasonal positions.

Camp Fire, Orca Council
3555 McKinley Ave.
Tacoma WA 98404
597-6234
This council, which has offices in Puyallup, Olympia and Aberdeen, employs 11 full-time and others on a seasonal basis. Programs include day care, self-reliance, career development and camping. The program specialist who handles the traditional clubs works extensively with the volunteers who actually lead the club activities. The program for the developmentally disabled employs both specialists and high school students who work with the program participants. There's also a small administrative staff. Internships are available in either administration or direct services; interns can work on a project basis or for an entire academic term. Contact: Gloria LaBelle, executive director.

Camp Fire: Snohomish County Council
11627 Airport Rd., #F
Everett WA 98204-3790
355-9734
This council runs most of the same activities as the Seattle organization, including clubs, residential and day camps and the self-reliance and career development programs. There is a special summer camp for the developmentally disabled. Permanent employment is less than 25, with additional positions available during the summer. David Surface is the executive director.

The Casey Family Program
2033 Sixth Ave., #1100
Seattle WA 98121-2536
448-4620
A privately endowed long-term foster care program that provides help for children in 13 states, this nonprofit is headquartered in Seattle. Most employees are social workers; a M.S.W. is required. All administration is handled at this office. Total employment is about 225, with 60 of those working in Seattle. Most openings are advertised in the Seattle papers and appropriate professional association publications. Mike Wagner, personnel director, will accept unsolicited resumes. Division offices (see below) select some staff members directly.

The Casey Family Program
300 Elliott Ave. W., #110
Seattle WA 98119
522-4673
Division director: Rosemary Unterseher.

The Casey Family Program
5712 W. Orchard, #B
Tacoma WA 98467
473-9680
Division director: Napoleon Caldwell.

Catholic Archdiocese of Seattle
Office of Lay Personnel
910 Marion St.
Seattle WA 98104
382-4570
Jobline: 382-4564
About 2,000 lay personnel are employed by the Archdiocese of
Seattle, which serves western Washington between Bellingham and
Vancouver. Many work in Catholic schools, some in parishes and
others at the Archdiocese offices (the chancellery), where the operations include a weekly newspaper, the *Progress*. Each office hires its
own staff. Some positions must be filled by Catholics. The jobline
includes positions at the chancellery, in schools, in Catholic colleges,
in parishes and in affiliated agencies like Catholic Community Services. If you are a teacher, you should also contact the Catholic School
Department. (See *"Employers: Schools, Colleges and Universities."*)

Catholic Community Services, Seattle/King County
P.O. Box 22608
Seattle WA 98122
323-6336
This social service agency, one of King County's largest, employs
1,000 and offers such programs as adoption, foster care, counseling,
in-home day care for the elderly and disabled, chore services, legal
services for the elderly and disabled and day care. Mary Hatch is the
personnel director.

Catholic Community Services, Pierce and Kitsap Counties
5410 N. 44th
Tacoma WA 98407
752-2455
Robert Stevens is the personnel director for this agency, which offers
counseling, children's programs (including foster care and help for
the developmentally disabled) and the family crisis program at the
headquarters as well as a downtown Tacoma program for senior
citizens, refugees and the Latino community and a Spanaway program on substance abuse.

Catholic Community Services, Snohomish County
1918 Everett
Everett WA 98201
259-9188

DeLayne McDanold is the human resources director for this office, which offers adoption, foster care, the Crisis Nursery emergency respite care, pregnancy outreach, counseling, chemical dependency programs, HOPAA (coordination of volunteer services for those suffering from AIDS), chore services and the Independent Living Program, which provides personal care for the elderly. The office staff includes about 50; the independent living program employs as many as 80 in field positions. Some positions require M.S.W. degrees. Most interns are candidates for master's degrees and work in counseling.

Center for the Prevention of Sexual and Domestic Violence
1914 N. 34th, #105
Seattle WA 98103
643-1903

Founded by an ordained minister, the center's mission is to end sexual and domestic violence by working through churches. Services include training, a speakers' bureau, sexual abuse prevention curricula and publications. The Rev. Marie Fortune heads a staff of nine. Most interns are pursuing religious studies; some come between undergraduate and seminary programs.

Central Area Youth Association
119 23rd Ave.
Seattle WA 98122
322-6640

Michael Preston heads this nonprofit's staff of 11, which uses 1,200 volunteers each year to deliver a variety of sports, tutoring, job-readiness and social programs for youth, including teen parents. Tutoring is offered citywide in nearly 90 locations. Many other programs are based in the Central Area. Job applicants should have youth social services experience. Unsolicited job applications are discouraged; written inquiries regarding unpaid internships are welcome.

Childbirth Education Association of Seattle
10021 Holman Rd. N.W.
Seattle WA 98177
789-0883

This is a small organization with no full-time staff; the two directors each work 30-hour weeks. The administrative staff is very small and turnover is limited. However, if you are a nurse or physical therapist interested in teaching prenatal courses, there are six to eight openings each year. CEAS also offers courses for new parents in mother-baby care, child safety and breast-feeding. It also trains hospital childbirth educators and sells a childbirth education textbook. Contact: Janet Whalley.

Childhaven
316 Broadway
Seattle WA 98122
624-6477
Because Childhaven deals with abused, neglected or drug-addicted infants and toddlers and provides parent education and crisis intervention, most staff members need specialized training and experience. A master's degree in social work, counseling or psychology is typical. Nursing and occupational therapy are examples of other specialized training required. Some part-time positions, however, are appropriate for college students, especially those considering careers in social services. For its four therapeutic day care centers in Seattle and King County, Childhaven also hires people with early children education. Patrick Gogerty is executive director of the agency, which employs 120.

Children's Home Society of Washington
P.O. Box 15190
Seattle WA 98115
524-6020
D. Sharon Osborne, president, heads this statewide agency, which provides child- and family-related programs in 22 locations. Total employment statewide: 250. The emphasis is on preventive and crisis-intervention services, so many staff members have specialized training and experience in social work or counseling. Many administrative functions—for example, accounting and public relations—are centralized in Seattle. Some functions such as fundraising occur both in the corporate headquarters and the seven regional offices. Charlotte Wolcott is the personnel administrator for the corporate headquarters. Regional offices hire their own staff. This is also the location of the Northwest regional office, headed by Teresa Rafael, regional vice president. She handles hiring for her staff and for the East King County office located in Bellevue. Linda Selsor, whose office is at the Seattle address, hires for the South King County program in Auburn and for the special grant-funded "Families First" program currently being offered in Auburn.

Children's Home Society of Washington
201 S. 34th St.
Tacoma WA 98408
472-3355

Children's Museum of Tacoma
925 Court C
Tacoma WA 98402
627-2436
This hands-on museum in downtown Tacoma employs nine; most positions are part-time. Internships and work-study assignments may be possible. Contact Jackie Gretzinger or Jacquie Boyd, directors.

Chinese Information and Service Center
409 Maynard Ave. S., Second Floor
Seattle WA 98104
624-5633
An Asian bilingual outreach program that serves newcomers who live within King County is one of the programs of this nonprofit. Another program: recreation and counseling for at-risk youth. Interpretation, information referral, training referrals, job-search assistance and advocacy are among other services offered. Of the 23 employees, many are social workers; the administrative staff is small. Interns are sometimes accepted; bilingual applicants are preferred. Contact: Rita Wang, executive director.

Church Council of Greater Seattle
4759 15th Ave. N.E.
Seattle WA 98105
525-1213
Direct service programs (housing for the homeless and emergency feeding, for example) and ministries (which includes advocacy work on community issues) are the emphases of this agency. Clergy also work in the chaplaincy program. However, most of the 25 positions do not require theological training. Executive director: the Rev. Elaine Stanovsky.

Citizens Education Center
310 First Ave. S., #330
Seattle WA 98104
624-9955
Established in 1979, this statewide group employs six. Volunteers and interns are welcome, especially in such areas as research, marketing and program support. The CEC's primary focus is education. One current program is "parent leadership training." The center staff trains

teams from school districts, which then return to their communities and provide parents with training. Another program is the Team Tutoring Project, a business and school partnership cosponsored by New Horizons and PIPE. Judith McBroom is the executive director.

College Planning Network
Campion Tower
914 E. Jefferson
Seattle WA 98122
323-0624
Doug Breithaupt is president of this organization, which offers publications, workshops and individual counseling about higher education. CPN's publications include two books, *The Pacific Northwest Scholarship Options Guide* and *Back to School* (for those re-entering college), and "Beyond High School," a newsletter for schools. The workshops focus on college financing and on finding the best program for your child (or yourself). The individual counseling is usually offered by a corporate sponsor. The paid staff of seven includes vice presidents of publications, programs and finance, a counselor and communications and research assistants. There are free-lance and contract opportunities. CPN also uses interns, work-study students and volunteers.

Community Health Centers of King County
677 Strander Blvd., #B
Tukwila WA 98188
575-0494
Six medical clinics for the low-income and homeless are operated by this agency, which employs about 50. The staff includes doctors in family practice and nurse-practitioners as well as administrative and support positions. Volunteers are welcome. Medical personnel is handled by Patricia Wendt, operation manager; administrative staff is hired by Jayne Leet, executive director.

Community Home Health Care
200 W. Thomas, Second Floor
Seattle WA 98119
282-5048
This private not-for-profit provides in-house health and social services in King and Snohomish counties. Programs include mental health counseling, independent living skills training, geriatric assessment and case management (for example, help with alternative living arrangements and chore services.) It employs about 300. Margaret Shepherd is executive director.

Concilio for the Spanish-Speaking of King County
157 Yesler Way, #400
Seattle WA 98104
461-4891

The full-time staff at this organization is small, usually less than five; besides the executive director, Rey Lira, the staff includes the editor of *La Voz* and the coordinator of Fiestas Patrais, an annual festival. Volunteers are welcome. Internships may be available. Fluency in Spanish is important.

Consumer Credit Counseling Service
4220 Aurora Ave. N.
Seattle WA 98103
545-4300

More than 40 work for this program, which was established in 1965 and now serves 12,000 people a year. It offers budget and debt counseling, debtor payment plans and workshops. Most positions are in data entry and as account representatives and counselors. Counselor applicants should have at least three years of work in credit (for example, in banking or retail) and a college degree. Interns are accepted only in the education department, which provides workshops on money management, surviving layoffs and wise use of credit. Unsolicited resumes from qualified counselor candidates are kept on file.

Corporate Council for the Arts
1420 Fifth Ave., #475
Seattle WA 98101
682-9270

Raising funds from corporations for professional visual and performing arts in the Seattle and Tacoma area is the responsibility of this organization. Its five full-time staff members include development and communications directors and a business manager. Internships are also available; typical assignments would be grantwriting, volunteer coordination, public relations or special events coordination. Peter Donnelly is president.

Crisis Clinic
1515 Dexter Ave. N., #300
Seattle WA 98109
461-3210

This nonprofit, which employs about 25 full-time in addition to part-timers, operates a 24-hour telephone service for people in emotional distress. It also offers a community information line, a referral to social, health and welfare services. Because all the data are comput-

erized, an important part of the Crisis Clinic staff is the data processing manager and the Resource Center, the employees who actually
gather and update the information. Other staff members include the
business manager, program administrators and the telephone room
supervisors (master's degree required). There's also a volunteer
coordinator. The volunteers who help staff the telephone lines receive
a 40-hour training course recognized for its thoroughness; many
human services students use their volunteer work at Crisis Clinic for
valuable practical experience. Volunteer work with the Crisis Clinic
is also valuable for those new to the Northwest and those considering
a career change to human services. Some volunteers work into paid
positions. The clinic also issues two publications: *Where To Turn*, a
annual list of 600 King County social service agencies, and *Where To
Turn PLUS*, a 250-page directory describing 500 agencies. See *"Job
Bulletins and Valuable Publications"* for more information. Roy
Sargeant is the Crisis Clinic executive director.

Crista Ministries
19303 Fremont Ave. N.
Seattle WA 98133
Personnel: 546-7525
Jobline: 546-7202
This nonprofit interdenominational Christian service organization
employs 900 in its radio stations, a nursing home, schools, camps,
conference centers, Third World relief and Christian job placement
service. Most openings are in nursing, teaching, missions, advertising
sales for the radio stations, administrative support, finance and
accounting. Personnel director: Roy Parnell.

The Defender Association
810 Third Ave., #800
Seattle WA 98104
447-3900
Jobline: Ext. 513
Robert Boruchowitz directs this nonprofit, which contracts with
governments to provide defense representation to 20,000 people
annually. Established two decades ago and often called the "public
defender," this group employs 135. Of the staff, 92 are attorneys.
Other professional staff members include paralegals, investigators
and social workers. The association recruits attorneys nationally,
especially through law school programs; each summer it brings clerks
to Seattle. Paralegals and investigators are recruited through university and community college programs, including the association
internships.

Diabetes Association of Pierce County
1722 S. J
Tacoma WA 98405
272-5134
This organization, which offers public education on diabetes, free diabetes screening and a referral service, employs only two. Ruth Ann Ruff is executive director.

Eastside Domestic Violence Program
P.O. Box 6398
Bellevue WA 98008
746-1940
EDVP's staff of 20 provides services to victims of domestic violence and offers community education regarding domestic violence. Interim director Aggie Sweeney handles personnel.

Eastside Mental Health
2840 Northup Way
Bellevue WA 98004
827-9100
A counseling agency, Eastside employs nearly 200. Most of the staff therapists have graduate degrees in social work, psychology or related fields. Openings are described in a book available (even to the public) in the staff lounge. Resumes can be directed to "Personnel." Ann Brand, Ph.D., is executive director.

E.M.M./Northwest Harvest
P.O. Box 12272
Seattle WA 98102
625-0755
Twenty work full-time for Ecumenical Metropolitan Ministry/Northwest Harvest, which functions as a center for food collection and distribution. It serves more than 300 hunger programs in Washington state from the Seattle office and satellites in Aberdeen and Yakima. Staff positions include jobs in administration and accounting, communications and development, food delivery and the warehouse. There's also a volunteer coordinator. Interns are welcome. Contact: Rosemary Boyle, office administrator. An affiliate is

Northwest Caring Ministry
P.O. Box 12272
Seattle WA 98102
625-7524
This agency offers referrals and advocacy on issues other than hunger.

Steven Bauck, the executive director, welcomes interns, especially M.S.W. candidates.

Epilepsy Association of Western Washington
8511 15th Ave. N.E.
Seattle WA 98115
523-2551
Information referral, especially for those recently diagnosed with epilepsy; counseling; public education; and advocacy, especially regarding job discrimination, are among the programs of this group, which employs eight. Most employees work in direct services, where degrees in psychology, sociology, social work or counseling are helpful. Interns are welcome. Lynn Pevey is executive director.

Family Services
615 Second Ave., #150
Seattle WA 98104
461-3883
At six locations in the Seattle area, this agency provides counseling, education and support services for families including Men Working Against Abuse, Employee Assistance Program, and programs for stroke victims, the bereaved, the aging and the homeless. A master's degree in social work or counseling is required for many of the 130 positions and all of the counseling positions. The small administrative staff includes community relations, human resources, development and accounting personnel. Interns are welcome; most work in counseling and so should be candidates for a master's degree. Information on openings is available from the receptionist. Gail Jackson is the human resources director and Ruth Ann Howell the president.

The 5th Avenue Theatre
1326 Fifth Ave., Second Floor
Seattle WA 98101
625-1468
The 5th Avenue has two operations: The 5th Avenue Musical Theatre Company, which presents a four-show season each year; and theater rental, for touring shows, lectures and other performances. The permanent full-time staff of 10 includes marketing, operations, box office and accounting people; in addition, there's the technical staff, mostly union, that handles sound, lighting and construction. Interns are welcome. Actors interested in the Musical Theatre Company productions should watch for the general audition call each summer. For information about administrative positions or internships, contact Marilynn Sheldon, general manager.

First Place
P.O. Box 15112
Seattle WA 98115-0112
323-6715
Carolyn Pringle is executive director of this school for homeless children, founded in 1989. Today the school, which enrolls as many as 50, employs 10. M.S.W. candidates supplement the counseling staff and some 60 volunteers help in the classrooms and with clerical tasks.

Food Lifeline
15230 15th Ave. N.E.
Seattle WA 98155
545-6600
This United Way agency, one of the area's largest food bank distribution programs, solicits contributions primarily from the food industry and then distributes the food to 240 food banks and emergency feeding programs. An affiliate of Second Harvest, a national food bank network, the agency also distributes U.S.D.A. commodities in King County. Food Lifeline's permanent staff, which is about 25, includes the administrative staff, food solicitors, a development director and a warehouse crew. Volunteers are used to pack food in sizes needed by food banks, to distribute special non-food donations (for example, Christmas trees) and with special events. Interns are welcome. For information, contact the executive director.

Fremont Public Association
3601 Fremont Ave. N.
Seattle WA 98103
632-1285
Jobline: 548-8331
Established in 1974 in the Fremont neighborhood, this private nonprofit now serves some 35,000 people throughout King County. Programs range from the annual Fremont Fair to a food bank, legal clinic, emergency and transitional housing, employment counseling, and home care and transportation for the elderly and disabled. It employs nearly 300, most as home health aides. The administrative staff includes about 50. The staff is supplemented with interns and volunteers. Kathy Crumlish is personnel director. For information regarding internships, contact the appropriate program director or David Barker, community fundraising director.

Frye Art Museum

P.O. Box 3005
Seattle WA 98114
622-9250
The legacy of meatpacking magnate Charles Frye, this museum has been described as the U.S.'s leading collection of 19th century German academic painting and small-scale American art. The museum and office staff is very small (about a dozen total); there are curators, accountants and support staff. Inquiries can be directed to the director.

Girl Scouts, Totem Council

3611 Woodland Park Ave. N.
Seattle WA 98103
633-5600
The Girl Scouts offer educational group activities for girls 5-17. This council includes offices in Bellevue, Renton, Bremerton, Everett, Bellingham and Port Angeles and employs about 60 on a permanent, full-time basis. There are also occasional seasonal positions. Interns are welcome. Typical positions include the field directors, who support the volunteers who actually lead the clubs. The program staff includes three specialists who develop council-wide activities. The Council also has an outreach staff to recruit participants from minority and immigrant groups. There are also special programs for the children of migrant workers. Pamela Sanchez is executive director.

Girl Scouts, Pacific Peaks Council

5326 Littlerock Road
Tumwater WA 98512
572-8950
Many of the same positions exist in this council, which maintains branch offices in Tacoma, Aberdeen and Longview to serve most of southwest Washington. Total employment: about 30. Interns are welcome. Contact: Cecilia Kayano, public involvement director.

Girls, Inc. of Puget Sound

708 Martin Luther King Jr. Way
Seattle WA 98122
720-2912
Formerly Girls Club of Puget Sound, this affiliate of the national group provides programs and classes for girls and boys in such subjects as career planning, health, leadership and community action, sports and self-reliance. It operates three centers in Seattle. Teen Connection offers health education for teenagers. Most of the 12 permanent staff members are program coordinators or center direc-

tors. There are some seasonal opportunities, especially with the summer day camps. Interns are welcome. Virginia Williams is executive director.

Goodwill

All Goodwill programs are autonomous, but 176 of them, including the one in Tacoma, belong to a national Goodwill organization. Many in this organization continue to focus on training and rehabilitation of the handicapped. Seattle Goodwill program, which does not belong to the national group, emphasizes job readiness.

Seattle Goodwill Inc.

1400 S. Lane
Seattle WA 98144
329-1000

The thrift stores that sell donated items provide nearly all the funding for Seattle Goodwill, which runs programs in Seattle, Lynnwood and Everett as well as Goodwill Literacy and a rehabilitation center in Seattle. Although many of those served by Seattle Goodwill are handicapped physically, the organization focuses on those who are unemployable as a result of education or drug problems, lack of work experience or criminal records. Of the 265 employees, all work full-time. About 110 are participating in nine-month training programs in such areas as cashiering, bookkeeping, word processing or computerized spreadsheet management. The balance are permanent staff in accounting, administrative, personnel, public relations, merchandise pricing and teaching. The small teaching staff handles the vocational training, high school equivalency training and English; it also trains volunteers to tutor through Goodwill Literacy. For more information about the permanent positions or the training programs, contact the personnel office.

Tacoma Goodwill Industries

714 S. 27th
Tacoma WA 98409
272-5166

Although hundreds are employed by Tacoma Goodwill through training programs, the administrative staff totals only about 80. The Tacoma program includes operations in Auburn, Puyallup, Olympia, Lacey, Longview and Yakima. Departments include administration, accounting, public relations, industrial operations (which includes the drivers, receiving workers, car detailing program and stores) and rehabilitation, where the staff trains and supervises clients in vocational programs. Many of the instructors are volunteers, often retired teachers.

Greenpeace Action
Campaign Office
4649 Sunnyside Ave. N.
Seattle WA 98103
632-4326
An international environmental organization that conducts public education and direct action, Greenpeace maintains a regional campaign office in Seattle. About 20 work here full-time; to learn of openings in Seattle or in Greenpeace's other regional, national or international operations, check the job board in the office. Greenpeace also has opportunities for canvassers, the people who go door-to-door soliciting volunteers, contributions and signatures for petitions. For information, call the Canvass office, 633-6027.

Hearing, Speech and Deafness Center
1620 18th Ave.
Seattle WA 98122
323-5770
Certified audiologists and speech pathologists are examples of the specialists employed by this program, which has a full-time staff of about 25. There's also a vocational placement program for the hearing impaired, an independent living skills program and a parent-infant program, which provides early intervention services for hearing impaired children from birth to age 3. Most employees, including those in the center's store for assistive devices, use American Sign Language. Contact: Edward Freedman, the executive director.

The Hope Heart Institute
556 18th
Seattle WA 98122
328-8600
This cardiovascular research and education institute was founded in Seattle in 1959. A locally-based organization, it employs 30 full-time. For the research staff, medical, veterinary medical or pathology degrees are typical; some technicians are also employed. The administrative staff includes a controller, database manager, development officer and support personnel. Internships may be available. Personnel contact: Patty Shepherd, administrator.

Intiman Playhouse
P.O. Box 19760
Seattle WA 98109
626-0775
Approximately 20 work full-time on the administrative staff of this theater, with another 15 or 20 joining the organization on a full-time

basis during the May-December season. There are also temporary and free-lance opportunities on a show-by-show basis for technicians and designers. Only the acting staff is union. Examples of positions: the production manager, who coordinates all aspects of a show ranging from scheduling the performances to supervising the construction of sets; the box office staff; and the costume staff. As in most nonprofits, there's also marketing, public relations and development people. Internships are possible.

Jack Straw Foundation
4261 Roosevelt Way N.E.
Seattle WA 98105
634-0919
Carmen Ray is the executive director of this group, which has two operations: Jack Straw Productions, a noncommercial audio production and training center; and KSER-FM, a Lynnwood radio station. In total, there are 12 employees, with many opportunities for interns and volunteers. Inquiries should be directed to the manager of the operation in which you're interested. Nancy Keith runs the radio station; at press time, a manager was being sought for Jack Straw Productions.

Jewish Family Service
1214 Boylston Ave.
Seattle WA 98101
461-3240
Established in 1892, this social service agency has offices in Seattle and Bellevue and two group homes for the mentally ill and developmentally disabled. The services offered to the Jewish community in the greater Puget Sound area include individual, couple, family and group counseling; senior services; emergency assistance; vocational guidance; refugee resettlement; Jewish family life education; child welfare services; volunteer training; and assistance for the disabled. The staff of 50 includes fewer than 25 full-time positions. Many of the part-timers are counselors. Interns are welcome; most are graduate students in clinical counseling programs. Personnel contact: (Mr.) Merrill Ringold, associate director.

Jewish Federation of Greater Seattle
2031 Third Ave.
Seattle WA 98101
443-5400
This organization raises funds for a variety of Jewish agencies, including Jewish Family Service, the Jewish Community Center, the Jewish schools, the Kline-Galland Home and for social services in

Israel. The staff totals 20. Interns are usually graduate students in public affairs or social work. Contact: Michael Novick, executive director.

Junior Achievement of Greater Puget Sound
600 Stewart St., #212
Seattle WA 98101
296-2600
Providing children and teenagers with economic-based educational experiences through business and school partnerships is the goal of Junior Achievement, which has a central office in Seattle and a branch in the Tri-Cities. The staff of 20 is supplemented by volunteers. The four departments include administration, development, marketing (which includes special events and recruiting 800 volunteers annually) and operations, which works with school districts to implement programs. JA will enroll approximately 30,000 children in 1992-93. There's limited turnover in the managerial staff, but occasional openings in the support positions. Contact: Gloria Studer, office manager.

Leukemia Society of America, Washington State Chapter
1402 Third Ave., #1100
Seattle WA 98101
628-0777
Community education and fundraising for research and patient care are the major projects of this office, which serves both Washington and Alaska. There are seven permanent staff. Interns are welcome in public relations and development. Executive director: Kathleen Brumwell.

Lutheran Compass Center
77 S. Washington
Seattle WA 98104
461-7835
Job counseling and referrals, transitional housing, a representative payee program for those unable to manage their own finances and shelters are among the services offered by this United Way and church-supported agency. It employs 35 full-time plus a part-time staff. Interns are welcome, especially in public relations or marketing. Openings are posted at the center. Inquiries regarding professional positions should go to Grace Brooks, program director; for support positions, contact Dee Matz.

Lutheran Social Services of Washington and Idaho
4040 S. 188th
Seattle WA 98188
461-6932
This office provides fiscal and administrative services for all Lutheran Social Services area offices across the state. Jerry Hecker is chief financial officer. Because the staff totals only six, job openings are infrequent. Opportunities are more likely to occur in area offices listed below.

Lutheran Social Services of Washington and Idaho
Northwest Area Office
6920 220th St. S.W.
Mountlake Terrace WA 98043
672-6009
Individual, marriage and family counseling, adoption services, respite care, refugee services, pregnancy counseling, divorce support groups, Divorce Lifeline, the Seamen's Center and a social ministry are among the programs of this agency, which serves King and Snohomish counties. The staff includes 28 plus 45 counselors, many of whom work part-time. Internships are possible for graduate students in social work or counseling. Resumes can be directed to Barbara Couilliard.

Lutheran Social Services of Washington and Idaho
Southwest Area Office
223 N. Yakima
Tacoma WA 98403
272-8433
This office primarily serves Pierce County. There are approximately 25 staff.

Lutheran Social Services of Washington and Idaho
Olympic Area Office
5610 Kitsap Way
Bremerton WA 98312
377-5511
This office serves the Olympic peninsula with a staff, including counselors, of approximately 25.

March of Dimes/Birth Defects Foundation
Western Washington Chapter
1904 Third Ave., #230
Seattle WA 98101
624-1373

"Healthier babies" is how the March of Dimes describes its mission. This national organization works through research, education and advocacy to reduce birth defects and low birth weight. Local programs include prenatal health care, school programs to help children understand handicaps and video training materials. This chapter also provides grants for agencies pursuing the same goals. The staff of 15 includes fundraisers, a program director and a communications director. Most openings are in fundraising. Interns are welcome. Bruce F. Baker is executive director.

Medina Children's Service
123 16th Ave.
P.O. Box 22638
Seattle WA 98122
461-4520
Adoption services, counseling for unplanned pregnancies and school-based services for pregnant teenagers, expectant fathers and teenage parents are the programs of this United Way agency, which employs 25. All staff members have master's degrees, either in social work or related fields. Internships are possible for graduate students in social work. Dini Duclos is executive director.

Mothers Against Drunk Driving (MADD)
1511 Third Ave., #511
Seattle WA 98101
624-6903
At press time this chapter employed only one full-time. Volunteers and interns are welcome. Its mission is advocacy for the victims and the families of victims of drunk driving crashes; and public, corporate and school education to promote the awareness of the dangers of drunk driving. Jeanette Greenfield is chapter administrator.

Multiple Sclerosis Association of King County
753 N. 35th, #208
Seattle WA 98103
461-6914
Rehabilitation and social services are among the programs of this nonprofit. There's an information referral service and classes for those newly diagnosed with multiple sclerosis, help from a social worker and volunteer peer counseling and respite services. Marlene Lasher is executive director of the association, a locally-based provider of direct services to those with multiple sclerosis. Not affiliated with the National Multiple Sclerosis Society. There are 10 staff members. Interns are welcome, especially graduate students in social work. Turnover is limited, but when openings occur, they're adver-

tised in Seattle papers, *Sound Opportunities* and through such professional groups as the National Development Officers Association.

Multi-Service Centers of North & East King County
P.O. Box 3577
Redmond WA 98073
869-6000

A community action agency that helps low-income residents of Bothell, Kirkland, Redmond, Bellevue and the Snoqualmie Valley, this nonprofit operates a food bank network, emergency and transitional housing, an eviction prevention program, a transportation program for the elderly and disabled and clothing banks. There's also an information referral service. Virtually all of the 110 staff work in direct services positions ranging from van driver to program director, food bank clerk to shelter staff. Volunteers are welcome. Internships may be available. Doreen Marchioni is executive director.

Municipal League of King County
810 Third Ave., #604
Seattle WA 98104-1651
622-8333

A nonpartisan citizens' organization that calls itself a "good government watchdog," the Municipal League employs six permanent staff members. Interns are welcome year around. League programs include researching and rating candidates for public office; ad hoc study committees on governmental issues; and work with such other civic groups as the Greater Seattle Chamber of Commerce and the League of Women Voters. New programs include a review and evaluation of political campaigns and a study of regional transportation issues. Contact: Jerry Agen, executive director.

Muscular Dystrophy Association
701 Dexter Ave. N., #106
Seattle WA 98109-4339
283-2183

Education and fundraising for patient services and research are the major responsibilities of this MDA office, the only one in western Washington. The office employs 10; most work either in fundraising or in the coordination of patient services. The patient services positions require a counseling or medical background. Interns are welcome. Contact: Sindee Preston, who directs activities in the south district, or Elsa Stevens, the director for the north.

Museum of Flight
9404 E. Marginal Way S.
Seattle WA 98108
767-7373
Located on the edge of Boeing Field, this museum incorporates the original Boeing factory. However, the museum is private, supported by the independent nonprofit Museum of Flight Foundation. Preservation of Pacific Northwest flight history is its mission. There are 60 full-time employees in addition to part-timers and volunteers. Interns are welcome. Staff positions include the restoration manager; the collections staff, which includes exhibits managers, archivists and registrars; a public program staff that designs educational programs; the special events manager, who rents the facility; the air show planners; the gift shop staff; and administrative and development staff. Resumes are accepted only for open positions.

Museum of History and Industry
2700 24th Ave. E.
Seattle WA 98112
324-1126
Established by the Historical Society of Seattle, this independent nonprofit museum focuses on Northwest history. The staff includes 30 full-time positions as well as part-timers, interns and volunteers. Examples: curators, who require extensive backgrounds in local history; the in-house exhibit staff; and the education curator. There's also a development director, the public relations staff, a volunteer coordinator and the manager/buyer for the museum store. Contact: executive director Wilson O'Donnell.

National Multiple Sclerosis Society, Western
Washington Chapter
2328 Sixth Ave.
Seattle WA 98121
728-1088
Community education, fundraising and direct services to MS patients and their families in 18 counties are the programs of this chapter, which employs nine in Seattle and two in its branch office in Tacoma. The Seattle staff includes development people, to handle the nine annual fundraising events; the patient services staff; a public relations director; and an education director. The Tacoma staff handles only services. Internships are possible. All hiring for both offices is done by executive director Norman Schwamberg.

Nature Conservancy
217 Pine St., #1100
Seattle WA 98101
343-4344
Preserving biological diversity by protecting habitats for rare and
endangered species is the goal of this national organization, which
has one office and 25,000 members in Washington. Programs include
the purchase of land for preserves, assisting private landowners in
preservation of habitats for endangered species and public outreach,
especially through a speakers' bureau. Employs 16. Internships are
possible. Elliot Marks is executive director.

Neighborhood House
905 Spruce St., #213
Seattle WA 98104
461-8430
About 100 are employed by Neighborhood House, which runs day
care centers, Head Start and senior programs as well as a variety of
services in Seattle's low-income housing developments. Besides the
permanent positions, there are part-time and seasonal jobs. Executive
director: Bob Swanson. Personnel director: Patricia Hudson.

New Beginnings Shelter for Battered Women
P.O. Box 75125
Seattle WA 98125
783-4520
This program provides transitional housing for women and children,
a 24-hour crisis line, counseling for those suffering from domestic
violence and community advocacy. The staff of 18 is supplemented
by volunteers, who complete a training program. Executive director:
Marcie Summers.

911 Media Arts Center
117 Yale Ave. N.
Seattle WA 98109
682-6552
Robin Reidy is executive director of this membership organization,
which has three full-time paid positions. Interns are welcome and can
sometimes work into paid positions. This is the only media arts center
in the state; it maintains a video-editing facility and screening room
and offers video and film workshops.

Nordic Heritage Museum
3014 N.W. 67th
Seattle WA 98117
789-5707
This museum in Ballard is devoted to the preservation and interpretation of Scandinavian heritage. The permanent staff is eight; interns and volunteers are welcome. Contact: Marianne Forssblad, director.

Northwest AIDS Foundation
127 Broadway E.
Seattle WA 98102
329-6923
Direct services to AIDS patients, fundraising, grant administration, advocacy services, technical assistance to smaller nonprofits and a volunteer program are among the activities of this organization, which employs 46. Direct services include case management, which requires specialized social work training; information referral; education; and work with 18 local housing agencies to provide patient housing. The fundraising staff includes a development director and manager, special events and walk coordinators, and a major donor specialist. The administrative staff includes a director, accounting manager, accounting specialist, human resources administrator, MIS manager and software support specialist. No unsolicited resumes are accepted; most openings are advertised in the Seattle papers. The paid staff is supplemented with nearly 650 volunteers. Interns are welcome and can work in such departments as education, communications, housing and direct services. To inquire about an internship, call and you'll be referred to the appropriate department head.

Northwest Chamber Orchestra
1305 Fourth Ave., #522
Seattle WA 98101
343-0445
Both traditional and contemporary chamber music are played by this group, which offers a dozen concerts during its August-May season. There are also summer concerts, a musical education program that tours elementary schools and elementary schoolteacher-training materials. The four-member permanent staff is supplemented by volunteers and interns. Contact: Sandra Schwab, interim managing director.

Northwest Education Loan Association
811 First Ave., #500
Seattle WA 98104
461-5300
Toll-free within Washington: (800) 732-1077
About 130 work for this nonprofit, which guarantees student loans. Its underwriting staff reviews the loan applications submitted to banks and educational institutions; its collections staff ensures that loans are repaid. Human resources manager: Sue Keil.

Northwest Folklife
Mailing Address
305 Harrison St.
Seattle WA 98109
684-7300
The private nonprofit corporation that produces the Folklife Festival at Seattle Center each Memorial Day weekend also runs catalog sales (of Folklife music and handcrafts), a teacher training program in ethnic culture, an ethnic music touring program and a festival consulting service. It also publishes the *Washington Festival Directory and Resource Guide* and produces Winterfest. There is little turnover among the five full-time permanent positions, but interns are welcome. Some internships later result in paid positions. There are also seasonal opportunities for part-time work in preparation for the festival. The weekend of the festival, there are both paid positions and 800 volunteer assignments. Unsolicited resumes are discouraged. Openings are advertised in the Seattle Arts Commission newsletter, and posted in the festival office, which is located at 158 Thomas St. Interested in an internship? Contact Scott Nagle, executive director, at any time.

Northwest Interpretative Association
83 S. King St., #212
Seattle WA 98104
553-7958
Mary Ellen Rutter is the executive director of this membership group, which publishes and sells interpretative materials for the National Park Service. It employs seven. An affiliated group is Pacific Northwest Field Seminars (telephone 553-2636), headed by Jean Tobin. She employs instructors as needed for the programs, which are intended to enhance individual knowledge and enjoyment of natural resources.

Northwest Renewable Resources Center
1411 Fourth Ave., #1510
Seattle WA 98101-2216
623-7361
The resolution of disputes over the use of natural resources is the mission of this group, which works at a policy level with tribes, state agencies, environmental groups and industry. Founded in 1984, the center is regional; it will consider projects in Washington, Oregon, Idaho, Alaska and Montana. The staff of six includes two mediators. Internships may be possible. Amy Solomon is the executive director.

Northwest Women's Law Center
119 S. Main St., #330
Seattle WA 98104-2515
682-9552
Advancing legal rights for all women is the mission of this group, founded in 1978. Besides litigation, it provides education and a telephone referral service. The center employs seven. Interns and volunteers are welcome. Contact Monique Tucker, office manager.

One Church, One Child
6419 Martin Luther King Jr. Way S.
Seattle WA 98118
723-6224
Gwendolyn Townsend is executive director of this group, which was established in 1989 to recruit African-American adoptive families for African-American children. Today the organization also offers parenting preparation for foster and adoptive parents of all races. The paid staff of four is supplemented with volunteers. Interns are welcome.

Pacific Northwest Ballet
4649 Sunnyside Ave. N.
Seattle WA 98103
547-5900
There are more than 50 nonperforming full-time positions at the ballet; interns are welcome. Positions unique to the performing arts include the company manager, who arranges for travel and touring; the production staff, which includes the stage manager and technical director; and the costume department. Crew positions are union. Human resources manager: Trish MacKinnon.

Pacific Northwest Pollution Prevention Research Center
1218 Third Ave., #1205
Seattle WA 98101
223-1151

Madeline M. Grulich is executive director of this group, which uses interns and an occasional volunteer to supplement the paid staff of four. Founded in 1990, the center offers grants and organizes conferences and roundtables on different kinds of pollution.

Pacific Science Center
200 Second Ave. N.
Seattle WA 98109
443-2001
There are 300 paid positions at this private not-for-profit educational and museum foundation; of those, about 120 are full-time. Interns are welcome. Once the U.S. Science Pavilion at the 1962 World's Fair, the science center promotes the understanding of science, mathematics and technology through interactive exhibits and programs. Positions include science demonstrators and explainers, the majority of the part-time employees, who demonstrate science principles and help explain exhibits; and the education department, which offers programs across the state. Openings, especially for demonstrators and explainers, are often advertised in the University of Washington *Daily*, a student newspaper available free on campus. Teenagers 14 and older are recruited for a summer volunteer program. Job openings are posted in the science center offices, located under the IMAX theater.

Pathways for Women
6205 222nd S.W.
Mountlake Terrace WA 98043
774-9843
Formed in the late 1970s, this United Way agency provides job-search help and runs an emergency shelter. The 15 employees include counselors and program directors (many with training in social work), an employment specialist, bookkeeper, fundraiser and support staff. Executive director: Anne Gordon.

Performance Support Services
1625 Broadway
Seattle WA 98122
328-5548
This group sponsors the Allegro Dance Festival to showcase local dancers and runs the Foundation for Choreographers, which helps dancers prepare for touring. In 1992 PSS also co-sponsored the Seattle Center Academy, a summer art festival for children. Executive director: John Vadino.

Planned Parenthood of Seattle-King County

2211 E. Madison
Seattle WA 98112
328-7734
Jobline: 328-7721

Providing quality reproductive health care to men and women in King, Island, Mason, Lewis and Thurston counties is the mission of this Planned Parenthood chapter, one of 188 affiliates across the U.S. It operates 11 clinics and a central office. About 95 work full-time for Planned Parenthood, with an additional 55 in part-time positions. Job openings are posted in the personnel office on East Madison, in each clinic, at the University of Washington and at community colleges and in community service centers. Applications are accepted only for open positions.

Planned Parenthood of Pierce County

813 S. K St.
Tacoma WA 98405
572-6955

Two clinics are operated by this chapter, with the possibility of more being opened in the future. The total staff is less than 25. Internships are possible. Openings are posted in the building and advertised in the *Morning News Tribune*. Unsolicited resumes are discouraged.

Planned Parenthood of Snohomish County

P.O. Box 1051
Everett WA 98206
339-3392

This chapter, which serves all of Snohomish County, operates two clinics, one in Everett and one in Lynnwood. The total staff is about 40. Openings are advertised in the Seattle and Everett papers. Unsolicited resumes are discouraged. For information about an internship, contact Barbara Smith, executive director.

Pratt Fine Arts Center

1902 S. Main St.
Seattle WA 98144
328-2200

This visual arts facility is supported mostly by user fees and tuition for the classes offered to adults and children. It employs 10 in addition to the artists who teach. There are work-study opportunities but no internships. Contact: Risa Morgan, executive director.

Program for Early Parent Support (PEPS)
4649 Sunnyside Ave. N.
Seattle WA 98103
547-8570
Anne O'Leary is executive director and Katie Bucy volunteer recruiter for this local parent-support organization, which employs fewer than 10. Volunteers are involved in many of its programs, which include neighborhood support groups for new parents, outreach to low-income parents and help for teen parents.

Washington State PTA Office
2003 65th Ave. W.
Tacoma WA 98466
565-2153
Programs in organizational leadership and personal development and programs to meet children's needs are offered by this office, which serves 800 parent-teacher groups representing 135,000 individual members. Some topics are covered as workshops; the PTA presents 150 seminars around the state each year. Jim Carpenter, executive director, heads the staff of eight, which includes a governmental relations director, meeting coordinator, archivist, bookkeeper and the membership services staff. There is limited turnover.

Puyallup Tribe of Indians
2002 E. 28th
Tacoma WA 98404
597-6200
More than 200 work for this organization, which provides social and medical services, housing, employment counseling and a property buying program for members of the Puyallup tribe and other Native Americans. Job openings are posted at several locations in the complex, including the personnel office, JPTA office and the reception area of the health authority, located at 2209 E. 32nd. Resumes can be submitted at any time to the appropriate personnel director: Dennis Johnson for the health authority and Dianne Ward for tribal administration. Internships are possible; approval of the tribal council is necessary.

Ruth Dykeman Children's Center
P.O. Box 66010
Seattle WA 98166
242-1698
Thomas E. Rembiesa is the executive director of this program, which serves emotionally and behaviorally dysfunctional youth and families.

Ryther Child Center
2400 N.E. 95th
Seattle WA 98115
525-5050
Frances Hume is the executive director of this private social service center, which runs alcohol and substance abuse programs for youth as well as a Parents Anonymous support group and parenting classes. Total employment: 140, with about 50 working part-time. Openings are advertised in the Seattle daily papers and in *Sound Opportunities*.

Salvation Army
Northwest Divisional Headquarters
P.O. Box 9219
Seattle 98109
281-4600
You need not be a Salvation Army member to work at this nonprofit, which provides emergency help for the needy (including alcohol/ drug abusers and abused women), counseling and holiday programs. The address above is for an administrative office where most positions are in finance, data processing and clerical support; to apply, contact the divisional secretary's office. For information about the adult rehabilitation program, which employs about 150 and operates the thrift stores, contact the address below. The social services program, which employs about 30, has limited openings; call 325-8101 for more information.

Salvation Army Adult Rehabilitation Center
P.O. Box 3756
Seattle WA 98124
587-0503
Personnel director: (Ms.) Ingbritt Honold

Seattle Art Museum
Human Resources Office
P.O. Box 22000
Seattle WA 98122-9700
654-3100
The Asian art collection started by Richard E. Fuller and his mother, the African collection bequeathed by Katherine White and a new Native American collection are examples of the works you'll see at the SAM. Founded in 1933 by Dr. Fuller, the museum today also includes collections of modern and contemporary American and European art. Total employment is about 200. Interns are welcome. Departments include education, which prepares programs that relate to special exhibitions and trains docents to work with the Seattle

public schools; curatorial, which develops the exhibits and contacts with local art collectors; public relations; media and publications, where the staff includes an editor, a graphic designer, audio-visual crews and photographers; museum services, including registrars and exhibition designers; security; maintenance; volunteer coordination; development; finance; administration; support services; library; and museum store. No unsolicited resumes are accepted. Openings are often advertised in the Seattle dailies and the *Seattle Weekly*. Inquiries regarding internships can be mailed to Cynthia Miles, human resources manager.

Seattle Children's Home
2142 10th Ave. W.
Seattle WA 98119
283-3300
Specialized care and treatment for mentally ill children, youth and young adults is provided by this nonprofit, which employs about 100. Besides administrative, computer and development positions, Seattle Children's Home employs occupational therapists, social workers, doctors and other medical specialists and special education teachers. Graduate degrees are necessary for those who provides direct services to patients. Internships are sometimes possible. Job openings are posted on the second floor of the administration building; resumes can be directed to Dan Green, personnel specialist.

Seattle Children's Museum
305 Harrison St.
Seattle WA 98109-4695
441-1768
The museum expects to enlarge its space by the mid-1990s. So, although there are at press time no new positions, there may be soon. Currently the staff, which focuses on children 8 and younger, includes 10 full-time and several part-time. Interns are welcome. There are also free-lance opportunities. Positions include an exhibit designer, a program developer (who puts together the educational activities), development, marketing and membership directors, a volunteer coordinator and the "floor staff," those who facilitate children's use of exhibits. Contact: Michael Herschensohn, director.

Seattle Children's Theatre
305 Harrison St.
Seattle WA 98109
443-0807
This Equity theater employs 25 as well as part-timers, free-lancers and interns. It has three major operations: the main stage theater,

which does six productions a year; an education program, which teaches children appreciation of the theater and introduces them to performing arts skills; and a touring program, which makes presentations in schools. The administrative staff includes business, development, public relations and marketing directors as well as the managing and artistic directors. The education director designs, organizes and markets the educational programs, including hiring the part-time faculty. The production stage manager, the union liaison, serves as the director's "right hand" and hires other stage managers. The production manager supervises construction of sets and props. The operations manager runs the box office and the theater facility. Contact: Thomas Pechar, managing director.

Seattle/King County Housing Development Consortium
318 First Ave. S., #200
Seattle WA 98104
682-9541
Organized much like a trade association, this group represents 20 nonprofit developers of low-income housing. Its members (which include Common Ground, the Fremont Public Association, Habitat for Humanity and the YWCA) provide housing for about 4,500. Established in 1988, the coalition does some fundraising for members and negotiates program changes (for example, in funding) that help its members. Its responsibilities also include matching volunteers with members. Executive director Carla Okigwe heads a staff of three. Interns, work-study students and volunteers are welcome.

Seattle Opera
P.O. Box 9248
Seattle WA 98109
389-7600
Established in 1964, this is the Northwest's largest opera. It employs about 50 in nonperforming positions; besides the full-time positions, there are part-time and seasonal opportunities. Kathy Magiera, administrative director, is the personnel contact.

Seattle Rape Relief
1905 S. Jackson
Seattle WA 98144
325-5531
Counseling, legal and medical advocacy, education and a 24-hour crisis line are the services of this group, which employs 11. Volunteers receive an 80-hour training program before starting on the crisis line. Co-directors are Ellen Hurtado and Ann McGettigan.

Seattle Repertory Theatre

155 Mercer St.
Seattle WA 98109
443-2210

You'll find part-time and full-time positions, free-lance opportunities and a formal internship program at the Rep. Many positions do not require a theater background. For example, free-lancers design the costumes for the theater productions and the costume shop employs cutters, stitchers, a tailor and a wigmaster. The production shop coordinates the design and construction of sets and the paints crew creates all the scenic painting. There's also a properties staff, which finds or builds the props used on stage; a public relations and advertising staff; the box office crew; and the "front-of-house" staff, the people who run the lobby and ushers. The administrative and development staffs are other examples of positions that do not require theater background. (It is, of course, helpful.) The Rep staff is supported by the Seattle Repertory Organization, a group of 400 volunteers. Assistance is also provided by interns, who usually join the Rep for a season (October through May) shortly after completing college. If you have a theater background and expect to make the arts your career, you can submit an inquiry regarding the Professional Arts Training Program (internship) to Laura Penn, associate manager. If you're interested in an administrative position, write Ben Moore, managing director.

Seattle Symphony Orchestra

305 Harrison St.
Seattle WA 98109
443-4740

Established in 1903, the SSO offers classical concert music in a variety of concert series. It employs 40 administrative staff. Internships are sometimes available and volunteers are always welcome. The operations department staff is responsible for negotiating contracts with musicians, renting halls and hiring guest artists. The SSO also has a systems department, which handles computer systems for ticketing, direct mail lists, internal reporting, desktop publishing and word processing and the library of music. The one-person education department coordinates the programs for children, workshops for teachers and the pre-concert lectures. The orchestra handles most of its promotion in-house, with staff in public relations, advertising, marketing and graphic design. Contact: Colleen Caesar, administration director.

Seattle Urban League, Inc.
105 14th Ave.
Seattle WA 98122
461-3792
This nonprofit, which strives to eliminate racism and the conditions that promote poverty, employs about 20. Job openings are usually posted in the League lobby. The most frequent openings are for project directors, job developers, program assistants, secretaries and counselors. R.Y. Woodhouse is president and Jackie Walker employment director.

Tacoma Urban League, Inc.
2550 S. Yakima
Tacoma WA 98405
383-2006
Thomas Dixon is president of this group, which employs about 30.

Senior Services of Seattle/King County
1601 Second Ave., #800
Seattle WA 98101
448-5757
Headed by Leo Desclos, Senior Services provides counseling, home sharing, nutrition, advocacy, home repair, home-delivered meals, adult day care, transportation, recreation and health services for senior citizens. It employs about 155. Volunteers are welcome. Internships are possible.

Stroum Jewish Community Center
3801 E. Mercer Way
Mercer Island WA 98040
232-7115
Forty work full-time and 200 part-time for this nonprofit, which offers 150 classes each quarter, a day care, preschool and summer day camp. Besides the administrative staff, the full-time positions include department heads for such programs as youth, preschool, Jewish enrichment, cultural arts, health and physical education, child care and adult education. The part-time positions include child care workers, lifeguards, instructors and the customer service staff that handles registrations. Job openings are usually advertised in the Seattle and Bellevue dailies and posted at the center. Volunteers are welcome; contact Ann Meisner, membership services director. Internships are possible.

Stroum Jewish Community Center, North End Branch
8606 35th N.E.
Seattle WA 98115
526-8073
This branch offers preschool, child care, summer day camp and some classes. It employs 10 full-time and about 50 part-time. For information regarding openings, volunteering or internships, contact the director.

Tacoma Actors Guild
1323 S. Yakima
Tacoma WA 98405
272-3107
Tacoma's resident professional theater company, TAG is the only Equity house outside Seattle. Founded in 1978, it presents six plays between October and May and in 1990 initiated a Summer Conservatory Program. The permanent staff of 10 includes the marketing and development directors, box office and finance managers and the managing and artistic directors. There's also a seasonal staff of 10, which includes the costume and technical crew, and opportunities for interns. Contact: Nancy Hoadley, company manager.

Tacoma Art Museum
1123 Pacific Ave.
Tacoma WA 98402
272-4258
Fewer than 20 work at this museum, which has a collection of French Impressionist paintings and the Sara Little Center for Design Research. Volunteers are welcome and internships are possible. At press time, a search was underway to replace director Wendall Ott, who had announced his resignation effective Sept. 30, 1992.

Tacoma Little Theatre
210 N. I St.
Tacoma WA 98403
272-2481
Managing director Peter Epperson has a small staff, but interns are welcome. Founded in the early 1900s, this community organization is the oldest theater in the west. It presents six shows during its September-June season in addition to the performances of the Young Actors Program.

Tacoma Symphony
917 Pacific Ave.
Tacoma WA 98402
272-7264
Five classical music concerts are offered October-March by this group, which also plays "Pops in the Park" each July. The staff includes Carlene Garner, executive director, a music director and an office manager. About 80 musicians are part of the symphony; auditions are held each August for open positions in the non-union group. Interested in an internship? Contact Ms. Garner.

Travelers Aid Society
909 Fourth Ave., #630
Seattle WA 98104
461-3888
About 15 work for this organization, which offers emergency and transitional services to the homeless and protective travel services to children, senior citizens and the disabled or ill. Travelers Aid also assists in inter-country adoptions. Many of the employees are social workers; for this position, a graduate degree in social work is required. More than 100 volunteers supplement the paid staff. Internships may be possible. Contact Bob Rench, associate director. Jane McKinley-Chinn is the executive director.

United Indians of All Tribes Foundation
1945 Yale Pl. E.
Seattle WA 98102
325-0070
A variety of job placement, youth, human services and economic development programs are run by this nonprofit, which employs about 80. Examples include pre-employment counseling and a job listing service, for the general public as well as ex-offenders; foster care licensing and placement; sexual abuse counseling; family counseling; substance abuse intervention programs; Head Start; high school equivalency classes and testing; Daybreak Star Printing; and the Daybreak Star art gallery and Indian dinner theater. For more information about paid positions or internships, contact David Young, program assistant.

United Way of Washington
615 Second Ave., #350
Seattle WA 98104
461-3717
This office's staff of three assists the 26 local United Way programs in the state of Washington. For job opportunities, look to the local

organizations listed below. United Way organizations operate autonomously; all hiring is handled at the county level.

United Way of King County
107 Cherry
Seattle WA 98104
461-7843

Raising and allocating funds, recruiting volunteers and advising nonprofit groups are some of the responsibilities of the Seattle-based United Way program. It works with some 150 member agencies that provide health and human services. About 25 per cent of its 80 employees work in planning and distribution, which serves as the liaison division between United Way and member agencies. The professional staff, most of whom are social workers (often with graduate degrees) also gather information for United Way's annual needs assessment. Fundraising is another large division, responsible for working with corporations and employee groups and with the training and support of "loaned executives," businesspeople whose time is donated to the annual campaign. United Way also has a marketing/information staff; a community resources department that recruits, trains and places volunteers; a management assistance program that provides specialized volunteer expertise to smaller agencies; volunteer board member training; a computer programming staff; and accounting and support services. Internships are available, especially for students doing field work. Unpaid summer internships may also be available. Human resources manager: John Mack.

United Way of Pierce County
P.O. Box 2215
Tacoma WA 98401-2215
272-4263

Twenty-six work for this chapter, which handles many of the same programs as the King County office. United Way of Pierce County also funds a volunteer center, the Center for Nonprofit Development. Most job openings are advertised. Interns are welcome. Contact: Marcia Walker, vice president, administration.

United Way of Snohomish County
917 134th St. S.W., #A-6
Everett WA 98204
258-4521
From Seattle: 742-5911

Eighteen work full-time for this chapter, which supports 54 member agencies. Besides the fundraising, fund allocation and advising responsibilities common to all United Way organizations, this chapter also is focusing on community-wide problem-solving. Its staff does needs assessments and works with other agencies to ensure the needs are met. It also works with business and industry to encourage volunteerism. Job openings are posted in the coffee area and advertised in the Everett *Herald* and sometimes the Seattle papers. Interns are welcome. Direct inquiries to Jack Healy, president.

United Way of Kitsap County
2135 Sheridan Rd., #D
Bremerton WA 98310
377-8505
Volunteer Action Center: 377-0059
Six staff members work for this chapter, which serves 33 member agencies. Turnover is limited. Interns are welcome. Personnel contact: Barbara Stephenson, executive director.

United Way of Thurston County
203 E. 4th, #221
Olympia WA 98501
943-2773
Three staff members work for this chapter, which serves 34 member agencies. Turnover is limited. Volunteers are welcome. David W. Brown is executive director.

Visiting Nurse Services of the Northwest
400 N. 34th, #306
P.O. Box 300317
Seattle WA 98103-9717
548-8100
Home health services in King, Snohomish and Skagit counties, including specialized nursing care, speech, physical and occupational therapy and medical social work are among the services offered by VNS, which was founded in 1929. Although loosely affiliated with the national visiting nurse program, the Northwest program is autonomous. VNS, which serves people of all ages, employs nurses (both visiting and private duty), therapists, medical social workers, a nutritionist and home health aides. The administrative staff is small. Many of the 650 employees are part-time. Internships are possible. Human resources manager: Courtney Larsen.

Washington Association of Churches
4759 15th N.E.
Seattle WA 98105
525-1988
Supported by 17 Protestant and Catholic denominations and 15

ecumenical organizations across the state, this association currently employs fewer than 10 full-time. The staff is supplemented with part-time employees, interns and volunteers. The association emphasizes ecumenical dialog, legislative advocacy, refugee advocacy, economic justice, civil rights and farm worker justice. Executive minister: John Boonstra.

Washington Business Week
P.O. Box 658
Olympia WA 98507
943-1600
Toll-free within Washington: (800) 521-9325
Beverlee Hughes is the executive director of this group, responsible for organizing week-long summer educational programs for high school students. The Business Week staff of three handles fund-raising, faculty and student recruitment, volunteer coordination, conference planning and development of the teaching materials. Volunteers are welcome; internships are possible.

Washington Campaign for Freedom of Expression
1402 Third Ave., #421
Seattle WA 98101
340-9301
David Mendoza is the executive director of this affiliate of a national advocacy group formed to protect and extend freedom of artistic expression and fight censorship. At press time, the office employed three. Volunteers and interns are welcome.

Washington Commission for the Humanities
615 Second Ave., #300
Seattle WA 98104
682-1770
This private group, funded in part by the National Endowment for the Humanities, supports the humanities and humanities education with several programs: its foundation, which provides grants; a speakers' bureau, which on a fee basis provides speakers for lecture series across the state; an exhibit touring service; the *Humanities Today* quarterly; and forums for community groups considering the establishment of humanities programs. The full-time staff of seven includes public relations, programs and finance directors, a volunteer coordinator, and support staff. Turnover is limited, but internships are available. Contact: Hidde Van Duym, executive director.

Washington Literacy
2209 Eastlake Ave. E.
Seattle WA 98102
461-3623
Providing reading training for adults is the emphasis at Washington Literacy, which helps develop community literacy programs. The staff is small; there are fewer than a dozen positions. Interns are welcome. Contact: Christine Cassidy, executive director.

Washington Occupation Information System
1415 Harrison Ave. N.W., #201
Olympia WA 98502
754-8222
Paul Bert is the executive director of this nonprofit, which researches and compiles data on occupations and education. Formed in the mid-1970s, the organization employs people in research, marketing and support. (See *"Counseling and Job-Search Help."*)

Washington Special Olympics
2150 N. 107th
Seattle WA 98133
362-4949
Organizers of year around athletic games for the developmentally disabled, the Special Olympics employs 13 in its state office. Each of the 12 area offices is also staffed by one. At the Special Olympics, most employees have specific functional experience; for example, in managing the area, regional and state games, fundraising, public relations or volunteer coordination. There are few opportunities for entry-level people, although internships are occasionally available. The ability to work with volunteers and good organizational skills are important for all employees. Contact: Bonnie Benofski, office manager.

Washington State Democratic Central Committee
506 Second Ave., #1701
Seattle WA 98104
583-0664
Even during presidential elections, this office staff is very small. Most positions require some experience in politics. Volunteers and interns are important members of the staff. Contact: Jeff Smith, executive director.

Washington State 4-H Foundation
7612 Pioneer Way E.
Puyallup WA 98371
840-4560

This private nonprofit raises funds for 4-H programs; the 4-H clubs themselves actually work with the cooperative extension staff in each county. John Engen is executive director of the foundation, which has a staff of three.

Washington State Jewish Historical Society
2031 Third Ave., #400
Seattle WA 98121
443-1903
Charna Klein is the executive director of this group, which employs two part-time. Volunteers and interns are welcome. Founded in 1980, this membership organization is a member of the American Jewish Historical Society. It maintains archives in cooperation with the University of Washington libraries, issues a monthly newsletter, organizes exhibits, presentations and workshops.

Washington State Nurses Association
2505 Second Ave., #500
Seattle WA 98121
443-9762
A professional association and labor union, this organization has a staff of 25. Openings are posted in its office.

Washington State Republican Party
9 Lake Bellevue Dr., #203
Bellevue WA 98005
451-1988
Lance J. Henderson is the executive director of this group, which divides its permanent staff of 12 into four divisions: finance, communications, administration and political (the division that supports campaigns statewide). There are also part-time and intern positions, especially during campaigns. Political experience, either paid or volunteer, is helpful.

Washington Trails Association
1305 Fourth Ave., #512
Seattle WA 98101-2401
625-1367
Supported by 2,500 members, this organization was founded about 20 years ago to preserve and enhance existing trails and to extend the trails network. Another purpose of the group is advocacy for trails and promotion of nonmotorized use of trails. The office has two paid staff members, executive director Jan Milligan, and magazine editor Dan Nelson. Each takes interns; for example, in administration and in journalism. The monthly magazine, *Signposts for Northwest Trails*, established in 1966, accepts freelance writing and photography.

Washington Women's Employment and Education
841 N. Central, #232
Kent WA 98032
859-3718
Committed to breaking down the barriers low-income women (and single-parent men) face in succeeding in education and careers, this nonprofit provides an intensive three-week program and then a year of followup as participants pursue training or job placement. The Kent and Tacoma offices each employ fewer than 10, including the publicist and accountant who split their time between the two offices. Both offices employ directors, education directors, employment specialists and transition coordinators. Volunteers handle many functions in both operations and interns are welcome. For more information about this office, contact Lynn Roberts, director.

Washington Women's Employment and Education
1517 Fawcett Ave., #250
Tacoma WA 98402
627-0527
Contact: Margo Fleshman, executive director.

WashPIRG
340 15th Ave. E.
Seattle WA 98112
322-9064
A citizen outreach lobby that works on environmental and consumer legislation, WashPIRG has 35,000 members across state. Its current project is the federal resource conservation and recovery act. Rick Bunch, executive director, heads the office staff of fewer than 10 and the field staff that ranges between 20 and 70. Volunteers and interns are welcome.

Wing Luke Asian Museum
407 7th Ave. S.
Seattle WA 98104
623-5124
This museum specializes in Asian and Asian-American folk art and history. Its staff is very small and all positions are part-time. Volunteers are always needed. A variety of internships (all unpaid) are available. Intern assignments can be designed to meet academic requirements; although most students work part-time in the museum for three months, internships ranging in length from two weeks to one year have also been arranged. Contact: Ron Chew, director.

Women's Funding Alliance
219 First Ave. S., #120
Seattle WA 98104
467-6733
A fundraising organization for several nonprofits that offer health and human services programs for women and children, this group has only two staff members. Volunteers and interns are welcome. Besides fundraising, WFA provides technical assistance (for example, on financial management, public speaking and payroll deduction plans) for its members. The alliance staff also promotes its members' programs through public speaking and advertising. Karen Campbell is executive director.

World Association for Children and Parents (WACAP)
P.O. Box 88948
Seattle WA 98138
575-4550
This organization recruits adoptive parents, provides home studies for adoption, provides support to adopting parents, arranges with child care agencies in the U.S. and abroad to place children for adoption and runs an Options for Pregnancy program. Janice Neilson is executive director.

YMCA of Greater Seattle
909 Fourth Ave.
Seattle WA 98104
382-5022
King County and part of Snohomish County are served by this branch of the Young Men's Christian Association, which has 16 offices in the service area. Besides six geographic districts, the organization includes the Metrocenter Y, which focuses on community development programs; camping services, which operates two residential camps; and the administrative office. Full-time, the Y employs about 200, with part-time and seasonal employees increasing the count to as many as 1,000. The Y also operates 250 guest rooms, providing opportunities for hospitality industry jobs. The child care program for school-age children is one of the Y's largest areas, offering both full-time and part-time job opportunities. The Y welcomes both volunteers and interns. Openings are posted in most Y offices and listed in *Sound Opportunities* and the United Way monthly. Contact: Sheila vander Lugt, human resources director.

YMCA of Snohomish County
2720 Rockefeller
Everett WA 98201
258-9211
This Y offers health and fitness, child care and preschool, and youth leadership programs in Everett, southeast Everett, Mukilteo and Marysville. The Y offers full-day and before- and after-school child care as well as a half-day preschool. There are leadership programs for junior and senior high school students. Other programs include a support group for pregnant teenagers and senior citizen fitness and travel activities. The Y employs 200, with about half working full-time. Interns are welcome. Contact: Debbie Anderson, personnel.

Kitsap Family YMCA
60 Magnuson Way
Bremerton WA 98310
377-3741
Activities for children and teenagers, before- and after-school care in school buildings, health and fitness programs and a program for the military are examples of what's offered by the Y. The permanent staff of six is supplemented with approximately 60 part-timers. Interns are welcome. Contact: Jane Erlandsen, associate director.

YMCA of Tacoma-Pierce County
Metropolitan Office
1002 S. Pearl
Tacoma WA 98465
564-9622
More than 120 are employed full-time at this Y; there's also a large part-time staff. Besides the Metropolitan office, the Y operates facilities in downtown Tacoma, Lakewood, Puyallup and Gig Harbor. Programs include health and fitness, day, residential and family camps, employment preparation, international programs and community school. Interns are welcome. Resumes should be directed to the president.

YWCA of Seattle-King County
1118 Fifth Ave.
Seattle WA 98101
461-4871
About 100 work for the Seattle YWCA. Job opportunities range from semi-skilled to professional and managerial and include employment counselors, administrators and teachers in the day care centers, summer day camp staff, maintenance and housekeeping workers and the administrative staff. The Y also employs counselors in its

emergency shelter and transitional housing and contract instructors for the health and fitness classes. Job openings are posted in the Y employment resource center.

YWCA-University of Washington
4057 Roosevelt Way N.E.
Seattle WA 98105
632-4747
This YWCA, which is not affiliated with the Seattle Y, employs three. Interns are welcome. Employment search, birth control and abortion referral and post-abortion support are the programs. Judy Rowley is the director.

YWCA of Kitsap County
P.O. Box 559
Bremerton WA 98310
479-5116
This Y offers a confidential shelter for battered women and their children; a child support program for custodial parents; a pro bono legal service run with the Kitsap County Bar Association; Operation Smart, an after-school program for girls aged 11-13; and a women's financial information service (open to women of all ages) co-sponsored by the American Association of Retired Persons. The staff of 12 is supplemented with volunteers, many of whom receive training in domestic violence programs so that they can work in the shelter, and with interns. Contact: Barbara Malich, executive director.

YWCA of Tacoma-Pierce County
405 Broadway
Tacoma WA 98402
272-4181
This Y operates a shelter, health and fitness center, youth programs, thrift store and career resource center. When openings occur in the staff of 45, they're advertised and announced in the resource center. Executive director: Venetia Magnuson.

YWCA of Thurston County
220 Union S.E.
Olympia WA 98501
352-0593
Pat McGreer is the executive director of this Y, which has two permanent staff members and two on contract for the displaced homemakers program. Other programs include advocacy for women and children, job search assistance, an interview clothes bank and community forums and workshops. Interns are welcome.

11. Employers: Business and Tourism Organizations

The Puget Sound area includes many business and tourism organizations that can serve as valuable resources in your job search. Some chambers of commerce offer directories of their members or major area employers. Most welcome nonmembers to meetings and educational sessions. Both chambers and convention bureaus offer literature about their communities. (See *"Job Bulletins and Valuable Publications."*) The larger organizations offer a variety of job opportunities. A reminder: none of these groups run employment services; don't expect them to provide job-search counseling or to circulate your resume to their members.

Greater Seattle Chamber of Commerce
600 University, #1200
Seattle WA 98101
389-7200
The Seattle chamber employs about 55 in its departments and affiliated programs. The affiliates, which have their own boards of directors and executive directors, typically have small staffs—often only the executive director and an assistant. Current affiliates include Business Volunteers for the Arts, King County Housing Partnership, Leadership Tomorrow, Partners in Public Education, Sports Council of Seattle and King County and Cruise Ship Alliance. Other departments include accounting, member services, communications, community relations, computer services, governmental affairs and trade development. Openings are posted in the reception area. Personnel contact: Bev Matthews.

Bellevue Chamber of Commerce
10500 N.E. 8th, #750
Bellevue WA 98004
454-2464
Advocacy for business, information (including publications and educational seminars) and networking are the three major goals of the

Bellevue chamber, which employs 13 to serve its 1,800 members. Departments include communications, issues (which interacts with local and state government), special events and membership (which includes commissioned salespeople to recruit new members). Internships are welcome. Contact: JoAnn Curley, administrative manager.

Everett Chamber of Commerce
P.O. Box 1086
Everett WA 98206
252-5181
The Everett chamber, which includes a convention and visitors bureau, employs 11. Besides the convention and visitors bureau staff, which "markets" Everett as a site for conventions and business meetings, the chamber employs an administration staff; and membership services, which recruits new members and plans special events, including educational forums. Turnover is limited. Interested in an internship? Write Tom Burns, president.

Tacoma-Pierce County Chamber of Commerce
950 Pacific Ave., #300
P.O. Box 1933
Tacoma WA 98401-1933
627-2175
The Tacoma chamber employs 18 in such departments as business and trade development, member services, neighborhood area councils, small business programs, government and community issues, communications and publications, computer services and business. Department managers usually handle their own hiring.

Other area chambers include:

Auburn Area Chamber of Commerce
228 1st N.E.
Auburn WA 98002
833-0700
Employs four. Internships possible.

Bainbridge Island Chamber of Commerce/Visitor Center
590 Winslow Way E.
Bainbridge Island WA 98110
842-3700
Employs one. Internships possible. Volunteers welcome.

Ballard Chamber of Commerce
2208 N.W. Market St.
Seattle WA 98107
784-9705
Employs one full-time, one part-time. Internships possible.

Bremerton Area Chamber of Commerce
P.O. Box 229
Bremerton WA 98310
479-3579
Employs five full-time, two part-time. Internships possible.

Edmonds Chamber of Commerce
P.O. Box 146
Edmonds WA 98020
670-1496
Employs one. Internships possible.

Enumclaw Chamber of Commerce
1421 Cole St.
Enumclaw WA 98022
825-7666
Employs one full-time, one part-time. Internships possible.

Gig Harbor/Peninsula Area Chamber of Commerce
P.O. Box 1245
Gig Harbor WA 98335
851-6865
Employs three year 'round. Seasonal positions and internships possible.

Greater Des Moines Chamber of Commerce
P.O. Box 98672
Des Moines WA 98198
878-7000
Employs one. Internships possible.

Greater Federal Way Chamber of Commerce
34400 Pacific Highway S., #1
Federal Way WA 9803
838-2605
Employs three full-time, one part-time. Internships possible.

Greater Greenwood Chamber of Commerce
P.O. Box 30715
Seattle WA 98103
789-1148
Employs one. Internships possible.

**Greater Issaquah Chamber of Commerce/
Issaquah Festivals**
155 N.W. Gilman Blvd.
Issaquah WA 98027
Employs four full-time, three part-time.

Greater Redmond Chamber of Commerce
P.O. Box 791
Redmond WA 98073
885-4014
Employs four full-time, one part-time.

Greater Renton Chamber of Commerce
300 Rainier Ave. N.
Renton WA 98055
226-4560
Employs two. Internships possible.

Kent Chamber of Commerce
P.O. Box 128
Kent WA 98035
854-1770
Employs three full-time, one part-time.

Kirkland Chamber of Commerce
301 Kirkland Ave.
Kirkland WA 98033
822-7066
Employs five.

Lake City Chamber of Commerce
2611 N.E. 125th, #102
Seattle WA 98125
363-3287
Employs one. Internships possible.

Lakewood Chamber of Commerce
P.O. Box 98690
Tacoma WA 98498
582-9400
Employs two.

Mercer Island Chamber of Commerce
7601 S.E. 27th
Mercer Island WA 98040
232-3404

Northshore Chamber of Commerce
10410 Beardslee Blvd.
Bothell WA 98011
486-1245
Employs four full-time, one part-time. Internships possible.

Olympia-Thurston County Chamber of Commerce
P.O. Box 1427
Olympia WA 98507
357-3362
Employs six full-time, two part-time. Internships welcome.

Port Orchard Chamber of Commerce
839 Bay St.
Port Orchard WA 98336
876-3505
Employs two. Internships possible.

Puyallup Area Chamber of Commerce
P.O. Box 1298
Puyallup WA 98371
845-6755
Employs four. Internships welcome.

Shoreline Chamber of Commerce
P.O. Box 55066
Seattle WA 98155
361-2260
Employs one. Internships possible.

South Snohomish County Chamber of Commerce
3400 188th St. S.W., #102
Lynnwood WA 98037
774-0507
Employs four full-time.

Southwest King County Chamber of Commerce
P.O. Box 58591
Seattle WA 98138
244-3160
Employs six.

West Seattle Chamber of Commerce
4151 California Ave. S.W.
Seattle WA 98116
932-5685
Employs one full-time, one part-time. Internships possible.

Woodinville Chamber of Commerce
17630 140th Ave. N.E., #A
Woodinville WA 98072
481-8300
Employs two. Internships possible.

Downtown Associations

Downtown Seattle Association
500 Union St., #325
Seattle WA 98101
623-0340
John Gilmore is president of this 10-employee organization, which promotes downtown Seattle vitality through such programs as "Easy Streets," the holiday carrousel and the summer Out to Lunch concerts. Housing and transportation are other concerns of the association staff and its committees of businesspeople. Internships are possible.

Bellevue Downtown Association
500 108th Ave. N.E., #210
Bellevue WA 98004
453-1223
Making downtown Bellevue vital, especially after 5 p.m., is one of the goals of this group, which employs four full-time.

Greater Bothell Association
P.O. Box 1203
Bothell WA 98041
485-4353
Winter and Independence Day festivals and co-op advertising are among the projects of this organization, which has only one staff member, program manager Randy Flesher. Internships are possible.

Convention and Visitors Bureaus

Seattle-King County Convention and Visitors Bureau
Administrative Office
520 Pike St., #1300
Seattle WA 98101
461-5800
This tourism development office, which is not part of the government-operated Washington State Convention and Trade Center, employs nearly 200. Some positions are part-time or seasonal. Despite the size of the staff, turnover is limited; unsolicited resumes are not accepted. When openings do occur, they are advertised in the Seattle and Bellevue papers and posted at Job Service Centers. An affiliate of the visitors bureau is:

Seattle-King County News Bureau
461-5805
Provides media relations liaison to out-of-state media, especially on tourism-related questions. Because the staff includes only three full-time employees, openings are infrequent. Internships, especially for students in journalism, public relations or marketing, are offered. Contact: Barry Anderson, news bureau manager.

Other convention and visitor bureaus:

East King County Convention and Visitor Bureau
515 116th N.E., #111
Bellevue WA 98004
455-1926
Employs eight. Internships possible.

Bremerton/Kitsap County Visitor and Convention Bureau
120 Washington Ave.
Bremerton WA 98310
479-3588
Employs seven. Internships possible.

Snohomish County Visitor Information Center
101 128th S.E., #5000
Everett WA 98208
745-4133, 338-4437
Employs two. Uses 45 volunteers. Internships possible.

12. Transportation and Child Care

When you're job hunting, especially if you're new to the Puget Sound area, you may need help getting to the interview. If you have children, you may need day care. For more information, you'll find these telephone numbers and publications helpful.

Transportation
How can you reach an interview by bus? You'll receive detailed help from:

METRO: 553-3000
King County rider information available 24 hours a day.

Community Transit: 778-2185, 353-RIDE
Snohomish County information available from 5:30 a.m. to 9 p.m. weekdays and from 8 to 4:30 weekends.

Pierce Transit: 581-8000
Pierce County information available from 6 a.m. to 6 p.m. weekdays and from 9 to 5 weekends.

Kitsap Transit: 373-2877
Kitsap County information available from 6 a.m. to 6 p.m. weekdays and from 10 to 2 Saturdays.

Intercity Transit: 786-1881
Thurston County information available from 7 a.m. to 7 p.m. weekdays, from 8 to 5 Saturdays and from 8:30 to 5:30 Sundays.

Directions
When you schedule an interview, don't hesitate to ask for directions. You'll find some companies are so accustomed to the question that they have taped instructions on their telephone systems.

A good map is also valuable. Some suggestions:

Thomas Bros. Maps, available from many map dealers and bookstores in King, Snohomish and Pierce county versions. The one-county spiral-bound edition is $15.95.

King of the Road Maps, available in many book, drug and grocery stories in several different versions. By mail the maps are $2.50 each. Contact King of the Road Map Service, 6325 212th S.W., #E, Lynnwood WA 98036, (800) 223-8852 or 774-7112.

Seattle Best Places includes a detailed map of downtown Seattle and *The Seattle Survival Guide* includes a list of downtown buildings with parking garages. Both are available in bookstores and from the publisher, Sasquatch Publishing Co., 1931 Second Ave., Seattle WA 948101, 441-6202.

Child Care
The Child Care Resource and Referral Network provides free telephone referrals to licensed day care statewide through 17 local offices. There are three serving King County and one each in Snohomish, Pierce, Thurston and Kitsap counties. Call (800) 446-1114 weekdays between 8 a.m. and 5 p.m. for the telephone number of the referral office handling your geographic area.

If you live in Seattle, the city's Comprehensive Child Care office, part of the Department of Housing and Human Services, offers referrals to day care providers who contract with the city. It also provides financial assistance for families that meet income guidelines. For more information, call 386-1050 between 8 a.m. and 5 p.m. weekdays.

The King County Child Care Program serves those who live outside Seattle but within the county as well as all King County employees. This office also provides financial assistance for families that meet income guidelines and use the providers on contract with the county. For information: call 296-1362 between 8:30 a.m. and 4:30 p.m. weekdays.

If you need financial assistance with your day care bill, help may also be available through:

The subsidized child care program offered by the state Department of Social and Health Services (DSHS). It serves three groups: those who are employed but earn less than 52 per cent of the state median income; teenage parents completing high school; and recipients of public assistance who are working or completing training programs. For more information, check the telephone book's blue pages for the state Community Service Office serving your ZIP code.

For Snohomish County residents, subsidies are available through the grant-funded Child Care Assistance Program offered by Volunteers of America's Family and Children's Services. Most participants are single parents completing educational programs or beginning their careers. For information: 259-3191.

13. Evaluating the Job Offer:
Is This Is the Right Job—and the Right Employer?

What's the right job—and the right employer—for you? Sometimes the answer to that question is obvious: you know exactly what you'd like to do and you've identified an organization that provides the best possible combination of compensation, challenge and working conditions.

Many of us, however, aren't that lucky. Some of us have specific jobs and specific employers in mind—but we're unsure which of our options would be best. Money is almost always a consideration, but as the next chapter points out, there's more to a compensation package than paycheck and vacation days.

What else should you evaluate? At least these three:

1. Growth opportunities;

2. Job security; and

3. The organization's culture.

Opportunities for professional growth are important. Does this firm have enough depth in your functional area to give you several promotional options? Or will you be a one-person department, with the opportunity to learn a little about everything? Some companies pigeonhole employees, so you'll risk becoming an expert on a very narrow topic. That makes changing jobs difficult. In other organizations, you won't develop particular kinds of expertise because your employer doesn't use it; for example, if you're the marketing manager in a firm that advertises only in the Yellow Pages, you'll learn nothing about producing magazine ads and radio commercials.

If your department is small, you may gain invaluable knowledge about many different functions in your field. For example, if you're the personnel manager, you may handle new employee orientation as well as screening applicants and evaluating different benefits packages. But you may never have the time or expertise to write an employee policy handbook, negotiate union contracts or analyze the cost of high turnover in certain divisions. Even if your firm grows, you may have to move to a different employer to focus on specialties within your field.

You'll also want to think about job security; start-ups and turnarounds can be exciting, but they sometimes fail with no warning, often without making the last payroll. Mergers and buyouts in firms of any size often mean consolidation or liquidation.

If you have a job offer from a start-up or turnaround, you'll want to consider:

The company owners' backgrounds and financial resources and the commitment of the investors. Are you confident the owners know what they're doing? Is the business plan realistic? Is the financing in place? Are the investors patient—and will they commit additional cash if necessary?

The product or service itself. Does it work? Is it marketable? Look for well-documented evidence, not just the owners' enthusiasm, a few initial sales and some favorable publicity. Remember that some companies inflate their sales figures by recognizing deals for which payment may never be made. And those complimentary newspaper stories? Most—even in the reputable *Wall Street Journal*—are based on the owners' conversations with reporters.

The possible upside. If you truly believe in this company, you may be a millionaire in five years. Even if the company doesn't make it, your investment of time might pay off handsomely. You may work with state-of-the-art technology, gaining experience a later employer will value highly. Or you may meet brilliant people who will serve as mentors and friends throughout your career.

Whether an organization's large or small, new or well-established, take a look at the culture. This is especially difficult if you're new to the area or industry and you have no "inside" sources. But it's a vital step: culture is probably the single most common reason that well-qualified employees don't like their jobs. For an executive position, it's even more important that you be comfortable with the culture of your new employer.

Some considerations:

Family ownership or control. The smaller the company, the more you'll want to know. Look, for example, at the physical health of the owners and soundness of their marriage. How aggressive are they? Are they just coasting, cashing in on years of work, or are they committed to more growth? Look at the other family members in the business; are they real contributors? Or will part of your job be picking up after them?

Top-down or bottom-up. Does top management issue decrees or does it listen to people at lower levels? How are budgets developed? Will you be asked to put together a plan—or expected to work within an arbitrarily set budget?

Decision-making. What does it take to get a decision: a conversation with your boss, a one-page memo or a 5,000-word analysis for the board of directors? Are decisions made quickly...or are proposals repeatedly referred to another committee or task force?

Channels. Will you have ready access to people in many different functions and at many different levels? Or does communication occur only through channels? For example, can you initiate contact with someone in another department—or will your department head call or memo the senior person in the other department? And can you speak directly to your boss' boss? If you're moving from an informal or small organization, you may be surprised at the rigid structure of some larger employers.

What happens when problems occur. Problems can't be avoided. Accidents happen. People make mistakes. Situations change. How does your prospective employer respond to problems? Do your boss—and the layers of management above him or her—focus on solving the problem and preventing a recurrence? Or do they worry more about finding a scapegoat?

Attitude about money. Some organizations are notoriously tight; you'll have to justify every charge to your expense account and wrench discounts from your suppliers. Other employers are careless. High-cost changes are made at the last minute or there's little attention to the expensive details that ruin budgets. Many public companies are driven by the requirement that they report quarterly earnings; spending is manipulated to make this earnings report better than the last one, regardless of market conditions.

Work ethic. Some organizations are nose-to-the-grindstone; you're expected to be hustling (or look as if you are) from dawn to dusk. Business trips always start on Sunday and end with late flights home on Fridays. Other employers are more laissez-faire; there's always a crowd around the water-cooler and most people take off early on winter Wednesdays to catch the ski bus. When deadlines aren't met...well, there's always tomorrow.

Your attitude about work ethics will be determined by three factors: your personal workstyle, your role within the organization and your boss. If you're stuck with a fairly monotonous job, you'll welcome those morning breaks around the donut wagon; if you're a manager always struggling with rush projects, you'll be frustrated by every interruption.

Now, how does your boss affect your attitude? Obviously, a workaholic boss is likely to expect similar commitment from you. You may also find yourself skipping lunches and working late if you work for a procrastinator who lets projects slide until the last minute; if you work for someone who promises everything—and then expects you to deliver; or if you're the detail person who doublechecks all of the department proposals.

What drives this organization. Many firms are sales-driven; that's what is valued. The way the salespeople are treated will often reflect this; although the organizational chart will show the vice presidents of sales, marketing, finance and operations on the same level, the vice president of sales may have significantly more influence. Many high-tech firms are engineering or product development-driven. Some advertising agencies are described as creative-driven. Before you accept an offer, try to determine where your department ranks on the corporate totem pole. This is especially important if you're coming from an organization where your department and function carried more clout than it historically has with your new employer.

A corollary: what counts in the organization. Some companies value industry experience; with others, it may be functional experience, where you went to school, credentials, personality...or family connections. In some organizations, seniority is important; people who've worked their way up through a variety of assignments have a great deal of influence.

14. Evaluating the Paycheck:
How Much Will This Job Pay? And How Much Will It Cost?

How much will a job pay? And how much will it cost you? These are two questions you need to consider throughout your interviewing process. As you job hunt, think not only of the salary you'll earn. Remember the fringe benefits like health and life insurance, vacation, sick leave and employee discounts. And remember to factor in the costs of the job, too: the union dues, health insurance costs, mandatory retirement contributions, parking, lunches and wardrobe. It's these benefits and costs that determine how much is actually left in your checkbook every month.

Let's start with the fringe benefits. As you progress through interviews with a prospective employer, you should be given a chance to ask about benefits. If possible, direct these questions to the personnel staff; these people are more likely to have the most current information and they are accustomed to being asked about benefits. Some important, common benefits:

401(k)
This allows you to reduce your taxable income—and thus, your income taxes—by making contributions to a retirement account. Often your contributions are matched by your employer.

Dependent care allowance
More and more employers are offering these allowances, which take advantage of a recent tax law change. Like the 401(k), this allows you to reduce your taxable income by setting aside money in a fund

that pays the people who care for your dependent children or elderly relatives. There are a number of restrictions, but in most cases, this program will save you tax dollars.

Health insurance
Some employers provide health insurance to employees at no or nominal (for example, $10 per month) cost. A few employers provide health insurance to employees and their families at no cost or sharply reduced rates. This is a significant benefit if you are currently paying for your own health insurance, either on an individual plan or as a dependent on your spouse or parent's plan.

Life insurance
Term life insurance is another common benefit. Some policies provide the equivalent of your salary at no charge to you, with additional insurance available at low rates for you and your family members.

Cafeteria benefits plans
Everybody gets health insurance, life insurance and two weeks of vacation—whether they want it or not. That's the way most benefit plans used to work. Today, many firms have switched to cafeteria plans that allow you to select what you need. You "pay" for the benefits with an "allowance" provided by your employer. If you want more benefits than your allowance covers, you pay the difference in cash. If you want less, you get the extra cash, often as a contribution to your 401(k).

Free parking
If your employer provides parking or if you're working in a suburban office park or a quiet neighborhood where unrestricted on-street parking is available, you may save hundreds of before-tax dollars.

Bus passes
Many employers offer bus passes at a discount. This can reduce your commuting costs to less than $1 per day. And the passes are good on the weekends, too.

Flextime
Reducing your travel time and the hours your children spend in day care or making time for college classes are three examples of the possible benefits of flextime, the program that allows you to work something other than an 8 to 5 shift. Some employers allow you to change your work hours daily; others expect you to select a shift and stick to it.

Comp time

Many of us work long hours in positions for which overtime is not paid. In return, some employers grant "comp," or compensatory, time off. Your boss may have a formal policy, where each hour after 5 earns you an hour of comp time. Most employers are more casual. Most managerial positions do not include comp time.

Four-day weeks

How would you like to work from 7 to 6 Monday through Thursday...and take every Friday off? Some companies do. In others, some employees negotiate special schedules, often in lieu of a higher salary. One possibility is long days at the beginning and end of the week and Wednesdays off.

Employee discounts

Employee discounts come in two forms. One is the discount on your company's products; for example, if you work for a clothing store, you can buy your suits at a reduced price. Some employers have also arranged discounts for their employees on other purchases; for example, at many firms, you can buy a computer at below-market rates. Many of these programs also allow you to finance the purchase at no interest and make your payments through payroll deduction.

Subsidized meals

Lunch for a couple of dollars in a downtown highrise? Yes, if you're eating in your employer's subsidized cafeteria. Special discounts for employees are typical in restaurants run by many firms.

Brown-bagging

If you'd rather pack your own lunch, check if your employer offers a lunchroom with refrigerator and microwave.

Now let's look at some of the hidden "costs" of a job. Remember, most of these costs are incurred with after-tax dollars.

Parking

If you work in downtown Seattle, Tacoma or Bellevue, and you must use your car for commuting, you're likely to be paying for parking. This can be $10 a month—or nearly $200. When you're visiting a prospective employer located in a highrise with garage, take a few minutes after the interview and ask the garage cashier how much monthly parking costs—and if it's readily available.

Long hours

If you expect to work long or irregular hours, consider how that will impact your use of public transportation and your child care expenses. You may find yourself spending more than you expected on taxis and late charges at the day care center. Or you may choose to commute by car and park in your building's garage; that's a cost to be considered.

Health insurance

As noted above, some companies absorb most of the cost of health insurance for employees and their families. Don't assume that all employers do so. Even if your new employer provides your insurance at no cost, you may pay $200 or $300 per month to cover your family. And you'll still have a deductible or co-payments.

Mandatory retirement contributions

Although many businesses provide basic retirement programs for their employees, this is not typical of government retirement plans. Most are employee-funded with mandatory payroll deductions. If you're interviewing with a state, county or city agency or with a public school, be sure to ask about retirement contributions.

Sick leave

Employers who offer sick leave as a benefit now must allow you to use your accrued sick days to care for an ill family member. As a result, some firms have eliminated sick leave allowances; if you're truly ill, you'll probably be paid for the days you miss...but you won't be able to take time off to care for a sick child.

Contributions

Try to discreetly inquire about your prospective employer's policy on charitable or political action committee (PAC) contributions. You may find that you're expected to pledge a certain portion of your paycheck to the boss' favorite charity or your industry's PACs. Some employers expect contributions of time, too; as part of some community relations programs, employees are encouraged to be active in professional, civic or charitable groups. Be aware that board membership in a civic or charitable group often carries with it the expectation of a significant cash contribution.

Gifts

Some firms celebrate birthdays with all-department luncheons and Secretaries' Day with bouquets for every word processor and administrative assistant. Sometimes the cost is covered by the managers' petty cash fund; in other organizations, you'll be anteing up.

Wardrobe

Getting dressed for the office costs money. The more formal your office, the more traveling you do, the higher your wardrobe costs will be. Besides the initial purchase, you'll have maintenance and repair: dry cleaning, laundry (especially if you're on the road for extended periods) and shoe repair. If you travel to extremely hot or cold areas, factor in the cost of clothes you might not otherwise buy.

Travel expenses

If your job will involve travel in your own car, ask about mileage allowances. If you'll be on the road overnight, ask about reimbursement for travel expenses. Unlimited expense accounts are rare these days, and some organizations (especially government agencies) pay nothing above a given daily allowance. The extras are your responsibility. To survive on some per diums in expensive cities like New York, you'll need to share hotel rooms with colleagues and eat dinner at McDonald's.

After-hours commitments

Besides the professional, civic and charitable activities mentioned earlier, you'll find that some positions involve significant time commitments for entertaining, management retreats, all-company breakfasts or dinners and travel (many cross-country trips begin with a Sunday flight). If you have young children, especially if you are single or if your spouse has similar commitments, consider both the cost and the challenge of arranging child care. Early mornings and weekends are difficult times to find child care, particularly at the last minute.

Indexes

More Help for the Seattle Job Search

Most readers find this a valuable tool when looking for work in the Puget Sound area. From time to time, Linda Carlson also teaches job-search classes and publishes updates of this book and other materials. For a class schedule, please call North Seattle Community College's Continuing Education office at (206) 527-3705. For information on book updates and other job-search material available after Jan. 1, 1993, send a self-addressed envelope to

Book Updates
Barrett Street Productions
P.O. Box 99642
Seattle WA 98199

Free Resume Critique

How good is your resume? What could you do to improve it? If you'd like the opinion of an expert, take advantage of our free resume critique offer for buyers of this book.

Since the publication of the first edition of **How To Find A Good Job In Seattle,** Linda Carlson has spoken to hundreds of job-seekers. The most common question: How to write an effective resume. If you have similar concerns, you can now receive a written critique of your resume--for free.

To obtain your critique, please send the following:

> one neatly typed copy of your resume (no handwritten resumes or rough drafts);
>
> the original (no photocopies) of this page; and
>
> as proof of purchase, your sales receipt for the book. (If your book was purchased by mail and you do not have a receipt, you may substitute a copy of your cancelled check.)

Send all material with a large self-addressed envelope to:

Free Resume Critique
Barrett Street Productions
P.O. Box 99642
Seattle WA 98199

You'll receive written comments within four weeks. Caution: marginal notes may be made on the resume you submit. Do not send in your only copy.

If you'd like critiques of a second version of your resume or a friend's resume, please enclose $25 per additional resume. Make checks payable to Barrett Street Productions.

(We're sorry; at this time, telephone and fax critiques are not available. Resumes submitted without proof of purchase or $25 fee will not be critiqued or returned.)

How To Save Money On Your Next Copy Of This Book

To make the next edition of **How To Find A Good Job In Seattle** even better, we'd appreciate your comments. You need not identify yourself, but if you do, we'll send you a discount coupon good for $5 off on another copy of this year's book—or the next edition.

Your completed survey should be sent to:

Barrett Street Productions
P.O. Box 99642
Seattle WA 98199

Please tell us where you bought your copy of **How To Find A Good Job in Seattle**:

___bookstore ___ by direct mail from_____

Other:_____

Your home ZIP code:_____

If you are not a Puget Sound area resident, do you plan to move here?

___ yes

        ___ within three months ___ within six months

        Other:_____

___ no

Please describe yourself:
___ college student/recent graduate
___ seeking professional/technical position
___ seeking middle management position
___ seeking secretarial/clerical/administrative position
___ seeking part-time, temporary or seasonal work
___ employed, seeking sales leads
___ job-search counselor
Other:_____

Your age:
___ younger than 25
___ 25-34
___ 34-45
___ older than 45

OVER, PLEASE

Your education level
___ high school graduate
___ vocational/technical training
___ some college
___ college graduate
___ postgraduate education

Your annual household income:
___ less than $10,000
___ $10,000-$24,999
___ $25,000-$40,000
___ more than $40,000

What did you find most valuable about **How To Find A Good Job In Seattle**?

Would you recommend it to friends?

How would you suggest we improve this book?

Your discount coupon should be sent to (please enclose a self-addressed envelope or address label):

Name_____

Address_____

Discount coupons are sent upon receipt of completed surveys only. Please submit the original of this page; **no photocopies can be accepted**. One coupon per household. Publisher reserves the right to limit recipients of coupons. Coupons are valid only on books ordered directly from publisher; discounts may not be combined.